KU-298-699

Book Reviews: Publishers are invited to submit books for review to the Editor.

Instructions to Authors: To facilitate editorial work and to enhance the uniformity of presentation, authors are requested to send a file of the paper to the Editor on e-mail. If the paper is accepted after refereeing then to prepare the contribution in accordance with the stylesheet information on the preceding two pages. Manuscripts will not be returned except for editorial reasons. The language of publication is English. The following information should be provided on the first page: the title, the author's name and full address, a title not exceeding 40 characters including spaces and a summary/ abstract in English not exceeding 200 words. Please use italics for emphasis, quotations, etc. Email to: sbr@kvl.dk

Drawings. Drawings, graphs, figures and tables must be reproducible originals. They should be presented on separate sheets. Authors will be charged if illustrations have to be re-drawn.

Style. CHK has selected the style of the APA (*Publication Manual of the American Psychological Association*, 5th edition) because this style is commonly used by social scientists, cognitive scientists, and educators. The APA website contains information about the correct citation of electronic sources. The APA Publication Manual is available from booksellers. The Editors reserve the right to correct, or to have corrected, non-native English prose, but the authors should not expect this service. The journal has adopted U.S.English usage as its norm (this does not apply to other native users of English).

Accepted WP systems:
MS Word and rtf.

Contents

The artists are Frank Ga' ~~DISCARD~~ *e poet is Bill Schiffer*

CYBERNETICS & HUMAN KNOWING
A Journal of Second-Order Cybernetics, Autopoiesis & Cyber-Semiotics

Cybernetics and Human Knowing is a quarterly international multi- and transdisciplinary journal focusing on second-order cybernetics and cybersemiotic approaches.

The journal is devoted to the new understandings of the self-organizing processes of information in human knowing that have arisen through the cybernetics of cybernetics, or second order cybernetics its relation and relevance to other interdisciplinary approaches such as C.S. Peirce's semiotics. This new development within the area of knowledge-directed processes is a non-disciplinary approach. Through the concept of self-reference it explores: cognition, communication and languaging in all of its manifestations; our understanding of organization and information in human, artificial and natural systems; and our understanding of understanding within the natural and social sciences, humanities, information and library science, and in social practices like design, education, organization, teaching, therapy, art, management and politics.

Because of the interdisciplinary character articles are written in such a way that people from other domains can understand them. Articles from practitioners will be accepted in a special section. All articles are peer-reviewed.

Subscription Information

For subscription send a check in $US (drawn on US bank) or £UK (drawn on UK bank or Eurocheque), made payable to Imprint Academic to PO Box 1, Thorverton, EX5 5YX, UK, or credit card details (Visa/Mastercard/Amex), including card expiry date. For more information contact Sandra Good. sandra@imprint.co.uk

Price: Individual $63 / £40.50. Institutional: $121 / £78
50% discount on complete runs of back volumes.

Editor: Søren Brier, Copenhagen Business School, department of Management, Politics and Philosophy, Blågårdsgade 23 B, room 326. DK-2200 Copenhagen N
sbr.lpf@cbs.dk Phone: (+45) 3815 2208
www.flec.kvl.dk/personalprofile.asp?id=sbr&p=engelsk

Associate Editor: Jeanette Bopry, Instructional Sciences, National Institute of Education, 1 Nanyang Walk, Singapore 637616
bopry@und.nodak.edu

Art editor: Bruno Kjær, Royal School of Library and Information Science, Aalborg Branch

Journal homepage: www.imprint-academic.com/C&HK
Full text: www.ingenta.com/journals/browse/imp

Cybernetics And Human Knowing. Vol. 10, nos. 3-4, pp. 5-8

Foreword: The *Oroborous* and the Glass Bead Game

Søren Brier and Ranulph Glanville

This double issue of *Cybernetics and Human Knowing* is dedicated to celebrating the life and work of Heinz von Foerster, cybernetician extraordinaire. He died on October 2nd, 2002. Mai von Foerster, his wife of over 60 years, died on June 22nd, 2003. They lived as a team and it is wrong to think of the work that appeared under the authorship of Heinz von Foerster without thinking of Mai's part in it. In life they were inseparable. Death did not separate them for long, either. It is fitting to start this introduction by recording this, and by commemorating Mai von Foerster, née Sturmer, along with her husband, Heinz.

We have attempted to make this issue a sort of *Glass Bead Game* in recognition of his ability to research and unite art with practical work; and in recognition of his teaching, rhetoric and existential conversation. Hermann Hesse envisages a system that has been able to combine science, arts, philosophy and poetry into one condensed expression—a new language of culture—and to build an institution around the development, preservation and communication of this new language of global culture. Von Foerster's work shares this character in the way he distilled messages into tiny, minimalist "crystals" that can be seen from many different perspectives. Reflecting both science and ethics, they were also little art works in themselves. The Biological Computer Laboratory he founded worked to this end, with von Foerster as the *Glass Bead Master* collecting creative scientists and scholars from all over the world.

Since, over the last ten years, von Foerster's written communication with the general public was mainly through the medium of the interview, we start off with an interview: "In Each and Every Moment I Can Decide Who I Am." This is a chapter from Bernard Poerksen's forthcoming book: *The Certainty of Uncertainty: Dialogues Introducing Constructivism*. Here Poerksen, in one of his last interviews with von Foerster, tries to get to the bottom of the wisdom of "the Socrates of Cybernetics."

In his paper "Action Without Utility: An Immodest Proposal for the Cognitive foundation of behavior," Karl Müller, from the Heinz von Foerster Society, abstracts from and recombines elements in several of von Foerster's papers to indicate how they provide a critique of rational choice theory, composing them to form a unified theory of cognition. Thus, the article both sums up von Foerster's work and generates new content previously only implicit in von Foerster's material.

Then we return to another interview (available in English for the first time) between von Foerster and Monika Bröcker. She calls this interview "Between the Lines: The Part-of-the-World-Position of Heinz von Foerster." The conversation focuses particularly on the implicit ethics in any contribution to a conversation and how we create ourselves in the way we speak to the other: to see oneself as a part of the universe, a participant and not an outside observer, to find "the matrix that embeds" as well as Bateson's "pattern that connects." Here is the great mystery of our role: deciding undecidable questions and thereby taking responsibility for the world. It is as difficult to speak of the true ethics as it is for the Taoists to speak of the true Tao.

Next, we publish Albert Müller's informative article about "Heinz von Foerster's Archives." This new archive, housed at the University of Vienna, is the richest source of further material for students of von Foerster and his theories and ideas. The photos from his scholarly life scattered throughout the pages and on the back cover of this issue, are by the courtesy of The Heinz von Foerster Archive, Institut fuer Zeitgeschichte, Universitaet Wien, Spitalgasse 2, A-1090 Wien/Vienna, Austria, which we thank for co-operating with us in creating this memorial issue.

Louis H. Kauffman's article "Eigenforms—Objects as Token for Eigenbehaviors" is a work in the von Foerster tradition. Kauffman contemplates the significance of this central idea from von Foerster's theory of cognition, and develops it into the position that objects are symbolic entities in network interactions, establishing solidity and stability from these interactions. Reflecting on our own reality we can see that this becomes a sign for our selves (an interesting connection to Peirce's semiotic and his model of the semiotic, dynamic network evolving meaning through time). Self-reflection occurs in language too, especially with the word *I*. With the lambda function, names can act on names and theory references. Between the person and the name we can create meta names, thus making a linguistic entry into the world of Gödelian sentences. As von Foerster says, "I am the observed link between myself and observing myself."

Ranulph Glanville, in his "Machines of Wonder and Elephants that Float through Air," explores the collection of papers in *Understanding Understanding: Essays in Understanding Cybernetics*. He analyzes the three machines familiar in von Foerster's work: Maxwell's Demon, Eigen Forms and the Non-Trivial Machine, to explicate von Foerster's implicit position, that, because we as observers are involved, he did not believe we could analyze and come to a complete understanding or depiction of the world. It will stay, in its everyday appearance to us, as a wonder, to be embraced and lived by deciding the rational-logical undecidable.

Marcelo Pakman writes about "Elements for a Foersterian Poetics in Psychotherapeutic Practice." He underscores the importance of how the second order cybernetic trend towards constructivism has influenced the therapeutic field, especially through family therapy. Pakman explores how much practice based in the theory can be seen to benefit from von Foerster's insights. He focuses on the poetics developed, assuming that strange and "irrational" behaviors are socially viable, requiring the therapist to look for the mechanism that makes them meaningful. In an intriguing model he combines ethics, pragmatics, aesthetics and politics as related to reflexivity, language and temporality. Then he investigates von Foerster's position on these, for instance, his "logic of becoming." Theory, as life, invents itself in an endless game.

Frederick Steier and Jane Jorgensen do research with the Museum of Science and Industry in Tampa contribute their paper, "Ethics and Aesthetics of Observing Frames." They use von Foerster's second order ethics and aesthetic imperatives to develop an understanding of science learning as an emergent co-improvisation between designers, researchers, interactors and visitors. They explore how "understanding" arises as a mutual interaction between different root metaphors, world hypotheses, frames and language games to become a reality as a social eigen-behavior, and how this conception develops as the dialogical interaction unfolds. It only stops when the eigen-behavior of one generates an eigen-behavior in the other as when one snake eats the tail of the other in the metaphor of the Oroborous: Reality equals community.

In the late 1970's, the now defunct *International Cybernetics Newsletter* began publishing a series on master cyberneticians. Bernard Scott's present contribution revisits the paper he wrote on Heinz von Foerster then, adding a critical and historical framework in which he highlights the emergence of second order cybernetics. As Scott points out, there was no mention in his original article of second order cybernetics, even though it was already established. In his epilogue he re-evaluates the influence of second order cybernetics and points to the work of Niklas Luhmann, the sociocybernetic group (RC51) under the International Sociological Association, and this journal itself as instances of how the torch has been passed on. It is good to be reminded of the considerable contribution von Foerster made before developing second order cybernetics.

In "Discovering Social Knowledge" Gerard de Zeeuw reflects on von Foerster's suggestion about how to deal scientifically with the study of social action, and its self-referring, self-descriptional and self-explanatory character. His concept of the collective container where members pre-construct and self-organize knowledge—and the mathematical tools he suggests using—appears much more exact than anything that previously existed in this area of study.

Stuart Umpleby writes about a crucial moment in the social development of cybernetics, especially second-order cybernetics, and the fate of the Biological Computer Laboratory. The story he tells gives a shocking insight into the unforeseen, invisible interactions between politics and science.

As usual, there are two columns. In the ASC-column former president, Pille Bunnell, reflects on the phrase "Standing on the Shoulders of Giants." Under the impression of the status of von Foerster as a giant she points out that part of being able to start a new lineage of ideas involves another important characteristic—the ability in life and theoretical practice to create spaces that invite others in, to produce the new world that living these ideas can generate. The regular column is by Ranulph Glanville and has a cybernetic appraisal of buffers and their conception as it theme.

There are also two reviews. Ole Thyssen has written a piece inspired by the book *Understanding Systems: Conversations on Epistemology and Ethics* by Heinz von Foerster and Bernhard Poerksen. Thyssen's personal account of his meeting with von Foerster sparks analysis of the themes in the book that both provide insight into von

Foerster's background and the essence of his methods. Thyssen praises the value of the "small Foersters" as von Foerster called his articles, and discusses the problems of collecting them within an overall framework. He points to some of the philosophical shortcomings of his own approach and shows where more work needs to be done. Hopefully, scholars will continue to explore various approaches in this journal.

Glanville reviews the same collaboration, *Understanding Systems: Conversations on Epistemology and Ethics*, formed from interviews between von Foerster and Poerksen. He praises the way the book brings some unity to the diversity of von Foerster's thought. The last of three interview books originally composed in German, this is the only one to appear so far in English. Von Foerster had hoped it would be titled after his notorious aphorism: "Truth is the invention of the liar." The text provides a cybernetic view on the relation between truth and falsehood, which matches the Cretan paradox on liars.

After the columns and reviews, we publish more personal memories from colleagues, friends and relatives, who give insight in to von Foerster as organizer, teacher, colleague, leader, friend and father. Frank Galuszka writes about the von Foersters' residence at Rattlesnake Hill, especially about painting there. He recollects memories of Open Air painting with Christina Waters in and around the von Foerster home, and their interaction with the von Foerster family and friends. Klaus Krippendorff shares a short piece on von Foerster's rhetorical genius, that wonderful practice so many of us have experienced, and how it embodies the theory of communication he shared with Maturana: "Anything said is said to an Observer." We move towards the conclusion of this double issue with a most charming piece: Cornelia Bessie's "The Man that Lived across the Hall." A tale about how she, as a teenager, came to teach von Foerster English and all that she received in return. The piece shows von Foerster's sense of play and the unique way he interacted with other "observers." We give the final words to Heinz and Mai's two surviving sons. We are fortunate that they have been willing to share insights into the von Foersters as parents. Their pieces provide a unique snapshot of life in the von Foerster household, how Heinz worked, and Mai's great contribution in supporting him and their children.

The front cover was created by Frank Galuszka, giving new life to the Oroborous that was the hallmark of Heinz von Foerster. The painting on the back cover, courtesy Frank Galuszka, the artist of this issue, is a view of Rattlesnake Hill. There are black and white reproductions of other paintings and drawings by Frank inside. Christina Waters provides the painting in Galuszka's paper. The poems are by Bill Schiffer. His way of combining the scientific and the existential as well as the oriental and the occidental seems to us to be so much in the spirit of von Foerster's work that we have chosen to publish them in this issue to make it a *Gesamtkunstwerk*.

We honour Heinz von Foerster, Viennese, Glass Bead Master, writer of the Oroborus, as a founding member of this journal and member of its editorial board. As editors of this special double issue devoted to the memory of the work and the person, Heinz von Foerster, known as the father of second order cybernetics, we would like to thank all those who have contributed to the present issue.

Cybernetics And Human Knowing. Vol. 10, nos. 3-4, pp. 9-26

"At each and every moment, I can decide who I am"

Heinz von Foerster on the observer, dialogic life, and a constructivist philosophy of distinctions

Bernhard Poerksen[1]

This dialog is an excerpt from the forthcoming book: *The Certainty of Uncertainty: Dialogues Introducing Constructivism* by Bernhard Poerksen. Translation by Alison Rosemary Koeck and Wolfram Karl Koeck. [2]

Heinz von Foerster (1911-2002) is held to be the "Socrates of cybernetics." Having studied physics in Vienna, he worked in various research laboratories in Germany and Austria, and after World War II also briefly as a journalist and as a consultant to a telephone company. At the same time, he wrote his first book, *Memory. A quantum-mechanical investigation.* (Publ. Vienna 1948) His theory of memory caught the attention of the founding figures of American cybernetics. They invited him; he immigrated to the USA in 1949. There, he was received into a circle of scientists that began to meet in the early fifties under the auspices of the Macy Foundation. He was made editor of the annual conference proceedings. The mathematician Norbert Wiener whose book *Cybernetics* had just been published, John von Neumann, the inventor of the computer, the anthropologists Gregory Bateson and Margaret Mead, the neuropsychiatrist Warren S. McCulloch, together with more than a dozen other intellectual enthusiasts, formed the group essentially contributing to the so-called Macy Conferences.

In 1957, Heinz von Foerster, meanwhile appointed professor, founded the Biological Computer Laboratory (BCL) at the University of Illinois, which he directed until his retirement in 1976. At this institution, he brought together avant-garde artists and original minds from all over the world. In the inspiring climate of the BCL, philosophers and electrical engineers, biologists (e.g. Humberto R. Maturana and Francisco J. Varela), anthropologists and mathematicians, artists and logicians debated epistemological questions from interdisciplinary perspectives deriving from both the sciences and the arts. They dealt with the rules of computation in humans and

1. Institut für Journalistik und Kommunikationswissenschaft, Universität Hamburg.
   Email: bernhard.poerksen@uni-hamburg.de
2. It is due to be published in February 2004 by Imprint Academic (PO Box 200, Exeter EX5 5YX, UK. http://www.imprint-academic.com) at £14.95.

machines and analysed the logical and methodological problems involved in the understanding of understanding and the observation of the observer. It is Heinz von Foerster's outstanding achievement to have brought into focus the inescapable prejudices and blind spots of the human observer approaching his apparently independent object of inquiry. His ethical stance demands constant awareness of one's blind spots, to accept, in a serious way, that one's apparently final pronouncements are one's own productions, and to cast doubt on certainties of all kinds and forms, while at the same time continually searching for other and new possibilities of thought.

The myth of objectivity

Poerksen: Every theory, every attitude, or worldview, rests on its own aphorisms and key statements that, if one probes their depths and thinks them through, encompass what is essential. Psychoanalysts follow Freud's thesis that humans are "not masters in their own house" because the subconscious reigns supreme there. The central formula of Marxism is: "Being determines consciousness." ("Das Sein bestimmt das Bewusstsein.") The behaviourist Skinner upholds the determinist thesis "Human behaviour is the function of variables in the environment." One of the key aphorisms of constructivism and your own world of ideas, it seems to me, may possibly be located in the writings of your friend, the biologist Humberto Maturana: "Everything said is said by an observer."

Von Foerster: The entree you have chosen seems very interesting to me — for there is always the question: With what claims and assumptions should we approach an area of thought? Where, how and when should we begin with the telling of a story? Moreover, what will happen afterwards? Will people pound their fists on the table and declare everything nonsense, or will they smile at you full of excitement? Considering Maturana's theorem in isolation and without all its implicit consequences will certainly not earn you special admiration. Nobody will exclaim: "Wow! What a revelation!" You might rather hear: "My God, if this is the fundamental tenet of his philosophy, then I prefer to go to the cinema or have a drink." This theorem, without its proper context, may appear ridiculous, annoying, or downright stupid.

Poerksen: What are some of the epistemological consequences — to formulate the question quite generally — if we take the statement seriously and try to build a system of thought upon it?

Von Foerster: One of the conclusions is that what a human being comprehends can no longer be externalised and be seen simply as given. The statement undermines our craving for objectivity and truth for we must not forget that it is a distinguishing feature of objective and true descriptions that the personal properties of the observer do not enter into them, do not influence or determine them in any way. They must not, it is claimed, be distorted or disturbed by an observer's predilections, personal idiosyncrasies, political or philosophical inclinations, or any other kind of club affiliation. I would say, however, that this whole concept is sheer madness, absolutely impossible. How can one demand a thing like that—and still remain a professor?! The moment you try to eliminate the properties of the observer, you create a vacuum: There isn't anyone left to observe anything—and to tell us about it.

Poerksen: The observer is the component that cannot be eliminated from a process of knowing.

Von Foerster: Exactly. There must always be someone who smells, tastes, hears, and sees. I have never really been able to understand, what the proponents of objective descriptions want to observe at all if they ban the human observer's personal view of things right from the start.

Poerksen: "Objectivity is a subject´s delusion," the *American Society for Cybernetics* quotes you, "that observing can be done without him."

Von Foerster: How can we get round the question: What can observers perceive who, according to the common definition of objectivity, are in fact blind, deaf and dumb, and who are not allowed to use their own language? What can they tell us? How are they to talk? Only an observer can observe. Without an observer, there is nothing.

Poerksen: If we, as you suggest, tie knowing inseparably to the knower, what sense and what function remains for the key concepts of realism, e.g. *reality, fact,* and *object*?

Von Foerster: If used at all, they will only serve as crutches, metaphors, and shortcuts. They may be used to state things and establish relations, without delving more profoundly into the questions involved. They will facilitate quick reference to specific points of relevance—a place, an object, a property, which are supposed to exist in the world—and to formulate corresponding statements. The danger lies in it being all too easy to forget that we are using crutches and metaphors and to believe that the world is *really* and *truthfully* represented by our descriptions. And that is the moment in which conflicts and hostilities and wars arise about the question what the facts are and who is in possession of the truth.

Poerksen: To take the knower—the observer—seriously also entails supplementing or even replacing ontological questions concerning the *What*—the object of knowing— by epistemological questions relating to the *How*—the process of knowing. What insights or perhaps what experiences have induced you personally to focus on the observer in your research and in your reflections? Was there an intellectual key experience?

Insights of a magician

Von Foerster: The experience occurred a very long time ago. At twelve or thirteen years of age, my cousin Martin and I—we grew up together like two inseparable brothers—began to practise magic. We invented our own acts, stunned the amazed grown-ups with our enthusiasm, and realised after a while that magic had nothing to do with mechanical things, false bottoms, tricks, optical illusions etc., which everybody is familiar with; the decisive thing was to create an atmosphere in which something unbelievable, something unexpected could happen, something nobody had ever seen. It is the spectator who invents a world in which girls are sawn apart and elephants float through the air. What instilled an awareness of the observer into me was the question: How can I create an atmosphere for a group of people, in which miracles may be seen? What sort of story must I tell, *how* must I tell it in order to make people accept it and make them work the miracles of the floating elephant and the sawn girl in their own individual ways? As a child or a youngster you simply perform your magic acts, you listen in amazement to what the grown-ups tell you about what they have seen, and perhaps you wonder what goes on in their brains. And this is what you later—when you are fifty, perhaps—describe as the *observer problem.*

Poerksen: Magicians are, if I am not mistaken, practising constructivists; they create visions and construct realities, which contradict the laws of gravity as well as the rules of probability and everyday life.

Von Foerster: This is the point. Magic, for me, was the original experience of constructivism: together with the other participants you invent a world in which elephants disappear and girls are sawn apart—and suddenly re-appear totally unharmed. What amused me and my cousin most was that the spectators who had apparently all seen the same event—the magic trick—often related quite different variations in the interval or after the show, which had nothing or very little to do with what we or other magicians had done. Mr Miller, Mr Jones, and Ms Cathy obviously created their own personal events. They saw girls sawn apart that were not, of course, sawn apart at all—neither had the elephants been made to vanish. These experiences drew my attention to the psychology of observing and the creation of a world: What happens, I asked myself, in the process of observing? Is that observer sitting in Hermann von Helmholtz's famous *locus observandi* and describing the world in a state of complete neutrality?

Poerksen: What do you think? What is the observer doing? What is going on?

Von Foerster: The customary view is: the observer sees the world, perceives it, and says what it is like. Observers supposedly occupy that strange *locus observandi* and watch—unconstrained by personality, individual taste, and idiosyncratic features—an independent reality. In contrast, I maintain that observers in action primarily look *into* themselves. What they are describing is *their* view of how the world appears to *them*. And good magicians are able to sense what kinds of world other persons would like to be real, at a certain moment, and they can help them to create these worlds successfully.

Poerksen: The magician's act, technically speaking, involves three components: the magician, the event, and the spectators. If we asked a solipsist, a realist, and a constructivist to describe what was happening, we would get quite different accounts. The solipsists would tell us that nothing of what they describe is real, but that everything is a chimera of our minds merely imagining the magician as well as a world that does not, in fact, exist. The realists would insist that observing is nothing but the mapping of reality onto the screen of our mind—and that the observers, the spectators, are deceived by the magician's trickery: they fall victim to an illusion that does not adequately represent the reality of what is independently existent. Your kind of constructivism occupies the middle ground between realism and solipsism: There is something there, you would probably say, something is really going on, and that seems beyond doubt; but it is just as certain that all human beings describe the reality of those events in their own ways and construct their very own worlds.

Von Foerster: I have an uncanny feeling that the language we are using at this moment in our conversation is playing tricks on us and producing all sorts of strange bubbles. You know what I want to talk about, and I know more or less, what I want to say. Still, I am not sure whether this kind of epistemological classification and this manner of linguistic embedding would enable other persons to grasp what you and I are getting at. This means: we must, for a moment, consider the language we use to express what we mean. The mere sentence "There is something there" seems to me to be poisoned by the presuppositions of realism. I am worried that the position you assign to me is holding some backdoor open through which that terrible notion of ontology may still gain entrance. Accepting this position, one may continue to speak of the existence of an external reality. And referring to an external reality and existence is a wonderful way of eliminating one's responsibility for what one is saying. That is the deep horror of ontology. You introduce the apparently innocent expression "there is..." which I once jokingly and somewhat pompously termed the *existential operator* and say with authoritarian violence: "It is so.... there is..." But why is what there? And who asserts that something is the case?

Poerksen: The fact that you reject any prefabricated terminology and show a noticeable aversion towards any clean and, as it were, unadulterated epistemological classification of your ideas, seems to me to be an important indication of a fundamental problem: How can we speak about the act of observing, the observer, and the observed, in a way that does justice to the dynamic processes involved?

Von Foerster: This is an incredibly difficult problem because we are working with a medium—language. Being tied to that medium, we are seduced to speak in a way that suggests the existence of a world independent from us. One of my great desires is to learn to control my language in such a way as to keep my ethics implicit, whether I am dealing with politics, science, or poetry, so that it is always evident that I myself am the point of reference of the observations I am offering. I would like to invent a language or form of communication—and perhaps it will have to be poetry, music, or dance—that would release something in another person, so that any reference to an external world or reality, to any "there is…" would be superfluous; any such reference, so I imagine, would no longer be needed. To do this successfully, however, one must be firmly anchored in that world. Moreover, one problem always remains: What other form can we invent that would also deal with the problem of form?

Poerksen: In my view, the actual question is: How can we speak or write in such a way as to make the observer-dependence of all knowledge visible whenever we speak or write? How can we show that our descriptions of the world are not the descriptions of an external reality but the descriptions of an observer who *believes* they are descriptions of an external reality?

Von Foerster: The problem is a dialogue between you and me that does not rely on any reference to something external. When I insist, for instance, that it is *you* producing this view of things, that it is not something out there, not the so-called objective reality, that we can fall back on, then a strange   foregrounding of you, the person speaking, is effected. Generalised expressions beginning with "There is…" are replaced by expressions beginning with "I think that…" We use, to say it somewhat pompously again, the *self-referential operator* "I think…" and abandon the existential operator "there is." In this way, a completely different relation emerges that paves the way for a free dialogue.

Poerksen: If you do not want to talk about subject, object, and the process of knowing—the observer, the observed, and the process of observing—on the basis of a form of language established in the academic world involving classic epistemological concepts, what ways of talking can we turn to?

Separation or Connection

Von Foerster: I cannot offer a general solution but I would like to present a short dramatic scene that I once wrote because it might help to escape the grip of predetermined forms. The scene is performed for an audience in a baroque theatre. The lights are dimmed, the impressive red velvet curtain rises, and the stage comes into full view. There is a tree, a man, and a woman, all forming a triangle. The man points at the tree and says: "There is a tree." The woman says: "How do you know that there is a tree?" The man: "Because I see it!" With a brief smile, the woman says:

"Aha!" The curtain comes down. I contend, this drama has been discussed, misunderstood, and even attacked for thousands of years, a drama that is well suited to illuminate the debates of questions of knowledge and the role of an external world. Whom do we want to trust, whom do we want to refer to? The man? The woman? Since primeval times, the undecidable question has been haunting us whether to side with the man or with the woman. The man affirms the observer-independent existence of the tree and the environment, the woman draws his attention to the fact that he only knows of the tree because *he* sees it, and that seeing is, therefore, primary. We must now ask ourselves which of these attitudes we are prepared to accept. The man relies on his external reference, the woman points out to him that the perception of the tree is tied to *his* observation. However, this little piece does not only deal, as might be suspected, with objectivity and subjectivity or different epistemological positions. Something else is much more important: The man separates himself from the world, the woman connects herself with what she describes.

Poerksen: This is, then, another contrast that comes into play here. It is not primarily concerned with the distinction between subjectivity and objectivity but with the question as to whether I connect myself to the world, or whether my epistemological position forces me to see myself as distinct from it, as a person observing it from an imaginary *locus observandi*.

Von Foerster: This is a good way of putting it. The man in my little drama looks at the passing and unfolding universe as if through a keyhole, at the trees, the things, and the other people. He does not have to feel responsible, he represents a sort of keyhole or peephole philosophy, he is a *voyeur*. Nothing concerns him because nothing touches him. Indifference becomes excusable. The woman insists that it is only a human being can see and observe. The attitude of the detached describers is opposed to the attitude of the compassionate participants who consider themselves as part of the world. Each one acts on the basis of the premise: Whatever I do, will change the world! I am the world, and the world is me!

Poerksen: What are the consequences of this experience or knowledge of connectedness?

Von Foerster: What we call the world is, all of a sudden, no longer something hostile but appears to be an organ, an inseparable part of one's own body. The universe and the self have become united. We have to shoulder responsibility for our actions; we can no longer retire to the position of the passive recorder who describes a static and supposedly timeless existence. We have been made aware that every action—even the mere lifting of an arm—may create a new universe that did not exist before. Knowing this—or better, sensing it and feeling it—excludes any kind of static vision; on the contrary, everything is now in constant flux, every situation is new, nothing is eternal, nothing can ever be as it once used to be.

Poerksen: I am quite in favour of this description of an observer-dependent universe. Nevertheless, objections immediately come to mind. We perceive the world as something that has developed and grown, and the experience of the stability of our human condition is definitely quite comforting. Its regularities seem reliable, they provide orientation, allow us to make plans and to face the future with certain expectations. What I want to say is: The attitude you describe contradicts our everyday experience and it is, in addition, psychologically unattractive.

Von Foerster (laughing): Absolutely right. I completely agree with you.

Poerksen: You agree with me? Do you not want to convince me of the correctness of an observer-dependent state of the world?

Von Foerster: For God's sake! I would not dream of trying to convince you because that would cause your view to vanish. It would then be lost. All I can attempt is to act the magician so that you may be put in a position to convince yourself. Perhaps I might succeed in inviting you to re-interpret, for a moment, the security you find so attractive as something undermining openness. For even security and stability of circumstances may get persons into great trouble at certain stages in their lives, when they, for instance, do not realise that the circumstances constraining them might be completely different ones, and that it is in their power to change them.

Poerksen: As you are unwilling to convince me, what is, then, for you, the purpose of a dispute or a conversation?

Von Foerster: I would like to answer with a little story about the world of Taoism, which has fascinated me since childhood. My uncle, Erwin Lang, was taken prisoner by the Russian forces soon after the outbreak of World War I and deported to Siberia. When the Russian Empire collapsed in 1917, he managed to escape to China. He finally reached the German settlement Tsingtau where he met the scholar Richard Wilhelm, the translator of the *I Ching*, who introduced him to the ideas of Taoism. Through his help and recommendation, Erwin Lang was accepted by a Taoist monastery at which he arrived after a two days walk. Still uncertain whether the War was over and the fighting had stopped, he asked one of the monks for newspapers. Of course, the monk said, we have newspapers; we have, in fact, an enormous library. My uncle was impressed and asked for a copy of the Austrian *Neue Freie Presse*. Certainly, the monk said, we have newspapers from all over the world. He took him to the archive in the monastery and, after a short search, produced the most recent issue of the *Neue Freie Presse* available. It was the issue of 15 February 1895. Of course, Erwin Lang was somewhat consternated and pointed out to the monk that the paper was more than 20 years old. The monk looked at him and said: "So what?! What are 20 years?" At that moment, my uncle began to understand Taoism: Time did not play any role in this world; topical news value was of no importance.

Poerksen: You are unwilling to convince me, and you refuse to discredit other, or antagonist, positions, but you use history and stories—your little parable seems a case in point—in order to make further possibilities of perceiving accessible.

Von Foerster: This interpretation is most welcome. My goal is indeed to present different perspectives that may, or may not, be taken up. To return to the beginning of our conversation: Whether we accept the theorem of my friend, Humberto Maturana ("Everything said is said by an observer"), and whether we consider ourselves connected with the world or separate from it—we are confronted by undecidable questions. Decidable questions are, in a certain sense, already decided through their given framework; their decidability is secured by specific rules and formalisms—for example, syllogisms, syntax, or arithmetic—that must be accepted. The question, for instance, whether the number 7856 is divisible by two, is easy to answer because we know that numbers with an even final number are divisible by two. Paul Feyerabend's notorious slogan, *anything goes,* does not apply here because the rules of arithmetic force us to proceed in a certain way in order to find an answer. Undecidable questions, on the contrary, are unsolvable in principle; they can never really be clarified. Nobody knows, I would claim, whether the man or the woman in my little drama is right, and whether it is more correct to consider oneself connected with the world or separate from it. This situation of fundamental undecidability is an invitation to decide for oneself. For this decision, however, one must shoulder the responsibility oneself.

Monologic and dialogic

Poerksen: Reviewing our conversation about the observer, I cannot help noticing that you keep returning to the interaction of human beings. To put it differently, as a kind of thesis: For you, observers are not isolated figures; they always exist in a field of relations, in a community. Your own ideas, too, always appear embedded in actual relationships, in personal experiences and personal thoughts.

Von Foerster: The observer as a strange singularity in the universe does not attract me, indeed; you are quite right there. This kind of concept will probably be of interest to a neurophysiologist or neuroanatomist, whereas I am fascinated by images of duality, by binary metaphors like dance and dialogue where only a duality creates a unity. Therefore, the statement that opened our conversation—"Everything said is said by an observer"—is floating freely, in a sense. It exists in a vacuum as long as it is not embedded in a social structure because speaking is meaningless, and dialogue is impossible, if no one is listening. So I have added a corollary to that theorem, which I named with all due modesty *Heinz von Foerster's Corollary Nr. 1*: "Everything said is said *to* an observer." Language is not monologic but always dialogic. Whenever I say or describe something, I am after all not doing it for myself but to make someone else know and understand what I am thinking or intending to do.

Poerksen: What happens when other observers are involved?

Von Foerster: We get a triple consisting of the observers, the languages, and the relations constituting a social unit. The addition produces the nucleus and the core structure of society, which consists of two people using language. Due to the recursive nature of their interactions, stabilities arise; they generate observers and their worlds, who recursively create other stable worlds through interacting in language. Therefore, we can call a funny experience *apple* because other people also call it *apple*. Nobody knows, however, whether the green colour of the apple you perceive, is the same experience as the one I am referring to with the word *green*. In other words, observers, languages, and societies are constituted through recursive linguistic interaction, although it is impossible to say which of these components came first and which were last — remember the comparable case of hen, egg, and cock. We need all three in order to have all three.

Poerksen: I do not want to over-interpret this transformation of a monologic idea, which is tied to a single observer, into a dialogic concept involving two or more observers in interaction, but it seems to me to contain some hidden anthropology; not a hierarchic one, to be sure, which would compare human beings with machines, animals, or gods, but an anthropology of relations, of interdependence, of You and I. When you relate one human being to another, you are reflecting on the essence of humanity and its potential: there is one human being and there is another — this seems to me to be your point of reference.

Von Foerster: Very well put, indeed. A human being is a human being together with another human being; that is what a human being is. I exist through another I, I see myself through the eyes of the Other, and I shall not tolerate that this relationship is destroyed by the idea of the objective knowledge of an independent reality, which tears us apart and makes the Other an object which is distinct from me. This world of ideas has nothing to do with proof, it is a world one must experience, see, or simply be. When one suddenly experiences this sort of communality, one begins to dance together, one senses the next common step and one's movements fuse with those of the other into one and the same person, into a being that can see with four eyes. Reality becomes communality and community. When the partners are in harmony, twoness flows like oneness, and the distinction between leading and being led has become meaningless. In my view, the best description of this sort of communality is by Martin Buber. He is a very important philosopher for me.

Poerksen: Buber is not just the protagonist of a dialogic philosophy but also a religious scholar and writer, and a mystic. For him, the dialogue between an I and a You mirrors the eternal dialogue with God.

Von Foerster: I feel deep respect for his religious beliefs and feelings but I am unable to share them, really, and perhaps would not like to, anyway. Should his religious orientation be the source of his incredible strength and depth, I can only admire him the more.

Poerksen: What were the seminal experiences that oriented you towards a dialogic life?

Von Foerster: Among the most important is an encounter with the Viennese psychiatrist and pastoral curer of souls, Viktor Frankl. He had survived the concentration camp but had lost his wife and his parents, and he practised again in the psychiatric institution in Vienna from where he had been deported years before. A married couple had also miraculously survived the Nazi terror, each partner in a different camp. Husband and wife had returned to Vienna, had found each other, had naturally been overjoyed to find the partner alive, and had begun a new life together. About a month after their reunion, the wife died of a disease she had contracted in the camp. The husband was absolutely shattered and desperate; he stopped eating and just sat on a stool in his kitchen. Finally, friends managed to persuade him to go and see Viktor Frankl whose special authority as a camp survivor was beyond doubt. Both men talked for more than an hour — then Frankl abruptly changed the topic and said: "Suppose, God gave me the power to create a woman completely identical with your wife. She would crack the same jokes, use the same language and the same gestures, — in brief, you would be unable to spot any difference. Do you want me to ask for God's help in order to create such a woman?" — The man shook his head, stood up, thanked Frankl, left his practice, and started up his life again. When I heard about this story, I went to see Frankl immediately — we were working together professionally on a radio programme broadcast every Friday, at the time — and I asked him: "Viktor, how was that possible? What did you do?" "Heinz, it is very simple," Frankl said, "we see ourselves through the eyes of the other. When she died, he was blind. But when he realised that he was blind, he was able to see again."

In the beginning was the distinction

Poerksen: Perhaps we could now, with a modest topical jump, leave all types of observers behind, and deal with the process of observing itself. Every observation, George Spencer-Brown writes in his famous treatise *Laws of Form*, begins with an act of distinction. More precisely: observations operate with two-valued distinctions one of which may be designated. Therefore, if I want to designate something, I have to decide about a distinction first. The choice of a distinction determines what I can see. Using the distinction between *good* and *bad* I can — wherever I am looking — observe other things than when I am using the distinctions between *rich* und *poor, beautiful* and *ugly, new* and *old* or *ill* and *healthy*. And so on. Consequently, observing means distinguishing and designating.

Von Foerster: Correct, yes. George Spencer-Brown formulates: "Draw a distinction and a universe comes into being." The act of distinction is taken to be the fundamental operation of cognition; it generates realities that are assumed to reside in an external space separated from the person of the distinguisher. A simple example: We draw a circle on a piece of paper; we create, in this way, two worlds, one *outside* and one *inside,* which may now be designated more precisely. In other words, if we follow George Spencer-Brown's argument, before something can be named or designated, before we can describe the space within the circle more exactly, the world has been divided into two parts: it now consists of what we have named, on the one hand, and what is obscured by the name, the rest of the world, on the other.

Poerksen: When you encountered these ideas—you wrote one of the first widely noted reviews of *Laws of Form* -, what fascinated you, in particular?

Von Foerster: What fascinated me, at the time, and still fascinates me now, is that the formal apparatus, the logical machinery, which Spencer-Brown developed, enables us to solve the classical problem of the paradox that has troubled logicians ever since the days of Epimenides. Epimenides, a Cretan, said: "I am a Cretan. All Cretans lie." He might as well have said: "I am a liar!" What do you do with someone who says: "I am a liar"?! Do you believe him? If so, he cannot be lying, he must have told the truth. If he told the truth, however, he lied, because he said: "I am a liar." The ambivalence of this statement is that it is true when it is false, and that it is false when it is true. The speaker steps inside what is spoken, and all of a sudden, the function turns into an argument of itself. Such a statement is like a virus and may destroy an entire logical system, or a set of axioms, and cannot, of course, be acceptable to honest logicians following the Aristotelean creed: "A meaningful statement must be either true or false." In the twentieth century, Bertrand Russell and Albert North Whitehead attempted to resolve the liar-paradox by simply prohibiting, as it were, self-referential expressions of this kind. Their theory of types and their escape into a meta-language, however, did not seem satisfactory to me. I have always thought, although I did not know an elegant solution, that language itself ought to be the meta-language of the logicians. Language must be able to speak about itself; that is to say, the operator (language) must become the operand (language). We need a sort of *salto mortale.* George Spencer-Brown has developed an operator that is constructed in such a way as to permit application to itself. His operator can operate on itself and, in this way, becomes part of itself and the world it creates.

Poerksen: How can these ideas be related to epistemology, in particular, to the observer, the central figure of our conversation?

Von Foerster: Whenever I want to say something about myself—and I maintain that everything I am saying is said about myself—I must be aware that speaking involves a fundamental paradox that has to be dealt with. George Spencer-Brown's formalism bridges the customary division between seeing and seen. The epistemology we might envisage against this background is dynamic, not static. It has to do with becoming, not being. Spencer-Brown refuses to start out from the supposition that a statement can only *be* true or false; the formalism invented by him reveals the dynamics of states. As in a flip-flop mechanism, the truth of an expression generates its falsity, and its falsity generates its truth, and so on. He shows that the paradox generates a new dimension: time.

Poerksen: I think it would be worthwhile to describe the philosophy of distinctions that has developed since the publication of *Laws of Form* in detail. Let me, therefore, ask you: What will happen, for example, when I introduce the distinction between *good* and *evil* into the world and make it the foundation of my observations?

Von Foerster: The distinction between *good* and *evil* and the universe created in this way may be used to form sentences and to make statements. Now, it is possible to say of an elephant or of a company director that they are good or particularly wicked. We can build up a calculus of statements, cascades of expressions, which deal with human persons, animals, directors, or elephants. What tends to be overlooked usually is that these distinctions are not out there in the world, are not properties of things and objects but properties of our descriptions of the world. The objects there will forever remain a mystery but their descriptions reveal the properties of observers and speakers, whom we can get to know better in this way. The elephants have no idea of what we are doing, the elephants are simply elephants; *we* make them good or wicked elephants.

Poerksen: Is it correct to say, as you claim, that the intrinsic properties of objects and things in the world do *not* become effective in our descriptions?

Von Foerster: In my view, objects correspond to the sensorimotor experience of a human being who suddenly realises that it cannot simply move everywhere, that there is something blocking its movement, something *standing in the way,* some *ob-ject.* This limitation of behaviour generates ob-jects. As soon as I have acquired enough practice and have experienced these ob-jects often enough, some stability in the experience of limitation has developed and I am in a position to give a name to the item of my sensorimotor skill and competence, call the *object* a cup, or glasses, or Bernhard Poerksen. This is to say: What I designate as glasses or cup is, strictly speaking, a symbol for my nervous system's competence to generate stabilities, to compute invariants.

Poerksen: What sort of truth status would you claim for this thesis? Is it an ontologically correct theory of object formation; are objects *really* constituted in this way?

Von Foerster: Let me return the question: What do you think? What would you prefer, what would you like better?

Poerksen: Are you suggesting it is a matter of taste?

Von Foerster: If *you* want it this way, then it may also be a matter of taste. If you, however, prefer to live in a world where the properties of your descriptions are the properties of the world itself, then that is fine.

Poerksen: People will condemn this as absurd.

Von Foerster: Naturally, this is one of the usual reactions to someone thinking along different lines. The persons that come up with objections of this kind will have to live with the consequences. They create this world for themselves. I am only myself, I am rolling along, I can only try to communicate what I like, what I see, what I find fascinating, and what I want to distinguish. Whether other people consider me a scientist, a constructivist, a magician, a philosopher, a curiosologist, or simply a brat—that is their problem; and it is due to the distinctions they draw.

Blind to one's own blindness

Poerksen: For you, the individual—socially anchored, of course—is evidently the central reality-creating instance. The sociologist Niklas Luhmann, however, who refers explicitly both to Spencer-Brown and your work, only speaks of the operation of observ*ing*—never the observ*er*. He wrote book after book on science, art, religion, politics, and economics, reconstructing the forms of observation and the central sets of distinctions at work in these social domains, to which everyone entering them must necessarily orientate.

Von Foerster: Let me just point out that society, too, is a relational structure; it is a framework according to which we may, but need not, think. In my work, however, the self and the individual are central and present from the start. The reason is that I can conceive of responsibility only as something personal, not as dependent on anything social. You cannot hold a society responsible for anything, you cannot shake its hand, ask it to justify its actions—and you cannot enter into a dialogue with it; whereas I can speak with another self, a you.

Poerksen: What you mean is, I think, that observers—human beings—can indeed decide what distinctions they want to make. My objection is that the world never is— in Spencer-Brown's terminology—an *unmarked space,* but that we are all pressured in many ways, and even condemned, to reproduce the distinctions and views of our own groups, of parents, friends, and institutions. To quote but a blatant example: the children growing up in a sectarian community will obviously absorb its reality.

Von Foerster: This is possible, no doubt. On the other hand, I remain convinced that these people, these individuals, can always opt out of such a network and escape from the sectarian system. They have this freedom, I would claim, but they are all too often completely unable to actually see it. They are blind to their own blindness and do not see that they do not see; they are incapable of realising that there are still possibilities for action. They have created their blind spot and are frozen in their everyday mechanisms and think there is no way out. The uncanny thing, actually, is that sects and dictators always manage to make actually existing freedom invisible for some time. All of a sudden, citizens become zombies or Nazis committing themselves to condemning freedom and responsibility by saying: "I was ordered to kill these people, I had no choice! I merely executed orders!" Even in such a situation, it is obviously possible to refuse. It would be a great decision, possibly leading to one's own death but still an act of incredible quality: "No, I will not do it. I will not kill anyone!" In brief, it is my view that freedom always exists. *At each and every moment, I can decide who I am.* Moreover, in order to render, and keep, this visible I have been pleading for a form of education and communality that does not restrict or impede the visibility of freedom and the multitude of opportunities but actively supports them. My ethical imperative is, therefore: "Act always so as to increase the number of choices."

Poerksen: But how can we re-invent ourselves at each and any moment? Surely, that is out of the question; the world—all the inescapable constraints on our lives—simply will not allow it. Here is my counter-thesis: In the act of observing, we reproduce either old orders or systems of distinctions, or we develop new ones from or against them. Therefore, the freedom and arbitrariness of constructions is massively reduced.

Von Foerster: It is certainly not my contention that the invention of realities is completely arbitrary and wilful and would allow me to see the sky blue at first, then green, and after opening my eyes again, not at all. Of course, every human being is tied into a social network, no individual is an isolated wonder phenomenon but dependent on others and must—to say it metaphorically—dance with others and construct reality through communality. The embedding into a social network necessarily leads to a reduction of arbitrariness through communality; however, it does not at all change the essentially given freedom. We make appointments, identify with others and invent common worlds—which one may give up again. The kinds of dance one chooses along this way may be infinitely variable.

Drop a distinction!

Poerksen: If I understand correctly, human beings are—together with others—capable of creating reality, in a positive sense. However, what are we to do about realities that we reject and do not want to create at all? Can we escape from them through negation?

Von Foerster: No, I do not think so. Ludwig Wittgenstein's *Tractatus-logico-philosophicus* made me see this clearly for the first time. There is the famous consideration that speaking about a proposition *"p"* and its negation *"non p"* means speaking of the same thing. The negation is in fact an affirmation. This is the mistake committed by my dear friends, the revolutionaries, who want to depose a king. They keep shouting loudly and clearly: "Down with the king!" That is, of course, free propaganda for the king who should, in fact, thank his enemies: "Thank you very much for mentioning me so frequently and for not stopping to call out my name!" If I negate a person, an idea, or an ideal, loudly and clearly, the final separation has not yet been achieved. The negated phenomenon will return and take centre stage again.

Poerksen: Who wants to get rid of something finally must neither describe it positively nor deny it, in order to achieve complete separation. What is to be done, then?

Von Foerster: Something different must be done. I suggest that certain distinctions are excluded because I have noticed in many discussions that their basis involves concepts that lead nowhere but only generate conflicts and hostilities. The negation of stupidity is no less stupid because it forces us to go on dealing with stupidity. To make these considerations clear I should like to speak, for a moment, about the *place-value logic* devised by the philosopher Gotthard Günther. In his papers, he analyses the emergence of a proposition, its logical place. Even talking about a king who is then either celebrated or shouted down by revolutionaries requires, according to Günther, a certain place. However, this place may be refused in order to prevent any talk about kings. In this way, a new kind of logic arises. The simple dichotomy of affirmation and negation is left behind; certain propositions are marked with a *rejection-value* in order to make clear that they do not belong to the category of propositions under discussion.

Poerksen: Can you describe this kind of place—the basis that is required by every proposition as the condition of its possibility—more precisely?

Von Foerster: I think the Russians understood this idea very well. I once took part in a conference in Moscow in the era of Khrushchev who sought to bring about a new kind of interaction between bureaucrats and humankind. One day I took a stroll in one of the small parks near the Lenin mausoleum. I saw the statues of the Great Russian military leaders cut in stone and sitting on huge pedestals, staring into the void with their large moustaches. Suddenly I saw a pedestal without a statue, empty. Joseph Stalin cut in stone had once stood on it. In this way, the present government expressed its rejection of Stalin. Had the pedestal been removed as well—the place of the logical proposition in Gotthard Günther's theory—this kind of negation would not have been possible. They were very well aware of that!

Poerksen: This means that we can get rid of concepts simply by stopping to mention them, relegating them to a domain of non-existence, taking away their pedestal and their foundation, as it were. They drop back into an amorphous and shapeless sphere, which is cognitively inaccessible to us because it is not marked by distinctions and indications. In this case, George Spencer-Brown's fundamental imperative must be changed from *"Draw* a distinction!" to *"Drop* a distinction!"

Von Foerster: This is an excellent new operator: "Drop a distinction!" However, this sort of approach seems to have been known to journalists in Austria for some time; they say there that the best way of demolishing an idea or a person is to stop mentioning them. The formula is: "Do not even ignore!" If you want to destroy a politician and president of a country it is best not to write about his extramarital contacts with interns and other women; this would be wrong because the mere mentioning of his name makes people aware again of his existence and may make them say: What a handsome man! It is much more effective to speak about the weather and the weather frogs. And the politician immediately disappears.

Mysticism and metaphysics

Poerksen: Let me attempt a brief résumé. In the process of reality construction, we draw distinctions, we negate distinctions, reject them, try to distance ourselves from them, and sometimes drop them completely in order to get rid of unwanted concepts. We are left with the tricky question what might exist behind the universe that we have constructed. What exists beyond the space we have created through our distinctions? Can you offer an answer, perhaps a very personal one?

Von Foerster: Let me tell you a little story about a personal experience of mine. A few years ago, I was invited to a large conference and participated in a workshop called *Beyond Constructivism*, organised by a charming French lady scientist. People asked me, too, what was beyond constructivism. My answer was: "Ladies and gentlemen, last night, after I had heard of this workshop, I could not go to sleep for a long time because the question troubled me considerably. When I finally did catch some sleep, my grandmother appeared to me in a dream. Of course, I asked her instantly: "Grandmama, what is beyond constructivism?" "Do not tell anyone, Heinz," she said, "I will let you in on the secret — constructivism!"

Poerksen: We can never go beyond our distinguishing and constructing of worlds.

Von Foerster: Exactly. The distinction creates the space. Without this basis, you cannot ask the question regarding the space and the world beyond the space.

Poerksen: Still, if we are to believe the reports of eastern mystics, there seem to be states of consciousness that are not constrained by the ordinary human forms of distinctions. Concluding your review of *Laws of Form,* you refer yourself to a "state of ultimate wisdom" and to the "core of a calculus of love in which all distinctions are suspended and all is one."

Von Foerster: That is indeed what I wrote; no more need be said because that is precisely what I wanted to say. I would be grateful if we could simply let that utterance be as it is and not take it to pieces as in an academic seminar.

Poerksen: It seems to me that you have developed a way of speaking that offers indications and hints at things you do not want to pursue any further once you have drawn attention to them.

Von Foerster: I am concerned with inviting people to look. If you are prepared to look, you may see, but you have to look first. This is what I want to make clear.

Poerksen: What do you want to show?

Von Foerster: That it is possible to show. Whatever someone sees is up to them.

Poerksen: I do not follow.

Von Foerster: I understand. However, in many cases, unanswerability and answerlessness generate insight.

Poerksen: What you call *answerlessness,* could just as well be the chiffre of a mystic: in this space of uncertainty we might again be able to envisage something absolute and "totally different."

Von Foerster: The very attempt to understand something completely ordinary immediately confronts us with puzzles and wonders that we usually pass by and leave unnoticed in our everyday lives. Most of these cannot be explained in any serious sense; in my view, we will never be able to penetrate them and remove or even destroy their awesome quality. The knowledge we have of our world is to me like the tip of an iceberg; it is like the tiny bit of ice sticking out of the water, whereas our ignorance reaches far down into the deepest depths of the ocean. Such a claim of principled inexplicability and awesomeness undoubtedly makes me a mystic. I would be a metaphysician if I claimed to have an answer to this inexplicability.

Cybernetics And Human Knowing. Vol. 10, nos. 3-4, pp. 27-50

Action without Utility.
An Immodest Proposal for the
Cognitive Foundations of Behavior[1]

Heinz von Foerster (first order author)[2]
Karl H. Müller (second order editor)[3]

In this article, several of Heinz von Foerster's papers have been recombined in order to demonstrate that during the late sixties and seventies he has developed a grand unified theory of cognition which is far more radical, complex and encompassing than subsequent or even contemporary approaches. Furthermore, the article demonstrates that working with a series of recombinative operators one is able to generate new contents out of already published materials. Finally, as a last leitmotif, Heinz von Foerster's cognitive action program turns out to be a devastating criticism of intentional action frameworks like Rational Choice and paves the way for a most promising alternative research path.

"What is Time?"[4] According to Legend, Augustine's reply to this question was: "If no one asks me, I know: but if I wish to explain it to one that asketh, I know not." Actions have a similar quality, for if not asked we all know what actions are but when asked, we find a multiplicity of different answers.[5] However, with a minimal change of the question[6] we could have made it much easier[7] for Augustine. If asked "What's the time?" he may have observed the position of the sun and replied: "Since it grazes the horizon in the west, it is about the sixth hour after noon."

A theory of action that is worth its name must not only be able to account for Augustine's or anybody else's intelligent conduct in response to these questions, moreover, it also must be able to account for the recognition of the subtle and

---

1. HLD$_1$: This article consists of a compilation of several articles by Heinz von Foerster, namely "Memory without Record" (1965), "What Is Memory that It May Have Hindsight and Foresight as Well?" (1969), "Molecular Ethology: An Immodest Proposal for Semantic Clarification" (1970), "Responsibilities of Competence" (1972), "Cybernetics of Epistemology" (1974), "Objects: Tokens for (Eigen-)Behaviors" (1976), "For Niklas Luhmann: How Recursive is Communication?" (1993). All articles except for the first one have been reprinted in Foerster (2003). Moreover, the article has been arranged in an unusual manner. The recipe for constructing this article, i.e., the generative rules for its multi-level design, have been assembled in the footnotes. Here, one finds a mixture of high-level descriptions (HLD) of the building of this article, of low level references (LLR) on the initial Foerster-sources, of footnotes from Foerster's published articles (HvF) or of mainly contemporary references which link the Foerster-papers with contemporary discussions in the fields of cognitive science and action theory. (KHM)

2. HLD$_2$: Heinz von Foerster assumes the role of a first order author of this article, being, quite naturally, the generator of his published work.

3. HLD$_3$: Karl H. Müller (Head of WISDOM, Maria Theresienstraße 9/5, A-1090 Vienna, Austria, mueller@wisdom.at) plays the role of an editor of edited work and, thus, of a second order editor. **All new parts to this article which have become necessary due to the new context of action and action theory are printed in italics.** In order to avoid confusion, italics within the articles of Heinz von Foerster have been omitted.

4. HLD$_4$: Continuing with high level descriptions on the evolution of this article, the final version has been the result of a metamorphosis in many steps, starting with a vague plan of using Heinz von Foerster's article "Memory without Record" and of transferring its main arguments to the arena of attitude research under the working title "Attitudes without Record" up to the final version.

fundamental difference in meaning of the two questions regarding time or action of before, a distinction that is achieved by merely inserting a syntactic operator – the definite article "the" – at a strategic point in the otherwise unchanged string of symbols. At first glance it seems that to aim at a theory of action which accounts for such subtle distinctions is overambitious and preposterous. On second thought, however, we shall see that models of action that ignore such aims and merely account for habituation, adaptation and conditioning do not only fall pitiably short of explaining anything that may go on at the semantic level, but also appear to inhibit the development of notions that will eventually account for these higher functions of cerebral activity.

Since an approach that attempts to integrate the enigmatic phenomenon of action into the even more enigmatic processes of cognition veers off under a considerable angle from well established modes of thinking about this problem, it may be profitable to develop the argument carefully step by step, first exposing and circumventing some of the semantic traps that have become visible in the course of this study, and then showing that even at the possible risk of losing track of some operational details a conceptual frame work is gained which, hopefully, allows the various bits and pieces to fall smoothly into place. At this moment it appears to me that this objective may be best achieved by delivering the argument in seven short "chapters."

- In the first chapter I shall state four theses which are central to the whole argument.
- *The second chapter will bring a complexity constraint which at first sight makes it impossible to defend my theses.*
- The third chapter will be devoted to an attempt to clarify some of the most frequently used terms in discussing action, memory and related cognitive concepts.

---

5. HLD$_5$: The current design of the article takes its basic organization from the "What Is Memory"-article, switches between Chapter 1 and Chapter 2 of the "What Is Memory"-paper by starting with a set of four theses (Chapter 1), adds a small section on complexity constraints from "Memory without Record" (Chapter 2), continues with a modified version on "Clarification of Terminology" out of "What Is Memory" (Chapter 3), brings in a powerful guiding metaphor from "Memory without Record" (Chapter 4), compiles core materials on neural organization from several Foerster-articles ("What Is Memory," "Molecular Ethology," "Objects: Tokens for (Eigen-) Behaviors," "For Niklas Luhmann") (Chapter 5), brings in Heinz von Foerster's solution of the complexity constraint from "Memory without Record" (Chapter 6) and ends with a short outlook on the high relevance of the Foersterian approach towards cognition for contemporary research ("Molecular Ethology," "Cybernetics of Epistemology," "Responsibilities of Competence").

6. HLD$_6$: The final version can be seen as a transformation of a set of articles by Heinz von Foerster plus recent addenda, using a "pandemonium" (Daniel C. Dennett) of recombination operators at various levels. For a list of these recombination operators like "adding," "deleting,"" merging," "breaking," "crossing-over," etc. see Müller 2000, on the multi-level pandemonium of operators, including the "I-operator" of the second order editor, see, among others, Dennett (1991, 1996) and on the organization of creative processes via recombinations, see especially Hofstadter (1981, 1985, 1995, 1997).

7. HLD$_7$: Finally, the beginning of each chapter gives a low level reference on the main source of the specific section. A detailed account of small operational transformations would have created a vast amount of footnotes far beyond the point of readability.

- In Chapter V I shall develop these four theses in details that are commensurate with the scope of this paper.
- *Chapter VI will offer a general hint for overcoming the complexity barrier introduced in the second chapter.*
- *In Chapter VII I finally shall venture to present several conjectures regarding the implications of cognitive foundations of behaviour for action-frameworks.*

Throughout this paper I shall be using examples and metaphors as explanatory tools rather than the frightful machinery of mathematical and logical calculi. I am aware of the dangers and misrepresentations and misunderstanding that are inherent in these explanatory devices, and I shall try to be as unambiguous as my descriptive powers permit me to be.[8]

1. Four Theses ...[9]

In the stream of cognitive processes one can conceptually isolate certain components, for instance

(i) the faculty to perceive,

(ii) the faculty to remember,

(iii) the faculty to infer,

(iv) the faculty to learn,

(v) the faculty to evaluate,

(vi) the faculty to communicate, or

(vii) the faculty to move

Functional Thesis: If one wishes to isolate these faculties functionally, one is doomed to fail. Consequently, if the mechanisms that are responsible for any of these faculties are to be discovered, then the totality of cognitive processes must be considered.

Local Thesis: If one wishes to isolate these faculties locally, one is doomed to fail. Consequently, if the mechanisms that are responsible for any of these faculties are to be discovered, then the totality of cognitive processes must be considered.

---

8. HvF$_1$: I should add that my use of the term computing (from "com-putare") throughout the article literally means to reflect, to contemplate ("putare") things in concert ("com") without any explicit reference to numerical quantities. Indeed, I shall use this term in this most general sense to indicate any operation (not necessarily numerical) that transforms, modifies, rearranges, orders, and so on, observed physical entities ("objects") or their representations ("symbols").

9. LLR$_1$: The introductory part has been taken with slight modifications from "What Is Memory":101-102. (The page numbering refers—with the exception of the "Memory without Record" article—to Foerster, 2003) The summary of the seven chapters within the introduction consists of a mixture of "What Is Memory":102 and additional notes. The final paragraph in the introduction has been taken, once again, from "What Is Memory":102. The first chapter is based on "What Is Memory":105-106 plus an extension of the initial thesis.

Genetic Thesis: If one wishes to isolate these faculties genetically, one is doomed to fail. Consequently, if the genetic mechanisms that are responsible for any of these faculties are to be discovered, then the totality of genetic processes must be considered.

Epistemological Thesis: If one wishes to describe these faculties in an *external stance*, one is doomed to fail. Consequently, if the mechanisms that are responsible for any of these faculties are to be discovered, the mode of description has to change into an *internal stance*.

Before going on with a detailed defence of these four by developing an integrated model of cognition, let me briefly suggest the inseparability of these faculties on two simple examples.

First Example: If one of these seven faculties is omitted, the system is devoid of cognition.

(i)   Omit perception: the system is incapable of representing internally environmental regularities.
(ii)   Omit memory: the system has only throughput.
(iii) Omit prediction, i.e. the faculty of drawing inferences: perception generates to sensation or memory to recording.
(iv)   *Omit learning: the system is bound to a fixed modus operandi.*
(v)   *Omit evaluation: the system is incapable of selecting.*
(vi)   *Omit communication: ....*
(vii) *Omit movement: the system is incapable of acting.*

Second example: If the conceptual linkages of action with the remaining six faculties are removed one by one, "nolens volens," action degenerates to a fictitious concept that is void of any content.

2. ... and a Complexity Constraint[10]

The four theses have to be maintained, however, despite a severe complexity constraint which results from the limited powers of the genetic machinery to determine the complexity of the cognitive architecture. In order to get a quantitative assessment of the complexity constraint, let us see whether or not the information that is needed to specify just the connection structure of the nervous system – not to speak of the specifications of the operational modalities of its elements – can be genetically determined. Fortunately, there exist good estimates for the information content of the genetic program. The most careful one, I believe, is still the one made by Dancoff and Quastler (1953). From various considerations, they arrived at an upper and lower limit for the amount of uncertainty H_G in a single zygote:

$$10^5 < H_G < 10^{12}$$

---

10. *LLR$_2$: Chapter 2 comes almost completely from "Memory without Record" 1967:412-413*

In other words, the program that is supposed to define the structure is, by a factor of, say, 10^{10} off the required magnitude of 10^{20} bits/brain. This clearly indicates that the genetic code which determined far more than just the nervous system is incapable of programming nets of the unrestricted generality of the human brain.

3. Clarification of Terminology[11]

I shall now turn to a more constructive enterprise, namely to the development of a crude and—alas —as yet incomplete skeleton of cognitive processes. However, before I attempt to suggest a solution for this problem, permit me to make a few preliminary remarks on the terminology used throughout this paper.

The hierarchy of mechanisms, transformational operations and processes that lead from sensation over perception of particulars to the manipulation of generalized internal representations of the perceived as well as the inverse transformations that lead from general commands to specific actions, or from general concepts to specific utterances I shall call "Cognitive Processes." In the analysis of these processes we should be prepared to find that terms like "action," "memory," "attitudes"—as convenient as they may be for referring quickly to certain aspects of cognition—are useless as descriptors of actual processes and mechanisms that can be identified in the functional organization of nervous tissue.

Furthermore, I would like to distinguish between the terms "external description" and "internal description." I wish to associate with the term "internal description" or "internal stance" a certain invariance of building blocks which are used for the description of cognitive mechanisms and for behaviours, actions or attitudes alike. Similarly, I wish to associate with the terms "external description" or "external stance" any description of the overt manifestations of results of cognitive operations which uses descriptive elements independent from the internal vocabulary.

Finally, there are two pairs of terms that occur and re-occur with considerable frequency in discussions of action, memory and related cognitive topics. They are (i) "storage and retrieval" and (ii) recognition and recall." Unfortunately, in my opinion, they are used freely and interchangeably as if they were to refer to the same processes. Permit me, therefore, to restore their distinctive features.

On the one hand, I wish to associate with the terms "storage and retrieval" a certain invariance of quality of that which is stored at one time and then retrieved at a later time.[12] On the other hand, I wish to associate with the terms "recognition and recall" the overt manifestations of *results* of certain operations, and I wish not to

---

11. *LLR$_3$: The third chapter has been selected from "What Is Memory":102 – 105.*
12. HvF$_1$: Example: Consider Mrs. X who wishes to store her mink coat during the hot months in summer, takes this coat to the furrier for storage in his vault in spring and returns in the fall for retrieving it in time for the opening night at the opera.
   Please note that Mrs. X is counting on getting precisely her mink coat back and not any other coat, not to speak of a token of this coat. It is up to everybody's imagination to predict what would happen if in the fall her furrier would tell her "Here is your mink coat" by handing over to her a sign on which is printed "HERE IS YOUR MINK COAT."

confuse the results of these operations with either the operations themselves nor the mechanisms that implement these operations.[13]

It could be that already at this point of my exposé the crucial significance of cognitive processes may have become visible, namely to supply an organism with the operations that "lift," so to say, the information from its carriers and to provide the organism with mechanisms that allow it to compute inferences from the information so obtained.

4. A Guiding Metaphor[14]

Perhaps, I should make my position clearer by continuing with a metaphor. Let me confess that I am a man who is weak in carrying out multiplications. It takes me a long time to multiply a two or three digit number, and, moreover, when I do the same multiplication over and over again most of the time I get a different result. This is very annoying. And I wanted to settle this question once and for all by making a record of all correct results. Hence, I decided to make myself a multiplication table with two entries, one on the left (X) and one on the top (Y) for the two numbers to be multiplied and with the product (XY) being recorded at the intersection of the appropriate rows and columns.

In preparing this table I wanted to know how much paper I need to accommodate factors X, Y up to a magnitude of, say, n decimal digits. Using regular-size Type for their numbers, on double-bond sheets of 8x11 inches, the thickness D of the book containing my multiplication table for numbers up to n decimal digits, turns out to be approximately

$$D = n \cdot 10^{2n-6} \text{ cm} \tag{1}$$

For example, a 100 x 100 multiplication table ($100 = 10^2$; $n = 2$) fills a "book" with thickness

$$D = 2 \cdot 10^{4-6} = 2 \cdot 10^{-2} = 0,02 \text{ cm} = 0.2 \text{ mm} \tag{2}$$

In other words, the table can be printed on a single sheet of paper.

---

13. HvF$_3$: Example: After arrival from a flight I am asked about the food served by this airline. My answer: "FILET MIGNON WITH FRENCH FRIES AND SOME SALAD AND AN UNDEFINABLE DESSERT."

My behaviour in response to this question – I believe – appears reasonable and proper. Please note that nobody expects me to produce in response to this question a real filet mignon with French fries and some salad and an undefinable dessert.

I hope that after my previous discussion of storage and retrieval systems it is clear that my verbal response cannot be accounted for by any such system. For in order that the suspicion may arise that I am nothing but a storage and retrieval system, first the *sentence*: "FILET MIGNON WITH FRENCH FRIES AND SOME SALAD AND AN UNDEFINABLE DESSERT" had to be "read in" into my system where it is stored until a querier pushes the appropriate retrieval button (the query) whereupon I reproduce with admirable invariance of quality (high fidelity) the sentence: "FILET MIGNON WITH FRENCH FRIES AND SOME SALAD AND AN UNDEFINABLE DESSERT." However, I must ask the generous reader to take my word for it that nobody ever told me what the courses of my menu were, I just ate them.

Clearly, something fundamentally different from storage and retrieval is going on in this example in which my verbal behaviour is the result of a set of complex processes or operations which transform my past behaviours into utterances, i.e., symbolic representations of these behaviours.

14. LLR$_4$: The guiding metaphor can be found in "Memory without Record" (1967):388-390.

Now I propose to extend my table to multiplications of ten-digit numbers. This is a very modest request, and such a table may be handy when preparing one's Federal Income tax. With our formula for D, we obtain for n = 10:

$$D = 10 \cdot 10^{20-6} = 10^{15} \text{ cm} \tag{3}$$

In other words, this multiplication table must be accommodated on a bookshelf which is 10^{15} cm long, that is, about 100 times the distance between the sun and the earth or about one light day long. A librarian, moving with the velocity of light, will, on the average, require a day to look up a single entry of this table.

This appeared to me not to be a very practical way to store the information of the results of all ten-digit multiplications. But, since I needed this information very dearly, I had to look around for another way of doing this. I hit upon a gadget which is about 5 x 5 x 12 inches in size, contains 20 little wheels, each with numbers from zero to nine printed on them. These wheels are sitting on an axle and are coupled to each other by teeth and pegs in an ingenious way so that, when a crank is turned an appropriate number of times, the desired result of a multiplication can be read off the wheels through a window. The whole gadget is very cheap indeed and, on the average, it will require only 50 turns of the crank to reach all desired results of a multiplication involving two ten-digit numbers.

The answer to the question of whether I should "store" the information of a 10^{10} x 10^{10} multiplication table in the form of a 8 x 11 in book 6 million miles thick, or in the form of a small manual desk computer, is quite obvious, I think. However, it may be argued that the computer does not "store" this information but calculates each problem in a separate set of operations. My turning of the crank does nothing but give the computer the "address" of the result which I retrieve at once—without the "computer" doing anything—by reading off the final position of the wheels. If I can retrieve this information, it must have been put into the system before. But how? Quite obviously, the information is stored in the computer in a structural fashion. In the way in which the wheels interact, in cutting notches and attaching pegs, all the information for reaching the right number has been laid down in its construction code, or to put it biologically, in its genetic code.

If I am asked to construct a "brain" capable of similar, or even more complicated stunts, I would rather think in terms of a small and compact computing device instead of considering tabulation methods which tend to get out of hand quickly.

In the literature on actions, it is my feeling that people seem to argue as if a person's actions were a search process in a storehouse with gigantic tables. To stay with my metaphor, the argument seems to be whether the symbols in my multiplication table are printed in green or red ink, or perhaps in Braille, instead of whether digit-transfer in my desk-computer is carried out by friction or by an interlocking tooth.

At this point, I have to admit that, as yet, my metaphor is very poor indeed because my computer is a deterministic and rigid affair with all rules of operation a priori established. This system cannot learn by experience and, hence, it should not have been brought up in a discussion on cognitive action. I shall expand my metaphor, then, by proposing to build an actor (computer, organism, etc.) that changes its internal organization as a consequence of interaction with its environment.

5. Cognitive Tiles, Recursive Formalisms, Tesselations, Double Closures, and Inter-Actions[15]

I shall develop the design of such an adaptive unit, starting with a minimal element capable of performing cognitive operations and continuing with the basic formalisms for minimal cognitive elements or, alternatively, for "cognitive tiles." Furthermore, I shall propose guidelines for the combination of cognitive tiles or, alternatively, for the process of tessellations as well as some hints on the dual closure as a result of vertical and horizontal tessellations. Finally, I shall conclude with a design overview for high-level processes involving two or more complex adaptive actors.

5.1. Minimal Cognitive Tiles

Figure 1 is a graphical representation of the design for a minimal cognitive system in form of a block diagram. I shall call this whole system a "Cognitive Element," for it represents a minimal case of a cognitive process, or a "Cognitive Tile," for it may be used in conjunction with other such tiles to form whole mosaics—or "tessellations"— which, as a whole, permit the high flexibility in representing relational structures not only of what has been perceived but also of the symbols —the "linguistic operators"— that ultimately are to convey in natural language all that which can be inferred from what has been perceived.

---

15. LLR5: The fifth chapter has been compiled from various sources and recombined in a very long mode of recursion. Section 5.1 has been taken from "What Is Memory":119 – 121, Part 5.2 has been recombined from "Molecular Ethology":138 – 141, "Objects: Tokens for (Eigen-) Behaviors":261 – 265 and "For Niklas Luhmann":316 – 317, Sub-Chapter 5.3 has been selected from "Molecular Ethology":154 – 157 and "What Is Memory":121, Part 5.4 is a recombination of "Cybernetics of Epistemology":242 – 244 and "For Niklas Luhmann":317 - 322 and Section 5.5 comes from "Objects: Tokens for (Eigen-) Behaviors":266 – 267as well as from "For Niklas Luhmann":321 – 322.

Figure 1: A Cognitive Tile

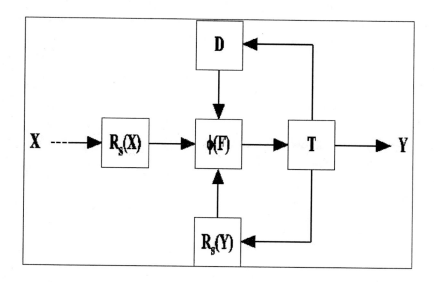

The various components of this cognitive tile are quickly explained. X stands for (external) sensory input, and Y for the output of the system as seen by an outside observer. Hence, this elementary component is a "through-put" system. However, because of its internal organization, this element is quite different from a simple stimulus-response mechanism with fixed transfer function. Sensory information X is operated on to yield relations $R_s(X)$ between observed activities with respect to the "self" (note subscript 's'), and is then used as input proper for the recursive function computer which may be operative at this moment with any of the functions F belonging to range Φ. Its output is fed back over two channels, one being the recursive loop with delay D to allow F to assess its earlier actions, the other carrying all the relational information of the system's own actions $R_s(Y)$ as they refer to "self," and operates on $\Phi(F)$ in order to set the recursive function computer straight as to this tile's internal goals.

This element incorporates all those faculties which I consider to be necessary components of cognitive processes: to perceive, to remember, to infer, to learn, to evaluate, to act. However, in this element none of these faculties can be isolated functionally: it is the interaction of all the processes here involved that "life"[16] the information from the input signal and translate it into action meaningful for this tile.[17]

5.2. Recursive Formalisms and Eigen-Values

After having introduced the building blocks of a cognitive tile, we are now prepared to define its basic operations. With due apologies to the reader who is used to

---

16. editor's note: enliven

a more extensive and rigorous treatment of this topic, these operations are two kinds and may be specified in a variety of ways.[18] The most popular procedure is first to define a "driving function" which determines at each instant the output state, given the input state and the internal state at each instant:

$$y = f_y(x, z) \tag{4}$$

Although the driving function f_y may be known and the time course of input states x may be controlled by the experimenter, the output states y as time goes on are unpredictable as long as the values of z, the internal states of the tile, are not yet specified. A large variety of choices are open to specify the course of z as depending on x, on y, or on other newly to be defined internal or external variables. The most profitable specification for the purposes at hand is to define z recursively as being dependent on previous states of affairs. Consequently, we define the "state function" f_z of the tile to be:

$$z = f_z(x^*, z^*) \tag{5a}$$

or, alternatively and equivalently

$$z' = f_z(x, z) \tag{5b}$$

that is, the present internal state of the machine is a function of its previous internal state and its previous input state; or alternatively and equivalently, the next internal machine state is a function of both its present internal and input states.

Those who are occupied with chaos theory and with recursive functions will recognize at once that these are the fundamental equations of recursive function theory. Those are the conceptual mechanisms with which chaos research is conducted; it is always the same equations over and over again. And they give rise to completely astonishing, unforeseen operational properties.

For the sake of brevity (lucidity) of the demonstration on these unforeseen operational properties, I propose to compress all that is observed—the output Y—into a single variable "Obs" and all coordinating operations by an acting unit—the relational domain of X and Z—into a single operator COORD. COORD transforms,

---

17. HvF$_4$: If forced to interpret some of this tile's functional components in terms of those conceptual components I would reluctantly give the following breakdown:

(i) Perception is accomplished by the elements that establish self-referential relations in the spatio-temporal configurations of stimuli and responses.

(ii) Memory is represented by the particular modus operandi of the central computer whose gross functional organization is determined and redetermined by evaluation of eigen-states or relations

(iii) Inference in this tile appears on three levels, depending on the type of function s, that are in range F and on the type of processes one wishes to focus on. Adductive inference is operative in the cumulative absorption of comparisons of past external and internal experiences that give rise to the functional organization of the central computer. Inductive or deductive inferences are computed by the central system concurrently with any new signal, the inferential mode being solely dependent on strings of earlier failures or successes and of some of this tile's internal dispositions to "disregard" false inductions.

(iv) Learning is accomplished by any change in the modus operandi of the cognitive tile.

(v) *Evaluation is performed through the channel T Æ Rs(Y)*

(vi) At the level of a minimal cognitive tile communication and movements are related to different types of outputs Y.

18. *KHM$_1$: It should be added that for reasons of simplicity the formalization of minimal cognitive tiles has been undertaken in a somewhat reduced form compared to the constitution of cognitive tiles as depicted in Figure 1. However, the two mutually dependent functions - driving function and state function – do form the basis in all of Heinz von Foerster's writings on non-trivial machines.*

rearranges, modifies, etc. the forms, arrangements, behaviours, etc. observed at one occasion (say, initially obs_0, and call it the "primary argument") into those observed at the next occasion, obs_1. Express the outcome of this operation through the equality:

$$obs_1 = COORD (obs_0) \qquad (6)$$

Allow the operator COORD to operate on the previous outcome to give

$$obs_2 = COORD (obs_1) = COORD (COORD(obs_0)) \qquad (7)$$

and (recursively) after n steps

$$obs_n = COORD (COORD (COORD \ldots\ldots COORD (obs_0)))\ldots. \qquad (8)$$

or by notational abbreviation

$$obs_n = COORD^{(n)} (obs_0) \qquad (9)$$

By this notational abbreviation it is suggested that also functionally (9) can be replaced by

$$obs_0 \rightarrow [\ COORD^{(n)}\ ] \rightarrow obs_n \qquad (10)$$

The remarkable feature of this expression is that it clearly shows the dependence of the present behaviour on the history of previous operations rather than on just its present state or to put this into more poetic terms, this system's present actions depend on its past experiences.

Two features should be noted here. First, no storage of representations of past events takes place here. Reference to the past is completely taken care of by the specific function that is operative. Second, an external observer who wishes to predict the behaviour of this system in terms of its input-output, revealed preference or stimulus-response pattern and who has no access to its internal structure may soon find to his dismay that he is unable to determine the elusive operator for after each experimental session the system behaves differently unless—by lucky circumstances —he finds a repeated sequence of inputs that will give him—by the very nature of that particular operator—repeatedly a corresponding sequence of outputs. In the former case, the experimenter will turn away with the remark "unpredictable," in the latter case he will say in delight "I taught it something!" and turn around to develop a theory of memory, learning, inference, action …

How can repeated sequences of behaviours enter into the recursive formalism? Let n grow without limit ($n \rightarrow \infty$):

$$obs_\infty = \qquad \lim_{n \rightarrow \infty} COORD^{(n)}(obs_0) \qquad (11)$$

or:

$$obs_\infty = COORD(COORD(COORD(COORD(COORD \ldots. \qquad (12)$$

Contemplate the above expression and note:

(i)   that the Eigen-values are discrete (even if the domain of the primary argument obs_0 is continuous). This is so because any infinitesimal perturbation $\pm\varepsilon$ from an Eigen-value Obs_i (i.e., $Obs_i \pm\varepsilon$) will disappear, as did all other values of obs, except those for which obs= Obs_i, and obs will be brought back to Obs_i (stable Eigen-value) or to another Eigen-value Obs_j (instable Eigenvalue Obs_j) In other words, Eigen-values represent equilibria, and depending upon the chosen domain of the primary argument, these equilibria may be equilibrial values

("Fixed Points"), functional equilibria, operational equilibria, structural equilibria, etc.

(ii)   that Eigen-values Obs_i and their corresponding COORD stand to each other in a complementary relationship, the one implying the other, and vice versa: there the Obs_i represent the externally observable manifestations of the (introspectively accessible) cognitive computations (operations) COORD.

(iii)   that Eigen-values, because of their self-defining (or self-generating) nature imply topological "closure" ("circularity").

The state of affairs allows a symbolic re-formulation of expression (12)

$$\lim_{n \to \infty} COORD^{(n)} \equiv COORD \qquad (13)$$

This result, that there emerge Eigen-values, is the only thing we can rely on. *It rests upon a theorem.* Among the many variants and paraphrases of this astonishing theorem I've picked Francisco Varela and Joseph Goguen's version (1979), for I believe I see an affinity here with sociological vocabulary. "In every operationally closed system there arise Eigen-behaviors." (Closure Theorem)

Let me make just a couple of more remarks about stable Eigen-behaviors. Consider the fascinating process that recursively sifts only discrete values out of a continuum of endless possibilities. Think of the operation of taking roots which lets one and only one number, namely "1," emerge from the endless domains of the real numbers. Can that serve as a metaphor for the recursiveness of the natural process, sometimes also called "evolution," in which discrete entities are sifted out of the infinite abundance of possibilities such as a fly, an elephant, even a Luhmann? I say "yes" and hope to contribute additional building blocks to the foundation of my assertion.

But consider also that although one can indeed make the inference from given operations to their Eigen-behaviors, one cannot make the converse deduction from a stable behaviour, an Eigen-behavior, to the corresponding generative operations. Therefore, the inference from the recursive Eigen-value "1" to the square root operation as the generator is not valid, because the fourth, the tenth, the hundredth root, recursively applied, yield the same Eigen-value "1." Can that serve as a metaphor for the recursiveness of the natural process, sometimes called the "laws of nature," of which there could be infinitely many versions that would explain a Milky Way, a planetary system, indeed, even a Luhmann? I say "yes" and turn for support to Wittgenstein's *Tractatus,* Point 5.1361: "The belief in the causal nexus is *the* superstition."

5.3. Tesselations

Although a cognitive tile consists of various components, I shall represent the entire tile by a single square or (rectangle): its input region denoted white, the output region black. (Figure 2a) I shall now treat this unit as an elementary computer—a computational or, alternatively, a cognitive tile T_i—which, when combined with other tiles T_j, may form a mosaic of tiles—a computational or cognitive tesselation. The operations performed by the ith tile shall be those of a finite state machine, but different letters, rather than subscripts, will be used to distinguish the two characteristic functions. Subscripts shall refer to tiles.

$$y_i = f_i\,(x_i,\,z_i) \tag{14}$$
$$z_i = g_i\,(x_i,\,z_i) \tag{15}$$

Figure 2b sketches the eight possible ways (for each of the parallel and the antiparallel case) in which two tiles can be connected.

Figure 2: Tesselations

Figure 2a: A Schematic Reduction of a Cognitive Tile to an Input (White)-Output (Black) Tile in Three Stages

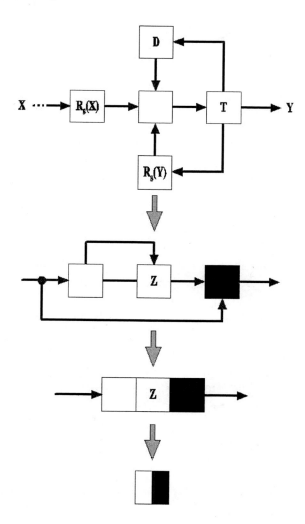

Figure 2b: Eight Elementary Forms of Tesselations for Two Cognitive Tiles [1, 2]

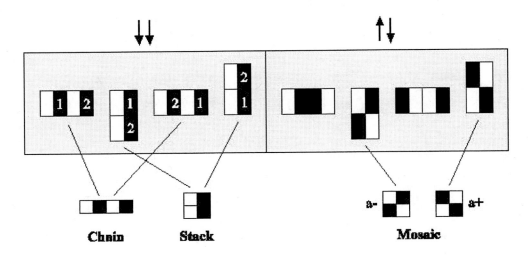

(I) Stack:	nT:	$y = \_f_i(x_i, z_i)$
(II) Chain:	T^n:	$y = f_n\,(f_{n-1}(f_{n-2}\,....(x^{(n)*}, z^{(n)*})\,...\,z^{**}{}_{n-2})z^*{}_{n-1})z_n$
(III) *Mosaic*:	$A = [a^+, a^-]$	nA^n [Stack] A^n [Chain]
	$[a^+, a^-], [a-, a+] = 0$	
	$[a^+, a^+], [a^-, a^-] \_ 0$	

Introducing a fourth elementary tessellation by connecting horizontally T → A → T, or TAT, we have

(IV) TAT $n(TA^nT)$ [Stack]

      $(TAT)^n$ [Chain]

 I shall conclude my remarks on tesselations with only a brief report on some properties as they may be relevant to this topic of aggregates of such tiles. John von Neumann (1964) was the first to realize the high computational potential of these structures in his studies of self-reproducing automata, and later Lars Löfgren (1961) applied similar principles to the problem of self-repair. We use these, however, in connection with problems of self-reference and self-representation.

 Two features of cognitive tiles permit them to mate with other tiles: one is its inconspicuous element T which translates into a universal "internal language" whatever the "output-language" may be; the other one is its essential character as a "through-put" element. Consequently, one may assemble these tiles into a tessellation, each cross white or black, corresponding to a single tile, while each square in a cross represents the corresponding functional element. Information exchange between tiles can take place on all interfaces, however, under observance of transmission rules. For instance, one tile may incorporate into its own delay loop pre-processed information from an adjacent tile, but eigen-state information of one tile cannot retroactively modify the operations of a "left" tile, although it can—via its own output—modify that of a "right" tile, and so on. When in operation, this system shifts kaleidoscopically from one particular configuration of cooperating sets of adjacent tiles to other configurations, in an ever changing dynamic mode, giving the impression of "clouds" of activity shifting, disappearing and reforming, as the task may demand.[19]

5.4. Double Closures

With the build-up of tessellation structures their functional complexity grows rapidly. One feature of these computational tessellations can be easily recognized, and this is that their operational modalities are closely linked to their structural organization. Here function and structure go hand in hand, and one should not overlook that perhaps the lion's share of computing has been achieved already when the system's topology is established. In organisms this is, of course, done mainly by genetic computation.

Remaining at the level of topology, Figure 3a reproduces a schematic overview of the organization of the nervous system. The black squares symbolize neuron bundles which can have an effect on the next bundle via spaces – a collection of synaptic gaps. The flow of signals along the bundle runs from left to right, starting with the sensitive surface and terminating in the motor surface, the changes of which are fed back via the exterior world—the "motor-sensory-synaptic gap"—to the sensory surface, thus closing the flow of signals through a circuit. A second circular flow of signals begins at the lower edge, schematizing the connection of the central nervous system with the neurohypophysis, which, in analogy to the motor surface, controls via the vascular system—the "endocrine-operational synaptic gap—the micro-environment of all synapses (shown by the minute threads in the spaces)[20]

19. KHM$_2$: Heinz von Foerster's approach on the process of tessellations is still highly intriguing. Among current versions, two programs become particularly relevant, namely William H. Calvin's hexagonal mosaics and Gerald M. Edelman's "neural groups." On the former see especially Calvin (1998), on the latter Edelman (1987, 1988 1989, 1992), Edelman and Tononi (2000) or Edelmann and Changeux (2001). On experimental evidence, see, for example, Rieke, Warland, de RuytervanSteveninck, and Bialek (1999).
20. HvF$_5$: If one, in the representation of Figure 3a, interprets the length of the edge of a square with the numbers of points of activity in the neuron bundle belonging to it, we would have had to sketch the whole system with 10^5 x 10^5 squares in order to do justice to the much larger proportion of interior compared with exterior surface. A square would then have to be represented by a point with a diameter of about 1 micron if the whole diagram were to be exactly the same size as the one given here.

Figure 3: Topology of Neural Nets

3a: A Schematic Representation in Two Dimensions

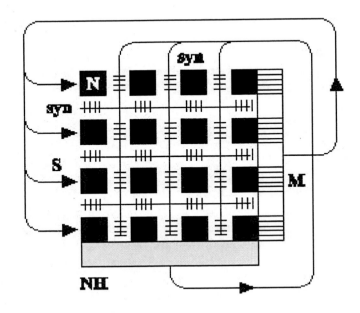

b: A Schematic Representation in Three Dimensions

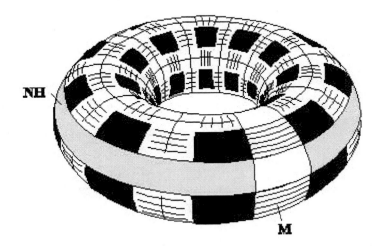

In order to express this functional scheme geometrically we can close circles of signals flowing in a right angle to one another by wrapping them around a vertical and a horizontal axis. A plane figure wrapped according to two right-angular axes is called a torus. Figure 3b shows a representation of the double closure of the stream of signals. The seam up front corresponds to the motor sensory synapric gap, the horizontal seam to the neurohypophysis.

Here, two systems — the sensory-motor system and the inner-secretoric neural system — control one another reciprocally: the operational functions of the one system become functions of the other: two recursive functors. Functors operate on a function and produce a function. Functors, too, have Eigen-values like the exponential function $y = e^x$ of the differential operator and on account of the extraordinary relationship of the exponential function to the trigonometric functions sin and cosin, sin and cosin are the Eigen-functions of the differential operator iterated fourfold.[21]

One can find the picture of double closures already in Warren McCulloch's article "A Heterarchy of Values Determined by the Topology of Neural Nets" (1945). His argument is as follows: He shows the recursion of neural activity where internal components are linked with external elements through the neural pathways via the environment. In this circuit the organization is hierarchical, for the presently external senso-motoric loops can exhibit the inner loops. He then introduces the diallels ("crossovers") that from lower circle can inhibit the upper: twofold closure. Thus, the senso-motoric and the inner-secretoric-neural circuits are organized in a double closure.[22]

5.5. Cognitive Inter-Action and Communication

Ontologically, Eigenvalues and objects, and likewise, ontogenetically, stable behaviour and the manifestation of a subject's "grasp" of an object cannot be distinguished. In both cases "objects" appear to reside exclusively in the subject's own experience of his sensori-motor coordinations, that is "objects" appear to be exclusively subjective. Under which condition, then, do objects assume "objectivity"?

Apparently, only when an actor or subject S_1 stipulates the existence of an actor or a subject, S_2, not unlike himself, who, in turn, stipulates the existence of still another subject, not unlike himself, who may well be S_1.

In this atomical social context each subject's (observer's) experience of his own sensori-motor coordination can now be referred to by a token of this experience, the "object" which, at the same time, may be taken as a token for the externality of communal space.

With this I have returned to the topology of closure where equilibrium is obtained when the Eigen-behaviors of one participant generate recursively those for the other; where one snake eats the tail of the other as if it were its own, and where cognition computes its own cognitions through those of the other.

---

21. HvF$_6$: One doesn't have to restrict oneself to mathematical expressions. Karl Menger developed these ideas for logical functions (1962), a generalization that is significant here.

22. HvF$_7$: I find that McCulloch's article on the circular organization of the nervous system is of such great significance that I'd like to draw the attention to one of its concluding sentences. "Circularities in preference instead of inconsistencies, actually demonstrate of a higher order than had been dreamed of in our philosophy. An organism possessed of this nervous system — six neurons — is sufficiently endowed to be unpredictable from any theory founded on a scale of values."

The word "inter-action," as well as "group practices," "social routines" etc. does imply the recognizability of regularities, of "invariants" in the temporal course of the social action. Here, among social scientists, one is probably not interested in whether the cosin or the sin appears as the Eigen-behavior of the system, but rather whether in a cultural domain a meeting between two members of this cultural domain is celebrated by a handshake or by a bowing.

One could even go further and be on the lookout for the emergence of invariants that arise when air is blown in a certain way through the vocal cords, whose vibrations then elicit hisses and grunt with which the meeting of two members of a cultural domain is celebrated and in the southern regions of this geographic area are heard as "Hi, y'all" and in the northern regions as "Hello there."

In all that I have said up until now I have tried to make it obvious that these invariants, these "Eigen-behaviors" arise through the recursively reciprocal effect of the participants in such an established social domain. Therefore, I'd like to turn to my proposal which can be summarized in three words: Communication is recursion. With the vocabulary developed throughout this article I can extend and sharpen this first version with a few words: Communication is the Eigen-behavior of a recursively operating actor that is doubly-closed onto itself.[23]

6. Tesselation as Solution of the Complexity Riddle[24]

At this point I would like to return to the complexity constraint introduced in the second chapter. One way out of this complexity dilemma is to assume that, de facto, only an extraordinary small amount in the structure of the nervous system is genetically specified, while the overwhelming portion is left to chance. Although the idea of leaving some space to chance-connections is not to be rejected entirely, it does not seem right to assume that only one hundredth of 1%, or less, of all neurons have specified connectivities. This assumption, for instance, would make neuroanatomy impossible, because the differences in brains would far outweigh their likenesses.

Another way out of this dilemma is to assume that the genetic code is indeed capable of programming a large variety of networks, each of which, however, involves only a small number of neurons, and each of which is repeated in parallel over and over again. Repetition of a particular structure in parallel requires very little information indeed, the only command being "Repeat this operation until stop." The

---

23. KHM$_3$: It must be noted that Heinz von Foerster's "grand unified theory of cognition" could serve as a much needed platform for a current wave of cognitive science-literature on consciousness, emotions, language and I's role in it, since for him, according to his guiding metaphor (Chapter 4), the broad stream of cognitive phenomena belongs to the computational domains and to generative computational mechanisms, should be analyzed in a bottom-up as well as context-sensitive manner, has to include, as one of its pre-requisites, the role of the observer and should lend itself to a process of self-description. For recent literature on the cerebral symphony, its deaf conductor and its blind observers, see for example, Ainslie (2001), Damasio (2003), Dennett (2003), Nørretranders (1998), Smith-Churchland (2002), Wegener (2002) or Wilson (2002).

24. LLR$_6$: The solution to the complexity riddle in Chapter 6 has been taken, like the complexity riddle itself, from "Memory without Record":413 -416.

various kinds of networks may then be stacked in the form of a cascade. In a very crude way, the appeal of this picture is that there is some resemblance to the various laminate structures that bare observed in the distribution of neurons in the outer folds of the brain. Let us see now what numbers we obtain if we assume that the whole system of parallel networks in cascade is specified by the genetic program.

I propose to consider a small elementary net that involves only 2n neurons, half of which are located in one layer, say L_1, and the other half in the adjacent layer L_2. The axons of neurons in L1 contact those in L_2, but there are no return pathways assumed in this simple model. Since the total number of neurons located in each layer is supposed to be large, say N, the complete connection scheme for the two layers is established by shifting the elementary network parallel to itself in both directions along the surface of the layers. The number of parallel networks is, thus,

$$P = N/n \tag{16}$$

Again, a connection matrix for the elementary network can be drawn with n rows and n columns, corresponding to neurons in layers L_1 and L_2, respectively, where, at the intersection of a row with a column, the absence or presence of a connection between the appropriate neuron in L_1 with a neuron in L_2 is indicated by a "zero" or a "one." Consequently, the number of nets is 2^{n2}, hence the uncertainty of this elementary network is

$$H_n = n^2 \tag{17}$$

Although P such nets are working in parallel between layers L_1 and L_2, the uncertainty for the whole network connecting these two layers is still only n2, because there is no freedom for even a single connection in any one of the P networks to change without the corresponding changes in all other nets, since their connectivity is determined by the connection matrix which functions as a genetic mould from which all P nets are cast.

I propose to assume that a different connection matrix controls the connections between the next pair of layers (L_2, L_3), and so on, in the cascade of C layers. The uncertainty of the system as a whole is, therefore,

$$H_S = nC^2 \tag{18}$$

And is assumed to be specified by the genetic code. Hence:

$$H_S = H_G \tag{19}$$

On the other hand, we have to accommodate in the whole system a totality of N* neurons which are distributed among C layers of nP neurons each:

$$N^* = nPC \tag{20}$$

Eliminating n, the number of cells in an elementary network, from the two equations above, we obtain a relation between the number of cascades and the number of parallel channels in each cascade

$$H_G = N^2 / CP^2 \tag{21}$$

or

$$P = (N^*/H_G) \cdot (1/C) \tag{22}$$

Assuming the various choices for triplets C, P, n which satisfy the above equation, it seems to me that, for an assumed genetic information of 10^8 bits/zygote, a system that, on the average, consists of 1000 layers ($C = 10^3$), each layer incorporating 30.000 elementary parallel networks ($P = 3.\ 10^4$) which involves 300 neurons each, is, in the crudest sense, a structural sketch of cortical organization which may, perhaps, not be dismissed immediately for being completely out of the question, quantitatively.

7. Conjectures[25]

I shall close with several conjectures in order to suggest that there are a variety of new avenues open of conceptualizing the grand spectacle of cognition in accordance with the initial four theses.

(i)   *There is a high propensity of falling victim to a* semantic trap which tempts one to associate with a conceptually isolable function a corresponding isolable mechanism that generates this function. This temptation seems to be particularly strong when our vocabulary suggests a variety of conceptually separable higher mental faculties as, for instance, "to learn," "to remember," "to perceive," "to recall," "to predict," etc. The hopelessness of a search for mechanisms that represent these mechanisms in isolation has a purely semantic basis. Memory, for instance, contemplated in isolation is reduced to "recording," learning to "change," perception to "input," action to "output," and so on. In other words, in separating these functions from the totality of cognitive processes one has abandoned the original problem and is now searching for mechanisms that implement entirely different functions which may or may not have any semblance to some processes that are subservient to the maintenance of the integrity of the organism as a functioning unit. *Thus, the semantic trap lures persistently into a substitution of an internal-unified mode of description by an external-isolationist mode.*

(ii)   *My theses on the four-fold unity of cognitive processes lead almost naturally to a new and most prominent role for partial and total ignorance with respect to cognitive mechanisms.* Consider, for example, the two conceivable definitions for memory:
(a) An organism's potential awareness of past experiences
(b) An observed change of an organism's response to like sequences of events.
          While definition A postulates a faculty (memory$_A$) in an organism whose inner experiences cannot be shared by an outside observer, definition B postulates the same faculty (memory$_B$) to be operative in the observer only — otherwise *she* could not have developed the concept of "change" — but ignores this faculty in the organism under observation, for an observer cannot "in principle" share the organism's inner experience. *Like in the tale of the emperor's new suit, behavioral sciences have tailored a huge amount of*

---

25. LLR$_7$: The final conjectures have been compiled from "Molecular Ethology":135-136, "Cybernetics of Epistemology":231, "Responsibilities of Competence":195-196, "Molecular Ethology":136, "Cybernetics of Epistemology" 236-240, "Objects: Tokens for (Eigen-) Behaviors":267.

conceptual clothes pretending to hide this dual ignorance without overcoming it. Recapitulating, once again, the cognitive architecture from Chapter 5, the level of ignorance for behavioural mechanisms is always considerably higher than the conventional wisdom of behavioral scientists. [26]

(iii)   In the same spirit, my next point deals with the structure of a complete and closed theory of the brain. If someone deals with this problem she will, without any doubt, use her brain. This observation is at the basis for my next working hypothesis: The laws of physics, the so-called "laws of nature" can be described by us. The laws of cognitive functions—or even more generally—the laws of biology must be written in such a way that the writing of these laws can be deduced from them, i.e., they have to write themselves.

(iv)   Phrased differently, a theory of the brain T(B) must be written by a brain: B(T). This means that this theory must be constructed so as to write itself: T(B(T)). Such a theory will be distinct in a fundamental sense from, say, physics since the observer is supposed to have a necessary place in it. A science of the brain in the sense of T(B(T)) is, I claim, indeed a legitimate science with a legitimate problem. *Moreover, experimental designs and test theories have to be modified substantially in order to be able to bring to light the generative cognitive mechanisms.*

(v)   Turning to new experimental designs, it is possible to establish, once and for all, the proposition that the motorium provides the interpretation for the sensorium and that the sensorium provides the interpretation for the motorium. The basis for this experiment lies in the common experience that it is extremely difficult, perhaps impossible, to squeeze oneself into the fourth dimension. No matter how much we stretch and twist, we remain stuck in the all-too-well-known three dimensions. The experiment requires a setting where hardly perceivable four-dimensional objects can also be grasped which means that they can be touched and handled. Thanks to friendly computers (which do not know of any dimensionality), the experiment can be carried out by giving to a test person manipulators which are online with a fast computer. According to the position of the manipulators, the computer computes two related two-dimensional projections of a four-dimensional body on the screen of a picture

---

26.   *KHM$_4$: In the light of the preceding discussion, the state of neural ignorance in a wide array of action approaches seems almost perfect. Simply consider the subsequent range of definitions of what attitudes are supposed to be. Attitudes (for an overview, see, e.g., Aiken, 2002) are conceptualized as*
an internal state (!) which affects (!!!) an individual's choice (!) of action toward some object, person or event" (Gagne/Briggs, 1974:62)
a relatively enduring organization of beliefs (!) around (!!!) an object or situation predisposing (!!!) one to respond (!!!) in some preferential (!) manner (Rokeach, 1968:112)
tendencies (!!!) to evaluate (!) an entity(!!!) with some degree (!!!) of favour or disfavour, ordinarily expressed (!) in cognitive, affective and (!!!) behavioural (!) responses" (Eagly/Chaiken, 1993:155)
a frame of reference (!) for organizing (!) information (!!!) about the world ..., attaining rewards and avoiding punishment ...., managing (!) emotional conflicts ...., expressing one's sense (!) of self (!!!), personal values (!), or (!!!) identity (!) ...., viewing oneself as being consistent (!!) ... and distinguishing (!) oneself from other people in a social group (Ostrom, 1994:116)

tube which—viewed by a person through a stereoscope—can be seen as three-dimensional projections of this body floating in space. The test person can control, via two manipulators with three degrees of freedom, the projections appearing on the screen whereby the right hand controls the three rotations in the xy, xz, and yz planes of our space, and the left hand the three in the fourth dimension, namely wx, wy, wz. As a conjecture, I expect that the realization that these strangely changing entities are nothing but the projections of one and the same object should be normally gained within 20-40 minutes if test persons themselves are permitted to use the manipulators compared to four to eight hours of sessions if it is the instructor who works with the manipulators.

(vi)   Through further developing the apparatus, the experiment should show, as another conjecture, the importance of motor-sensory correlation for the processes of cognition even more clearly: entry into the fourth dimension could be carried out via senso-motoric contractions of the muscles of the neck, the arm, or the upper part of the leg, i.e., through motor-participation not showing 3D, but only 4D consequences.

(vii)   As a concluding conjecture, I shall turn to traditional theories of action and their action schemes[27] in general and to the Rational Choice-paradigm (RC) in particular[28], currently the most prominent representative in the field of action theory and action schemes. RC can be considered as the prime offender of my initial four theses. It cannot be projected or transferred to the neural realm, neither from its composition nor from its formalisms. From the viewpoint of neural composition it is easy to see that the building blocks of an RC-action scheme miss most of the necessary elements of minimal cognitive tiles. The input domain is extremely reduced, the state composition is absent, memory and inference play no relevant roles. In terms of formalisms, the Rational Choice approach lacks the core ingredients for neural operations, namely recursion and dynamic closures. In a strong sense, the RC-formalism presupposes, aside from perfect amnesia, a perfect correspondence between evaluation results and action. Seen with the guiding metaphor in Chapter 4, the RC-formalism resembles much too much a storing device and a storehouse concept of cognitive action.

With these conjectures I have returned to the topology of closure where cognition computes its own cognitions through those of the *reader*.[29]

---

27. KHM$_5$: On action schemes, see, for example, Bunge (1999), Dretske (1988), Holland (1995, 1998), Kauffman (2000), Rescher (1994, 1998), Schank and Abelson (1977), or Schank and Kass (1994). On constructivist approaches towards action, see, e.g., Müller (1991 or 2002).

28. *KHM$_6$: RC-action schemes are, following Gary Becker, based on the following building blocks: "The combined assumptions of maximizing behavior, market equilibrium, and stable preferences, used relentlessly and unflinchingly, form the heart of the economic approach as I see it." (Becker, 1990: 5) Not only that, RC-action schemes are able, still following Becker, to shed new light on many non-economic processes like marriage, fertility, and the family (ibid., 169ff.), or on social interactions (ibid., 251ff.).*

29. KHM$_7$: This sentences concludes the list of footnotes.

References

Aiken, L. R. (2002). *Attitudes and related psychosocial constructs. Theories, assessments, and research*. Thousand Oaks, CA: Sage Publications.

Ainslie, G. (2001). *Breakdown of will*. Cambridge: Cambridge University Press.

Becker, G. S. (1990). *The economic approach to human action*. Chicago: Chicago University Press.

Bunge, M. (1999). *The sociology-philosophy connection. With a foreword by Raymond Boudon*. New Brunswick, NJ: Transaction Publishers.

Calvin, W. H. (1998. *The cerebral code. Thinking a thought in the mosaics of mind*. Cambridge: The MIT Press.

Damasio, A. (2003). *Looking for Spinoza. Joy, sorrow, and the feeling brain*. London: William Heinemann.

Dancoff, S. M., & Quastler, H.(1953). The information content and error rate of living things. In H. Quastler (Ed.), *Information theory in biology* (pp. 263-273). Urbana, IL: University of Illinois Press.

Dennett, D. C. (1991). *Consciousness explained*. Boston: Little Brown.

Dennett, D. C. (1995). *Darwin's dangerous idea. Evolution and the meanings of life*. New York: Simon and Schuster.

Dennett, D. C. (2003). *Freedom evolves*. London: Allen Lane, The Penguin Press.

Dretske, F. (1988). *Explaining behavior. Reasons in a world of causes*. Cambridge, MA: The MIT Press.

Eagly, A. H., & Chaiken, S. L. (Eds.) (1993). The psychology of attitudes. Fort Worth, TX: Harcourt Brace Jovanovich.

Edelman, G. M. (1987). *Neural Darwinism. The theory of neural group selection*. New York: Basic Books.

Edelman, G. M. (1988). *Topobiology. An introduction to molecular embryology*. New York: Basic Books.

Edelman, G. M. (1989). *The remembered present. A biological theory of consciousness*. New York: Basic Books.

Edelman, G. M. (1992). *Bright air, brilliant fire. On the matter of the mind*. New York: Basic Books.

Edelman, G., & Tononi, G. (Eds.) (2000). *A universe of consciousness. How matter becomes imagination*. New York: Basic Books.

Edelman, G. M., & Changeux, J. P. (Eds.) (2001). *Brain*. New Brunswick, NJ: Transaction Publishers

Foerster, H. v. (1967, orig. 1965). Memory without record. In: J. C. Eccles, L. Kruger, H. Hyden *et al.*, *The anatomy of memory. Learning, remembering, and forgetting* (2nd ed., pp. 388-433). Palo Alto, CA: Science and Behavior Books.

Foerster, H. v. (1969). What is memory that it may have hindsight and foresight as well? In S. Bogoch (Ed.), *The future of the brain sciences* (pp. 19-64). New York: Plenum Press.

Foerster, H. v. (1970). Molecular ethology: An immodest proposal for semantic clarification. In G. Ungar, *Molecular Mechanisms in Memory and Learning*. New York: Plenum Press.

Foerster, H. v. (1972). Responsibilities of competence. *Journal of Cybernetics, 2*, 1-6.

Foerster, H. v. (1974). Cybernetics of epistemology. In W. D. Keidel, W. Handler, & M. Spring (Eds.), *Kybernetik und Bionik* (pp. 27-46). München: Oldenburg.

Foerster, H. v. (1976/2003). Objects: Tokens for (eigen-)behaviors. (Paper presented on occasion of Jean Piaget's 80th birthday at the University of Geneva on June 29, 1976. Reprinted in Foerster, 2003, pp. 261-271.)

Foerster, H. v. (1993). For Niklas Luhmann: How recursive is communication? (R. Howe, Trans.). *Teoria Sociologica, 2*, 61-88.

Foerster, H. v. (2003). *Understanding understanding. Essays on cybernetics and cognition*. New York: Springer.

Gagné, R. M., & Briggs, J. L. (1974). *Principles of instructional design*. New York: Holt, Rinehart & Winston.

Goguen,J., & Varela, F. (1979). Systems and distinctions: Duality and complementarity. *International Journal of General Systems, 5*, 31-43.

Hofstadter, D. R. (1982). *Gödel, Escher, Bach. An eternal golden braid* (4th ed.). Harmondsworth: Penguin.

Hofstadter, D. R. (1985). *Metamagical themas. Questing for the essence of mind and matter*. New York: Basic Books.

Hofstadter, D. R. (1995). *Fluid concepts and creative analogies. Computer models of the fundamental mechanisms of thought*. New York: Basic Books.

Hofstadter, D. R. (1997). *Le ton beau de Marot. I praise of the music of language*. New York: Basic Books.

Holland, J. H. (1995). *Hidden order. How adaption builds complexity*. Reading: Addison Wesley.

Holland, J. H. (1998). *Emergence. From chaos to order*. Reading: Addison-Wesley.

Kauffman, S. (2000). *Investigations*. Oxford: Oxford University Press.

Löfgren, L (1961). *Kinematic and Tesselation models of self-repair*. TR 8. Contract NONR 1834(21). University of Illinois: Electrical Engineering Research Laboratory Engineering Experiment Station.

McCulloch, W. S. (1945/1988). A heterarchy of values determined by the topology of neural nets. In W. S. McCulloch, *Embodiments of Mind* (pp. 40-45). Cambridge, MA: The MIT Press. (Originally published 1945)

Menger, K. (1959). Gulliver in the land without one, two, three. *Mathematical Gazette, 43*, 241-250.

Menger, K. (1962). Function algebra and propositional calculus. In M. C. Yovits, G. T. Jacobi, G. D. Goldstein (Eds.), *Self-Organizing Systems (pp. 525-532)*. Washington, D.C: Spartan Books.

Müller, K. H. (1991). Elementare Gründe und Grundelemente für eine konstruktivistische Handlungstheorie. In P. Watzlawick & P. Krieg (Eds.), *Das Auge des Betrachters. Beiträge zum Konstruktivismus. Festschrift für Heinz von Foerster (pp. 209-246)*. München: Piper.

Müller, K. H. (2000). Wie Neues entsteht. *Österreichische Zeitschrift für Geschichtswissenschaften, 1*, 87-128.

Müller, K. H. (2002). On socio-economic embeddedness. In R. J. Hollingsworth, K. H. Müller, & E. J. Hollingsworth (Eds.), *Advancing socio-economics. An institutionalist perspective* (pp. 59-81). Lanham, MD: Rowman & Littlefield.

Neumann, J. v. (1964). The theory of automata: Construction, reproduction and homogeneity. In A. Burks (Ed.), *John von Neumann's Collected Works* (pp 1-49). Urbana, IL: University of Illinois Press.

Nørretranders, T. (1998). *The user illusion: Cutting consciousness down to size.* Harmondsworth, UK: Penguin Books.

Ostrom, T. M. (1994). Attitude theory. In R. J. Corsini (Ed.), *Encyclopedia of psychology* (2nd ed. pp. 116-118). New York: John Wiley.

Rescher, N. (1994). *Philosophical standardism. An empiricist approach to philosophical methodology.* Pittsburgh, PA: University of Pittsburgh Press.

Rescher, N. (1998). *Complexity. A philosophical overview.* New Brunswick, NJ: Transaction Publishers.

Rieke, F., Warland, D., de RuytervanSteveninck, R., & Bialek, W. (1999). *Spikes. Exploring the neural code.* Cambridge, MA: The MIT Press.

Rokeach, M. (1968). *Beliefs, attitudes, and values. A theory of organization and change.* San Francisco: Jossey-Bass.

Schank, R. C., & Abelson, R. (1977). *Scripts, plans, goals, and understanding. An inquiry into human knowledge structures.* Hillsdale, NJ: Lawrence Erlbaum Associates.

Schank, R. C., & Kass, A. (1994). *Inside case-based explanation.* Hillsdale, NJ: Lawrence Erlbaum Associates.

Smith-Churchland, P. (2002). *Brain-wise. Studies in neurophilosophy.* Cambridge, MA: The MIT Press.

Wegner, D. M. (2002). *The illusion of conscious will.* Cambridge, MA: The MIT Press

Wilson, T. D. (2002). *Strangers to ourselves. Discovering the adaptive unconscious.* Cambridge, MA: The Belknap Press of Harvard University Press.

View From Rattlesnake Hill
Frank Galuszka. Oil

Cybernetics And Human Knowing. Vol. 10, no. 2, pp. 51-65

Between the lines:
The part-of-the-world-position of Heinz von Foerster

Monika Bröcker[1]

My voice tells me: "That is how it all is." And the echo of my voice tells me: "That is how you are."
Antonio Porchia

Heinz von Foerster was a wonderful loving and caring friend and teacher to me. I learned a lot from him. During our numerous conversations it was especially fascinating for me to learn about what was most central and implicit in all his actions, namely his position of considering himself as part of the world. This position shall be illustrated by the following slightly edited extracts of our book that resulted from our conversations: *Part of the World. Fractals of Ethics – A Drama in Three Acts.*[2]

Implicitness

Heinz

As you know, it is for me of decided importance to separate ethics from morality once and for all. Morality, as you will remember, is characterized by two points for me. The first being that every statement, every rule, every law of morality is directed at the other. The Decalogue is a good example: "Thou shalt not kill," "Thou shalt not covet thy neighbor's wife," et cetera. The second point being that the authorities, who postulate these laws, are themselves not subject to these laws.

The self-organizing nature of the first point is clear, for in a society in which murders are committed continually, one wants to protect oneself from such a fate and therefore states, "Thou shalt not kill." Similarly, if every husband must fear that his neighbors want to sleep with his wife, he wants to put an end to this nonsense by saying "Thou shalt not ...," et cetera, et cetera. The second point, the independence of the lawmakers from their laws, has its origin in the attempt to enforce obedience to the law through threats of punishment. ...

If you were to read the tons of literature that have been written about ethics in the last decades, you would soon be agreeing with Wittgenstein: "It is clear that ethics cannot be articulated." But that only shows that I am not the only one who has difficulties in speaking about ethics. Due to the impossibility of describing it,

---

1. Monika Bröcker holds a Masters of Science degree in Communication. She is a freelance scientist, author, business consultant, trainer and coach. She was trained at the Brief Therapy Center of the Mental Research Institute in Palo Alto, California and at the Brief Therapy Family Center in Milwaukee, Wisconsin. From 1998-2002 she worked intensively with Heinz von Foerster in Pescadero, California. Currently she is working on her Ph.D. Her main research interests are cybernetics, constructivism, ethics, systemics, family therapy and the theory and practice of learning organizations. Monika can be reached at hvf@earthlink.net.
2. Teil der Welt. Fraktale einer Ethik. Ein Drama in drei Akten. Carl-Auer-Systeme Verlag, Heidelberg, 2002. Translated into English by Barbara Anger-Díaz. We intend to publish the American version of the book shortly.

numerous attempts at speaking about ethics have failed. I would like to avoid such an attempt.

Instead, a little experience: Many years ago Mony Elkaïm, a lively family therapist, full of ideas, invited me to a New York hospital to tell other therapists something about constructivism. I had prepared myself nicely, had printed out enough handouts for the participants and arrived punctually early in the morning at the lecture hall agreed upon. Mony Elkaïm introduced me and said: "Ladies and gentlemen, here we have the pleasure of hearing Heinz von Foerster, who, I am sure, prepared himself very nicely for the topic of constructivism. But permit me now to express a particular curiosity of mine, and to ask Heinz von Foerster a personal question: "Dear Heinz, do tell me: What do you devote yourself to with particular intensity at this time?" I was taken by surprise. I was quite unprepared for something like that and thought for a moment. Then I heard myself say the following: "The problem that I concern myself with now, in all my conversations, whether they are about science or therapy, or whether they are private conversations, is that of learning the art of mastering my own language, so that ethics is implicit." Whereupon everyone laughed and said: "What do you mean by that?" I did not know either, what I had meant by that, and said: "I simply do not want to articulate ethics. Ethics must be implicit; as if one read between the lines, but not in the lines."

That was the moment in which I had made the idea of an implicit ethic clear to myself for the first time. That is where it struck me for the first time that the problem of articulating ethics had to do with the limits of language or with the structure of language, or with the way in which language functions. And later I remembered a very beautiful statement by Wittgenstein. It bears the number 4.121. "What expresses itself *in* language, we cannot express *through* it."

"What expresses *itself* in language, *we* cannot express through it."
Ludwig Wittgenstein

That means that when I say something, something else comes along with it; and that other thing that comes along, I cannot express through the mere use of language. Well, maybe if I translate it into musical terms: "Whatever we can express in music, does not lend itself to being expressed through music." Perhaps if I take the idea of the poem, for instance this beautiful Goethe poem:

Wanderer's Song at Night II
Calm is over all the hill-tops, in all the tree-tops you can hardly feel a breath.
The little birds are hushed in the wood. Wait, soon you will be calm too.

In only a few words it speaks of calm; however, some other things express themselves along with it.

So that is what I mean when I say: "Ethics is implicit in what I say."

I consider that to be a very important insight. "What expresses itself in language, we cannot express through it." That means that I did not just say: "Calm is over all the hill-tops," but by having drawn upon these hill-tops, I created the image of calm. That is not in the language, for language consists only of these words. Something there is not expressed through language itself, but rather, through my speaking, these things occur.

There is a second example that might be of interest. That is the famous Erickson method. Milton Erickson was capable of speaking two languages at the same time. One of them being normal language. There he engaged with the patient: How was he doing; how was the trip; was everything all right at home. Quite normally he asked: "Did you get here okay? Did the bus take the correct route?" et cetera, et cetera. Now he put accents onto different words, either with a movement of the eye, with a nod of the head, with a wave of the hand, or with any other gesture, so that suddenly one word became emphasized. These words, put together, made up a new sentence. That was the second language with which he could talk to his patients. There he could make statements that he would not have been able to make at all through the use of normal language. Perhaps sentences expressing a kind of privacy, intimacy, depth. So here I have a comparison: That through speaking and emphasizing different points one can say something that later on one cannot say again merely through language. Or the matter of reading between the lines: That is exactly what I mean.

I use Wittgenstein's metaphor in order to give expression to the difficulty one has with ethics; namely, that in the statements one now wishes to use to speak about ethics, ethics is not contained at all. Ethics is to be found between the lines and must then be interpreted by the hearer. So the difficulty of speaking about ethics lies within the limits of language. I just remembered that perhaps the best analogy to the problem of speaking about ethics appears in Chinese philosophy, where they have the difficulty of speaking about the Tao. ...

Metaphysics

Part of my position is that metaphysics be given a solid and clearly visible grounding, and that metaphysics not be continually thrown out of the window because of many people's misuse of it for the sake of selling ideas otherwise unmarketable. ...

Monika
How did you come upon the idea that metaphysics plays a role in ethics? Where does the term come from?

Heinz
It is this matter of "in principle undecidable." Without noticing it, we constantly decide questions that are in principle undecidable. That is why people always get into each other's hair, for everyone claims "I am right." Very few people see that there exists a freedom when one gives an answer to in principle unanswerable, undecidable questions; that you make a decision when you decide either so, so, so or so. Many people do not even notice that they have made a decision. And therefore they think

that they possess the real truth. They did not notice that there was a freedom in deciding the game that they want to play from now on.

Monika

But what do the undecidable questions have to do with metaphysics? Where is the bridge?

Heinz

I call the human activity, in which we decide undecidable questions, a metaphysical activity. Namely, I give the name of metaphysics to that activity by which people, for some reason that they cannot articulate, decide undecidable questions. The interesting thing is that we have such undecidable questions. Well, how come? Why do we have that? That could only have come about through language. Only language produces such questions as: "For God's sake, how can I decide now?" Suddenly one is pinched by a difficulty that could only have been generated by language; because I pose a question, which, upon closer contemplation, is undecidable.

Monika

And what is language? What do you mean by language?

Heinz

There you can take language to mean all sorts of things. I now use language as if we were talking; as if we knew, what language is. For the trick is: at the very moment at which I go to define language, I already make the assumption that language is something known, since, after all, I am defining it with language.

Monika

Undecidable questions—where does this distinction come from?

Heinz

What is your problem with respect to undecidable questions?

Monika

My problem is: From where…? Who for the first time said, that there are undecidable questions, as opposed to decidable questions? Which questions fall into the category of questions that in your opinion are undecidable? What questions are decidable? Or is it that perhaps all questions are undecidable?

Heinz

Quite possible. I am not an academician. An academician could probably research the problem of the decidability of questions in much greater depth. I only know from my own education when it was that I first came upon the decidability of questions. And that was in the discussion about propositions within an axiomatic system; whether they can be decided; whether they can be deduced from the axioms or not. The game is a real chess game, or Chinese checkers, or Bridge. You come up with a bunch of statements, all of which you believe to be semantically independent. These statements are the rules for the game. In philosophy one calls them "axioms."[3] One has a group of axioms then, from which certain propositions can now be developed. Euclid, for example, was able to develop the entire plain geometry with his five axioms. Incredible, what that man was able to see there! This game was so contagious, that people began to ask: "Can we use that for other domains as well?"

My story now is the following—the academic story might well look very different—my story is that the philosophers of the 19th century, who concerned themselves with the formalization of logic, engaged in similar experiments and built axiomatic systems, with the help of which one can deduce, whether any given proposition is decidable or not.

Deciding turns out to be as follows: Can I declare a proposition, which occurs in such and such a logical context, as a valid deduction from the five, six or ten axioms at hand? If I can do so, it becomes a decidable proposition. Then I can show whether it is false or true. The question is: Can certain propositions, which I now invent, be proven to be true or false within this axiomatic system? Can I decide, whether I can come down from the big system of axioms to this proposition and say: "Yes, I can say it is true or false"?

Russell believed that he had developed a logical system, in which all propositions that you can make are in fact deducible. That is, you can state that they are false or true. Whereupon Kurt Gödel, a young lad from Vienna, said: "Dear Berti, you are mistaken! Within your gigantic machine, the Principia Mathematica, there are propositions that you cannot deduce from your system. That is to say, there are nondeducible propositions in the system." That is the famous Gödel Proof.

So this game of axiomatization, decidability, deducibility, et cetera, fascinated me. Already as a young man of fifteen, sixteen, seventeen I found these questions interesting, and there I noticed: "But Heinzerl, what your mother says about spinach is just as undecidable as what Gödel says about Russell. It is not that complicated at all. How does she know that spinach is good? Because she likes spinach? Yet she says: 'Spinach is good.' I don't like it at all. Now, how can one decide, whether spinach is good or not?" There it was that I saw: "It is an in principle undecidable question." Of course one might say: "I ask 100,000 people; 52,200 people say 'it is good', 37,000 say 'it is bad', and the remaining don't know whether it is good or bad." Then one can say: "For this reason I have now decided. Because I have invented a rule for a game according to which one can decide, whether spinach is good or bad." But already

---

3. Heinz explains how the definition of an axiom was altered by the philosophers of the Vienna Circle: "According to the classical perception, [axioms] are usually statements that neither require nor are capable of an explanation. This original perception of axioms changed over time. I was particularly influenced by the philosophers of the Vienna Circle, who said: 'Axioms are not statements, that neither require nor are capable of proof. Axioms are rules of a game that one invents, that one puts on the table, as if one were to play chess or bridge, and that one then follows.'"

when I was very small I noticed that I was constantly hit over the head with undecidable questions, of which I could say: "But Uncle So-and-so, that cannot be decided at all." So already as a small child Heinz was a disgusting pest. I retained this pest-like quality until I became a great professor and had to utter clever stuff.

Monika
That is just like our continual discussions about the soup.

Heinz
Exactly. Look, several times already you have pointed to my strange formulation: "This soup is good." And there you say: "Well, why? The soup is not good at all. You like it." And I said: "That's right." "Well, but then you cannot say, that the soup is good. For when you maintain that 'the soup is good', and I do not like it, I either feel bad or think that your taste nerve is wrong. Then we fight about whether the soup is good or bad. However, when you say: 'I like the soup' no one can counter that. Suddenly you avoid a clash, a disturbance."

Monika
And the undecidable questions lead you to two main questions: "Am I a part of the universe?" and …

Heinz
No, that does not lead there, but rather, is a position, that I consider to be a good point of entry for this sort of question. That is a completely personal strategic idea, as with chess: Which are the first moves? And there one usually moves the pawn out of the first row from d2 to d4. One could, of course, jump with the knight and make an opening by means of the knight. In many instances I find the opening easy when I first say: "There are undecidable questions. And now, ladies and gentlemen, just watch: If we make a decision regarding this question—namely, whether I am a part of the world or not—totally different positions evolve." And what I always find surprising is that people make a decision regarding this undecidable question, without noticing that they are doing so.

I call this domain, where one does not know as yet: "Should I accept this or that as my position?" metaphysics. I call that human being a metaphysicist, who consciously says: "I know that I have this choice before me. I make the decision. For example, I am an observer, who looks at the world through a peephole, and reports what he sees there." Or: "I don't possess a peephole. I am a part of the world. Whatever I do, I do to the world, and whatever the world does, it does to me." To decide who is right is total nonsense. One could, of course, play a game: Design experiments that shall decide, whether the peephole man or the fellow man, i.e., the one who plays along, who takes part, is right. I, however, maintain that the answer to this question is already contained in the experiment. Therefore I maintain that experiments that are supposed to decide independently of this decision do not exist. …

My own interpretation, independent of all philosophers, is: I, Heinz von Foerster, know what a metaphysicist is: one who decides for himself questions that are in principle undecidable.

Monika
But then everyone is a metaphysicist.

Heinz
That is what I claim! Without knowing it, we are all metaphysicists. I point out to my friends that when they, unbeknownst to themselves, make decisions about in principle undecidable questions, they become metaphysicists, whether they want to or not. ...

Togetherness and Circularity

Contemplate the human with the human,
and you will see the dynamic duality,
the human essence, together:
here is the giving and the receiving,
here the aggressive and the defensive power,
here the quality of searching and of responding,
always both in one, mutually complementing in alternating action,
demonstrating together what it is: human.
Now you can turn to the single one
and you recognize him as human for his potential of relating.
We may come closer to answering the question "What is human?"
when we come to understand him as the being in whose dialogic,
in his mutually present two-getherness,
the encounter of the one with the other is realized and recognized at all times.
Martin Buber

Again and again, Martin Buber brought to our attention the circumstance that I actually only come about, originate, in the "you." The moment I say "you," I become "I."

I become aware of myself through the existence of the other. Being together, togetherness is what makes for the human condition. Only through reciprocity, through being with one another, two-getherness, as Buber always calls it, am I actually born. ...

Monika
And how is that related to ethics?

Heinz
Whenever we speak about something that has to do with ethics, the other is involved. If I live alone in the jungle or in the desert, the problem of ethics does not exist. It only comes to exist through our being together. Only our togetherness, our being together,

gives rise to the question: "How do I behave with the other, so that we can really always be one?"

Monika
Doesn't the question, "How do I behave towards myself?" ever come up?

Heinz
No. I only am through the other. When I accept that, the other becomes "I." Perhaps that is understandable!?

Monika
Yes. How does this ethical position grow out of a cybernetic or a cognitive theoretical basis?

Heinz
I have the feeling that it is like a round dance, where some dancers reach out to one another and dance around in a circle. And there you can name these dancers: One of them is Cybernetics, the other's name is Ethics, the other is Cognition, the other I, the other You, Anyone. These are mutually-created perspectives, that mutually support each other, and that by contemplating, thinking, feeling, help us find a leading thread in this incredibly fascinating, almost impenetrable world. Certain positions or views are then called cybernetics. And in my opinion, cybernetics fits in very well, for in my feeling circularity, which serves as the basis for cybernetics, always emerges in these phenomena.

As soon as I speak of "you," that you, as well, speaks of "you" about me. Then I am the other's "you." These contemplations always entail circularity. Therefore, one could avail oneself of cybernetics, which has circularity as its basis; as a possibility for language to come to terms with these phenomena. Even cognition emerges, as has been found out, not only through my looking, but also through my acting. ...

The Logic of Change

The recommendation that I would make regarding change is that change essentially consists of descriptions of conditions. That is, one description of the condition and the second description of the condition are different; and it is that difference that I regard as change. That is to say, change does not reside where one thinks it does, but it is where one describes it. In my play, change is a problem of description. The main problem of change is that one says: "X is no longer the same," that is "X is not X." From a logical point of view, that is totally crazy. Why is X not X? One actually wants to say: "Suddenly X is different."

So the question is: Did X change or did my description of X change? It is my recommendation, that the point of view that it is a matter of description be accepted. For if I don't accept the position of description, but rather, the position that change has taken place with X, I come upon contradictions and paradoxes, since I cannot claim that X is no longer X. It's nonsense. Change manifests itself in the descriptions. The question, whether or not X is now different, no longer comes up.

A joke that illustrates that goes as follows: Two people meet. One says: "Hello, Mr. Müller, how changed you are." Whereupon the other says: "Well, my name isn't Müller at all." "Oh, so your name is no longer Müller either?" In my opinion, that is an important illustration of what we call "change."

The second question is: "Why is what I now see as different, the same? Mr. Müller now has a stroke. Before the stroke, he is such and such. After the stroke he is different. Is he still Mr. Müller? Is he someone else? This kind of problematic is eerie.

So I would always like to see the problem of change from the point of view of description. ...

Chuang Tzu, the Chinese Taoist in the fourth century B.C., had a beautiful parable: "The essence of change is constancy."

Monika
Would you elucidate that?

Heinz
The odd thing, what is paradoxical about change, transformation, is that one believes that one is talking about the same that is now different. Why is the same different? That is a paradoxical situation, for we still claim: "It is the same." So the strange thing is that I compare a condition, which I now see, with a condition that I remember having seen before. That is, I compare two inner images: One image that I believe to have seen before with another image, which I believe to have seen now. These two images are descriptions. It now depends completely on me, what parts of these descriptions I can no longer agree with. The chair is no longer a chair, but an elephant. The elephant is no longer an elephant, but a camel, et cetera, et cetera.

The idea behind this saying of Chuang Tzu is that one always believes that it is the same thing of which one speaks. If I say of something, "It has changed," I assume that we are talking about the same thing. I say: "Mr. Meier is very different now"; assume, therefore, that it is still Mr. Meier and has not suddenly turned into Mr. Müller, after Mr. Meier had a stroke. So Meier is constant, for otherwise I could not have talked about change. That is how I see the problems of change.

Monika
...and identity.

Heinz
And identity. The two are complementary. The problem of identity is just as difficult. The description of the situation always being the same, makes for the identity problem. So, interestingly enough, there is an invariance in my description.

One may dig a little deeper now and ask: "What are we talking about? Are we talking about descriptions or about what is being described, that is to say, of the described?" Two very different philosophers can now argue with one another. One of them says: "You can only describe, what you see." The other says: "You can only see, what you describe." Those are two positions that in my opinion are in principle undecidable. Now one of them might ask: "Heinz, how can you claim such things?" Whereupon I propose to the critic of this statement to conduct an experiment to decide, which position is the acceptable one and which is the non-acceptable position. And I claim that this experiment already carries within itself the answer to the decision to be made; that the experiment always contains a built-in bias towards the delivery of this or that answer.

The Position as the Beginning

Monika
You say: "When I change, the universe changes as well, for I am a part of the universe." Systemic thinking assumes an interdependence of individual and all other processes of change. How are processes of change connected in the universe? How are individual, social and overall ecological—or, as I believe Bateson says, overall systemic—processes of change related to one another? How am I to understand this process? What is this—as Bateson says—"mind" or "the pattern which connects"? Why do my actions have repercussions on everything else? Why is it that there is an effect on the cosmos when I move?

Heinz
Now, would you please describe to me the cosmos before and after you have moved? The so-called effects on everything else again occur in the descriptions. This question only makes sense if you separate yourself from the cosmos. When you are one with the cosmos, then this one-ness is a different one, when parts of it change.

Monika
When a tree falls in the woods and I don't notice it here, the change with the tree in the woods has nothing to do with me; it has no repercussions on me.

Many people do not worry about certain environmental problems when they are not directly affected by them. How can I raise my consciousness, so that even very distant events, that are independent of my person, can have an effect on me?

Heinz
You need to leave out the insertion "independent of me." This part of your sentence should disappear, for it is very difficult to prove, merely linguistically. It is all hidden in language. First I say: "Here there is an occurrence that is independent of me," and then I would like to teach someone that I am dependent on it after all. Therefore, the insertion "independent of me" should no longer appear. One would have to say:

"Make it clear to yourself—'the pattern which connects'—that we are all continually connected with one another!"

Monika
Why?

Heinz
It's got nothing to do with "why." That we are all connected is the position that I assume.

Monika
But how do you arrive at that position? On the basis of what perceptions, insights, or philosophies do you say, "We are all connected to one another"? Is it cybernetics or systems theory that leads you to it? You can say: "I say that because I am a constructivist."

Heinz
No, no, no!

Monika
I always thought that you derived your statement "I am a part of the universe" from your cybernetic theories.

Heinz
I would say: That is a fundamental position. It is in the beginning that these decisions stand. "I'd like to see myself as separate"—this peephole idea—or: "I would like to see myself as a part of the universe."

Monika
Well, why would you like to see yourself as a part of the universe? I would like to know if in cybernetics, in systems theories, in chaos theory, or in other theories I can find a theoretical foundation for this thought.

Heinz
Yes, you would like to deduce this basic position, which I hold to be an important decision, from other ideas.

Monika
Or substantiate it theoretically. Let us say that I would like to give this statement or this position a theoretical foundation, so that other people may also say: "Aha, that makes sense, for systems theory says, that all of these change processes are interdependent." For then it may become easier for these people to comprehend this position.

Heinz

You mean for pedagogical reasons. That is, how can I now promote this idea, convince others that this idea has a certain charm, and that other ideas have a different kind of charm?

Monika

That would be one possibility; for pedagogical reasons. But also for an intellectual understanding; that I simply want to know it. It is just one of hundreds of positions, but why does this one make sense?

Heinz

Well, the others make sense too. In my opinion it is a problem of decision-making.

Monika

But now, very concretely: My question is whether there are any stated views in systems theory or cybernetics that could substantiate the statement "I am a part of the universe"?

Heinz

I would rather say it the other way around: From this position certain statements of systems theory then arise, as for example Bateson's mantra "the pattern which connects" with Heinz von Foerster's footnote "the matrix which embeds."[4] All these connective ideas emanate from a fundamental position, which this thinker has accepted for himself, perhaps in many instances without naming it as such; a fundamental position, which then invites him to utter these statements, these propositions, these views. I would say that these thoughts, these statements are consequences of a position, which many of these thinkers have adopted, without making it clear to themselves, that they have done so. I think that if I still had the opportunity to speak about these thoughts with Bateson and say: "Look here, Gregory, don't we both have this position...?" he would perhaps say: "Yes, Heinz, that is a consequence." And I would say: "Gregory, for me it is the beginning. Your idea of 'pattern which connects', et cetera, all of that flows from your central position: That you don't want to separate yourself from all of us and from the cosmos, but that you consider yourself to be a part of this whole world." ...

---

4.   Later in our book Heinz states: "Now Gregory had the idea of pattern; and pattern comes from pater, and is thus a paternal, masculine arrangement. I have always been interested in women. So I find this predominantly male focus in 'the pattern which connects' not fitting for me. I prefer to think of a woman and therefore rather of 'a matrix which embeds'. After all, you've got to have a bed, or a context, in which these different ideas can constitute a pattern, then develop and become a crystal. I offer as a complementary thought to Bateson's 'the pattern which connects' 'the matrix which embeds'. Matrix is really a womb. That is my twist of the view; instead of the rather male point of view of pattern, I look at it from a female point of view of a matrix: something that embeds, something in which something can grow; something in which something originates. It is a play on words, not to be taken too seriously. It is only an invitation to invent a complement. Language does a lot with me; it constantly offers me snippets, from which I then have to drag myself out of. So when someone says to me: 'pattern', I ask: 'Why pattern? Why not matrix?'"

A particular line of questioning, which you have developed, appeals to me,
and I would like to answer to it very precisely,
namely
you ask whether one can deduce the idea that "I am a part of the world" from other insights in a variety of
scientific fields which concern themselves with such problems of connection, such as cybernetics,
systemics, et cetera, or must I first stipulate the sentence "I am a part of the world," and then deduce from
it the details of cybernetics, of ethics, of systemics?
My answer is the following: For me, Heinz von Foerster, today, my position is the following: I personally
cannot deduce the idea that I am a part of the world as a consequence of other theoretical statements
because I take it as a major premise.

Monika

But how does your position come about?

Heinz

That is a historical question. That is the question as to how Heinz von Foerster arrived at these ideas. After all, he did not always state it. At one time he said this, at another that. Finally, today he sits up there and says: "For me that is the central position. From this position I can deduce systemics, I can deduce ethics, I can deduce cybernetics, et cetera." It is the question about Heinz von Foerster's years of development from a high school student to a skeptic, who sits on Rattlesnake Hill, who earlier on thought such and such, and who in the end claims that: "For me, Heinz von Foerster, now in the year 2002, the idea that I am a part of the world is a central idea."

The second question is: If I want to develop a logical or a philosophical system, where do I begin? In my philosophical system, when someone says to me, "Heinz von Foerster, write a logical system," I begin with the basic statement: "I am a part of the world"; to be precise, I start with the experiment: "Do we want this or do we want that?" In the case of this in principle undecidable question, I have decided to declare myself a part of the world. When I do that, I can let all kinds of consequences flow from this position. They are called cybernetics, ethics, systemics, et cetera, et cetera. For me it is such that the other statements, circularity, connectivity, all of these theorems that appear in cybernetics, systemics, et cetera, are consequences of this central position.

We are faced with two questions here: The historical question and the systemic question.

If I am supposed to derive this position from something, I can only do it with Heinz von Foerster's developmental history; by elaborating on the formation of the human being Heinz von Foerster; by telling how it is that in the course of his life he came upon these insights. Then I could say: "I, Heinz, have had this education. I, Heinz, have had these hopes. I, Heinz, have had these experiences and these insights. I, Heinz, have spoken with these interesting people. I, Heinz, finally arrive at the idea that from this position I can easily develop the remaining problems of cybernetics, of systemics, of ethics." So that is my answer to the possibility of development.

Monika
Are there then analogies, metaphors, parables, examples, are there insights, perceptions, positions, in the many theoretical disciplines, with which you have occupied yourself in the course of your life, such as cybernetics, biology, epistemology, and anthropology that could support your position, substantiate it, enrich it with new perspectives?

Heinz
Yes, certainly; of course. I would start exactly with this statement and develop from it the positions that may be found in cybernetics, in biology, in the theory of organizations, et cetera. If you are interested in the concrete scientific influences, in how this position influenced basic ideas of cybernetics, basic ideas of systemics, basic ideas of Gregory Bateson and of family therapists, et cetera, I can easily explain it to you. If you feel like it, I can tell you about how Bateson, for example, understands explanations, how Bateson understands relationships. These are all those positions.

Monika
Wonderful!

Heinz
All right. So then the beginning of the story will be that I pronounce the postulate of the world, which is: "I and the world are one." There I will speak about the two possibilities for making a decision, for it is important that it is a choice, and not a consequence. For if it were a consequence, it would be a necessity. I, however, claim: It is not a necessity. It is a position that we can elect from all sorts of other positions. And it is my personal position, which I now propose be accepted. Once this position is accepted, I will not deduce it from something else, but use it to illuminate other things in such a way, that they can be traced back to this position. And I do not see it the way you like to see it. You would like to see the cosmological principle substantiated or supported by other thoughts that show up in cybernetics, in systemics, in physics. For me it is different. For me it is like this: You start with the free choice. For me they are not substantiations, but illuminations that come from this central principle. I would have liked Heinz von Foerster develop himself to the point of reaching this position, and then, from the top of a mountain, from the Himalaya, roll down on the other side, and tell about the incredible richness of a garden, of a flower bed, of a forest that emerges. ...

Meaning

What I have noticed most clearly is the close connection of the thoughts that we discuss here to the teachings of the Tao. ...

[Chuang Tzu] wrote a whole series of parables, similes and hints which I gobbled up with the greatest enthusiasm as a young man.

Again and again I found the point where he says: "We have to understand that we are one with nature. It is not a matter of different parts flying around in the universe. The essence of our idea is that we are one. One arises out of the other, and the other arises out of the one."

And that certainly is a beginning standpoint that I also try to express: I consider myself to be part of the world.

Then I noticed another point with great amusement: With Chuang-Tzu I find strategies similar to those in our conversations, where you push me to finally say, what ethics is, and where I always escape and hide behind Wittgenstein's "It is clear that ethics cannot be articulated," or similar excuses. When disciples ask him, what the Tao is, Chuang-Tzu answers: "Whoever inquires about Tao, will never understand it, and someone who gives an answer to this question, has never understood it."

I would like to hold on to this idea. When you ask, "What is ethics?" you will never understand it. And the one who gives an answer to this question, has never understood it.

In this sense I found it amusing that there exist parallels between the nature of the Tao and the position of the funny Heinz von Foerster from Vienna, from the third district; who somehow also absorbed these ideas, while coming from a very different direction. Probably it is related to the fact that already as a very young person I came in contact with these ideas, these stories, the fairy tales that are told about the Tao.

Now comes the question concerning consequences. I noticed the following: When we began these conversations, we talked about first wanting to lay the foundations, then to talk about my life, and then to draw the consequences. But that is still the old way of thinking! That is from A to B, from B to C and finally to D, that is to the consequences.

After having been amused by the parallelism to Taoism, I have now seen: This entire development, the foundations and the consequences are the consequence. The program is its own consequence. That is to say, it is a closed position that always leads back to itself. A Taoist position is actually expressed in what my house manager, Mrs. Grill, always said: "Heinz, all of that will come back upon you."

You, the past, the present and the future are all a one and only one-ness, from which you cannot, will not, or should not step out.

Our conversations themselves are the answer to the question concerning consequences. ...

Eastern Slope
Frank Galuszka, 2002. 24 x 18" Oil

Cybernetics And Human Knowing. Vol. 10, nos. 3-4, pp. 67-72

Heinz von Foerster's Archives

Albert Müller[1]

The article seeks to give a very rough overview on research material and archives concerning Heinz von Foerster's life and work, mainly focussing on the Heinz von Foerster archive in Vienna.

Urbana

When Heinz von Foerster became professor emeritus of the University of Illinois in 1976 and when, on his retirement, the research unit founded in 1957 and directed by him since then had to be closed, he had already made two important decisions regarding the documentation of his life's work.

Firstly, he encouraged that a micro-fiche edition be made of all the work which had been written at the Biological Computer Laboratory. This micro fiches-publication encompassing some 50,000 printed pages was edited by one of his students, Kenneth L. Wilson. As *the* monument of the wide-ranging studies done by the BCL they have been distributed all over the world. (cf. Wilson, 1976)

Secondly, he had his papers and those of the Lab filed and then donated them to the university archives of the University of Illinois at Urbana, where they were stored in 30 boxes. The University Archives produced a finding aid, which can be accessed by Internet. (cf. http://web.library.uiuc.edu/ahx/uasfa/1106026.pdf). Further 22 boxes refer to the Biological Computer Laboratory itself. (cf. http://web.library.uiuc.edu/ahx/uasfa/1106017.pdf) A smaller part of his papers, among them documents concerning his own publications and lectures, further personal pieces of correspondence and documents Heinz von Foerster took with him to Pescadero, California where he and his wife Mai moved to when he retired.

Lost material

This was not the first time Heinz von Foerster parted, or was forced to part, with documents, material or artefacts concerning his work and his personal life. When he as a young man left his parents' Viennese home in the 1930s he left behind some personal things, photographs for instance, things which he repossessed after the death of his brother, the jazz-musician Uzzi Förster. During the Second World War's bombing of Berlin most of Heinz von Foerster's valuable library was destroyed. In the final days of the war a railroad car containing Foerster's laboratory equipment and scientific notes was destroyed in a tank attack. I mention this here only to demonstrate

1. Dr. Albert Müller, Institut für Zeitgeschichte der Universität Wien, Spitalgasse 2, A-1090 Vienna, Austria. The author would like to express his gratitude to Camilla R. Nielsen, who carefully read and corrected a first draft of this paper.

how vulnerable and therefore incomplete and inconsistent the estate of a scientist (or of any person for all that matter) might be.

Pescadero

But let us return to the 1970's. Under rather difficult conditions Heinz von Foerster managed to build a house in the small town of Pescadero and went about quite successfully continuing his scientific work in an increasingly worldwide context. Now the very centre of his scientific work was no longer a university institution but his own home. In the cellar of his house he furnished a special room, which he used to refer to as his "archive". It was the place where he could store research material and correspondence in more or less the same way as he had at the BCL. Whereas Foerster's library – an essential part of the Rattlesnake Hill "Gesamtkunstwerk"– extended throughout the entire house, current correspondence was conducted in his study, which, in addition to a large writing desk, was equipped with a reference library. The archive in the cellar also served as a kind of storage room for already finished work and as a place for more formal work steps (for example, there was a place for the small Xerox machine with the help of which Heinz von Foerster produced his lovingly designed re-prints of his publications and handouts, a fax-machine and an old Atari computer for writing texts and letters).

Vienna

In 2000 Heinz von Foerster donated the larger part of this archive-room to the Department of Contemporary History (Institut für Zeitgeschichte) of the University of Vienna where this collection of documents has been processed for use in scientific research and documentation. The main reason why von Foerster decided to bequeath his archives may well have been the strong attachment he often claimed to have felt for the city of Vienna, his hometown, which he had departed from in 1948 for the United States. This close relationship was not just based on family and friendships but also on the very fact that Foerster saw the roots of his scientific work and his general "world-view" lying in the intellectual and cultural tradition of Vienna. Foerster's son Thomas von Foerster donated his copy of the "Logisch-philosophische Abhandlung" (Wittgenstein, 1921) for which he, as a student, had produced a register and short interpretation which he attached to the volume and which survived all the dangerous decades. This book in particular and the work of members of the "Vienna Circle" exerted a lasting influence on the student Heinz von Foerster and continued to inform his thinking throughout his whole life. (Foerster, 1996a). Another reason that Heinz von Foerster decided to donate his archive to the institute in Vienna was his long-standing cooperation and friendship with Karl H. Müller and Albert Müller (the author of this article, which, among other things, led to a joint publication (Foerster, 1997) and publications on the occasion of Foerster's 85th and 90th birthdays. (Müller et al., 1997)

The Austrian ministry of science provided financial support for the project "Heinz von Foerster-Archiv" at least until the February 2000, when a new government was formed. Since then the department of culture of the city of Vienna has (on a quite modest level) become the main sponsor of the project.

Years ago now Heinz von Foerster declared that his archive should be brought to Vienna in the event of his death. On account of a permanent illness as of 2000 it became impossible for him to make use of the material by himself and to take care of it at all. He thus suggested that the material be immediately moved to Vienna.

Activities

In Vienna the material was looked through, sorted, roughly catalogued to produce a first finding aid, packed into about 100 boxes and set up in the rooms of the newly built Department of Contemporary History. The archive more or less took over the order Heinz von Foerster had used. The next step was to begin preparing an online-catalogue whose first version was launched in 2001 (cf. www.univie.ac.at/heinz-von-foerster-archive) A second version about twice the size of the first one will be published by the end of 2003. The precise cataloguing and description requires accurate page-by-page inspection basis and is, therefore, immensely time consuming.[2] These exact descriptions will also provide the basis for future digitalization projects. The catalogue is presently in German. An English version will be prepared immediately once the precise cataloguing of the material has been completed. The material itself could be described as multilingual: English and German are the main languages, but also we find pieces in Italian, French, Spanish or Portuguese.

During his last trip to Vienna in autumn 2001, where he was honoured by the Victor Frankl Prize and the Ring of Honours of the City of Vienna, Heinz von Foerster had a chance to see *his* archive and was able to take part in the opening ceremony.

Contents

It seems worthwhile to briefly sketch the holdings of the Viennese Heinz von Foerster-archive and how these might be used in the future.

One of the archive's holdings is the so-called Do books series, i.e., diary- or calendar-like notes made on a regular basis, usually daily. These notes covering the period from 1964 to 1989 rarely include private or personal utterances, as associated with the classical diary-genre. Its contents consist of often abridged notes about telephone calls, travel plans, talks, meetings and so on. Given the regularity and the considerable period of time these Do Books cover they constitute a sort of chronological "backbone," supporting the interpretation of other holdings of the

---

2. Sorting and rough cataloguing was done by Albert Müller and Karl H. Müller. Detailed Descriptions were provided by Nicole Finsinger, Andrea Brenner and Susanne Kratochwil. Barbara Heller-Schuh and Ralf Heller prepared the first version of the online-catalogue.

archive, some of which are undated. The Do Books also provide insight into the contacts Heinz von Foerster had with other scientists.

Another holding of the archive consists of a rather small but extremely interesting collection of documents going back to his pre-emigration period and related to his activities as a journalist and a 'science-writer' (*avant le lettre*) when he worked for the radio broadcast of the US occupation force in Austria ("Radio Rot-Weiß-Rot") from 1946 to 1948. This section of the archive contains a number of short manuscripts of radio broadcasts, radio essays, radio interviews and group discussions, which Heinz von Foerster had been responsible for and many of which dealt with scientific themes. Here we find, for instance, a review of Erwin Schrödinger's "What is Life" (Schrödinger, 1944), a book that also played an eminent role in one of Heinz von Foerster's most influential articles on self-organizing systems (cf. Foerster, 1960)

One further more or less "insular" holding of the archive are the documents on the McCulloch edition. Heinz von Foerster (cf. Foerster, 1989) not only wrote introductions to several chapters of the four-volume edition of the collected papers of his admired and beloved mentor, Warren Sturgis McCulloch, but was seriously engaged in the editing and the production process of this monumental piece of work, which Rook McCulloch was responsible for (McCulloch, 1989). The documents not only contain galley-proof copies of the four volumes but also correspondence with scientific commentators and sketches for the cover design made by Heinz von Foerster. These documents merit greater attention, since this publication nowadays is a kind of *rarum*. Due to a highly unfortunate twist of fate, the publishing house went out of business soon after the four volumes and had been printed and only a few copies were distributed to libraries and customers.

The holding "publications" contains—catalogued according to different publication projects—on the one hand manuscripts and proofs, and on the other hand correspondence with publishing houses, journal editors, translators and so on. Although the material is quite voluminous, this does not mean that each and every one of the about 200 publications (not counting reprints here) of Heinz von Foerster is to be found in the archives. Sometimes manuscripts or correspondence refer to publications projects which were never to see the light of day. I would like to mention here one highlight in the large series of publication-related material: the documents related to the publication of the famous Macy-conferences on cybernetics, edited, and co-edited together with Margaret Mead and Hans Lukas Teubner, respectively (cf. Foerster, 1949). The circumstances under which Heinz von Foerster was appointed editor of the conference volumes have been described several times (cf. Foerster, 1993). The archives contain correspondence between editors and authors, manuscripts and copy-editing material and so on. These documents (including material e from other archives) represent an important building block in the reconstruction of the history of the Macy conference, which, as one of several birthplaces of cybernetics, has been of special interest for science studies (cf. e.g., Heims, 1993; Hayles, 1999).

The section "lecture notes" first of all in great detail documents Heinz von Foerster's worldwide activities in this field. He used to prepare a single folder for each lecture in which he collected all the related material, from notes or manuscripts, letter exchange with organizers of a conference, travelling documents such as tickets or hotel bills to notes from the discussion of a lecture. We cannot determine on the basis of this material what exactly was said in a given lecture. Heinz von Foerster tended to spontaneously change or vary or expand themes of his lectures in front of a given audience, even if he had prepared a detailed manuscript. Heinz von Foerster also prepared many hand-outs to accompany his lectures. In only one single instance the archive holds an audio document of a series of five lectures. These so-called 'Stanford Lectures' were already published on a CD-ROM on the occasion of Foerster's 90th birthday (cf. Grössing et al., 2001 — further audio-material has been published by the Carl Auer Verlag, cf. Foerster, 1996b, and by the supposé-Verlag, cf. Foerster, 1999). The archive also has video tapes of one lecture series, which could be used as a basis for a DVD-edition in the future. Among many other aspects, all of the material taken together gives impressive insight into the rapid spread of constructivist and systemic thinking in the 1980s and 1990s.

Heinz von Foerster's lecturing and teaching activities after his retirement — especially at San Jose State University, California — are not part of the lecture notes series, but are documented in a special section of the archive. There we not only find lecture notes but also pieces of correspondence with students, students' papers and so on.

Most of the different sections of the archive contain letters and correspondence thematically related to these different sections. In addition, there is a collection of correspondence. Speaking in general terms, we can say that the archive does not hold complete series of letter exchanges. Especially with regard to his own outgoing correspondence, Heinz von Foerster did not proceed very systematically, whereas he normally did keep incoming letters. Part of the correspondence is in a chronological order, while another part of it is sorted alphabetically according to the names of the persons he corresponded with. The collection containing copies of the letters he sent covers only a very short period of time.

Very closely related to the research process itself is a collection of calculations, most of which refer to projects from the 1950's to the 1970's. Among them we find calculations concerning the mitotic indices-project, the so-called "doomsday"-project (on demographic forecasts), the cybernetics of taxation, on muscle activity and many more. The holding with the heading 'calculations' illustrates how much detail Heinz von Foerster invested in his work on the mathematical background of his research findings.

Finally I would like to mention a special collection of the archives. Whoever reads texts by Heinz von Foerster will notice how fond he was of using instructive illustrations from quite different contexts. Not only technical sketches or diagrams of mathematical functions but also cartoons or reproductions of pieces of art can often be found as part of an article. In the 1950s Heinz von Foerster started to create a collection of slides, which he used regularly in lectures and talks. Some of them also served as illustrations in publications. A large numbers of these slides have survived in the archive. The collection again shows impressively the immense breadth of Heinz von Foerster's interests and his special gift for visualizing complex and abstract findings.

The Heinz von Foerster archive in Vienna is supplemented by a research collection most of which consists of oral-history tapes, photographs and so on (most of it produced by Albert Müller and Karl H. Müller). This additional collection also contains copies from the collection of papers on the von Foerster family, owned by Dr. Gerda Janouschek.

On the basis of these very short remarks we can safely say that the Heinz von Foerster Archive Vienna, along with the papers of other most famous scientists – just to mention Warren McCulloch (American Philosophical Society, cf. http://www.amphilsoc.org/library/mole/m/mcculloc.htm), Norbert Wiener (MIT, cf. http://www.aip.org/history/ead/mit_wiener/19990053.html), Gordon Pask (Paul Pangaro, Palo Alto, cf. http://www.pangaro.com/Pask-Archive/Pask-Archive-listing.html) or Gregory Bateson (UC Santa Cruz), one of the most interesting sources for research on the history, the intellectual background and the development of cybernetics, constructivism and systemics.

The archive can be easily accessed. For further information please contact albert.mueller@univie.ac.at

Literature

Foerster, H. von (Ed.) (1949). *Cybernetics: Transactions of the Sixth Conference*. New York: Josiah Macy, Jr. Foundation.

Foerster, H. von (1960). On self-organizing systems and their environments. In M. C. Yovits & S. Cameron (Eds.), *Self-organizing Systems* (pp. 31-50). London: Pergamon.

Foerster, H. von (1989). Preface. In R. McCulloch (Ed.), *The collected works of Warren S. McCulloch* (pp. i-iii). Salinas: Intersystems Publications.

Foerster, H. von (1993). *KybernEthik*. Berlin: Merve Verlag.

Foerster, H. von (1996a). Der Wiener Kreis – Parabel für einen Denkstil. In F. Stadler (Ed.), *Wissenschaft als Kultur: Österreichs Beitrag zur Moderne* (pp. 29-48). Wien: Springer.

Foerster, H. von (1996b). *Eine Theorie von Lernen und Wissen vis-à-vis Unbestimmbaren, Unentscheidbarem und Unwißbarem* (Audio Cassette Recording). Heidelberg: Carl Auer.

Foerster, H. von (2002). Der Anfang von Himmel und Erde hat keinen Namen. Eine Selbst-Erschaffung in 7 Tagen (3rd ed., A. Müller& K. H. Müller, Eds.) Vienna 1997. Berlin: Kadmos. (1st ed. published in 1997 by Doecker, Vienna)

Foerster, H. von (1999). 2 x 2 = grün (2 Audio CDs, K. Sander, Ed.). Cologne: supposé-Verlag.

Grössing, G., Hartmann, J., Korn, W. & Müller, A. (Eds. (2001). *Heinz von Foerster 90. I: Bio-Graphie als Picto-Graphie, II: A constructivist epistemology* (cd-rom), Vienna: Edition Echoraum.

Hayles, N. K. (1999). *How we Became Posthuman. Virtual Bodies in Cybernetics, Literature, and Informatics*. Chicago: University of Chicago Press.

Heims, S. J. (1993). *Constructing a social science for postwar America: The cybernetics group, 1946-1953*. Cambridge, MA: The MIT Press.

McCulloch, W. S. (1989). *The collected works of Warren S. McCulloch* (R. McCulloch, Ed.). Salinas: Intersystems Publications.

Müller, A., Müller, K. H., & Stadler, F. (Eds.) (1997). *Konstruktivismus und Kognitionswissenschaft. Kulturelle Wurzeln und Ergebnisse. Heinz von Foerster gewidmet*. Wien: Springer.

Schrödinger, E. (1944). *What is life?* Cambridge: Cambridge University Press.

Wilson, K. L. (Ed.) (1976). *The collected works of the Biological Computer Laboratory*. Peoria: Illinois Blueprint Corporation. (collection is on microfiche accompanied by a short print introduction)

Wittgenstein, L. (1921). Logisch-philsophische Abhandlung. *Annalen der Naturphilosophie, 14*, 185-262.

Cybernetics And Human Knowing. Vol. 10, nos. 3-4, pp. 73-89

Eigenforms — Objects as Tokens for Eigenbehaviors

by Louis H. Kauffman[1]

This essay is a discussion of Heinz von Foerster's concept of an eigenform, wherein an object is seen to be a token for those behaviors that lend it (the object) its apparent stability in a changing world.

I. Introduction

This essay is a contemplation of the notion of eigenform as explicated by Heinz von Foerster in his paper [4]. In that paper Heinz performs the magic trick of convincing us that the familiar objects of our existence can be seen to be nothing more than tokens for the behaviors of the organism that create stable forms. This is not to deny an underlying reality that is the source of these objects, but rather to emphasize the role of process and the role of the organism in the production of a living map that is so sensitive that map and territory are conjoined. Von Foerster's papers [4,5,6] in the book [3] were instrumental in pioneering the field of second order cybernetics.

The notion of an eigenform is inextricably linked with second order cybernetics. One starts on the road to such a concept as soon as one begins to consider a pattern of patterns, the form of form or the cybernetics of cybernetics. Such concepts appear to close around upon themselves, and at the same time they lead outward. They suggest the possibility of transcending the boundaries of a system from a locus that might have been within the system until the circular concept is called into being, and then the boundaries have turned inside out. As Ranulph Glanville has pointed out "The inside is the outside is the inside is the..."

Forms are created from the concatenation of operations upon themselves and objects are not objects at all, but rather indications of processes. Upon encountering an object, after that essay of Heinz, you are compelled to ask: How is that object created? How is it designed? What do I do to produce it? What is the network of productions? Where is the home of that object? In what context does it exist? How am I involved in its creation?

Taking Heinz's suggestion to heart we find that an object in itself is a symbolic entity, participating in a network of interactions, taking on its apparent solidity and stability from these interactions. We ourselves are such objects, we as human beings are "signs for ourselves," a concept originally due to the American philosopher C. S. Peirce [9]. In many ways Heinz's eigenforms are mathematical companions to Peirce's work. We will not follow this comparison in the present essay, but the reader familiar with Peirce is encouraged to do so.

---

1. Math Department., University of Illinois–Chicago, Chicago, IL. Email: kauffman@uic.edu.

Heinz performed a creative act that invites each of us into an unending epistemological investigation. The key to this act is the stance of an observing system. In an observing system, what is observed is not distinct from the system itself, nor can one make a separation between the observer and the observed. These stand together in a coalescence of perception. From the stance of the observing system all objects are non-local, depending upon the presence of the system as a whole. It is within that paradigm that these models begin to live, act and converse with us. We are the models. Map and territory are conjoined.

In this paper, sections 2 and 3 discuss the nature of object, leading from the descriptions and assumptions that we use in the everyday world to the somewhat different concepts of object that occur in scientific work, particularly in the physics of the very small. We indicate how the concept of object arising as eigenform (i.e. as token for the interaction and mutual production of the observer and the observed) intermediates among these points of view.

Section 4 gives an exposition of the form of Heinz's model. Once this mathematical model is on the table, one can discuss how it is related to our concept of "object." This section contains examples of fractal and geometric eigenforms.

Section 5 is a recounting of a conversation of the author and Ranulph Glanville in which Ranulph asked "Does every recursion have a fixed point?" In the language of the present essay this is the question "Does every process have an eigenform?" The obvious answer is no, but the answer that comes from Heinz's model is yes! There is always an ideal eigenform. The challenge is to integrate that form into the context of one's living.

In section 6 we point out that the construction of eigenforms in the sense of Heinz's model can be accomplished without an idealized excursion to infinity. The method was invented by Alonzo Church and Haskell Curry in the 1930's. This method is commonly called the "lambda calculus." The key to lambda calculus is the construction of a self-reflexive language, a language that can refer and operate upon itself. In this way eigenforms can be woven into the context of languages that are their own metalanguages, hence into the context of natural language and observing systems.

In section 7 we consider naming and self-reference and return to Heinz's definition of "I." The concept of section 7 is essentially related to the lambda calculus where names can act on names and their referents. We discuss how self-reference occurs in language through an indicative shift welding the name of a person to his/her (physical) presence and shifting the indication of the name to a metaname. More could be said at this point, as the indicative shift is a linguistic entry into the world of Godelian sentences and the incompleteness of formal systems. We emphasize the natural occurrence of eigenforms in the world of our linguistic experience and how this occurrence is intimately connected to our structure as observing systems.

Section 8 is an appendix discussing the relationship between eigenforms and the structure of quantum mechanics. Eigenvectors in quantum mechanics are, in this view, particular examples of eigenforms. From the world of observing systems, quantum mechanics is a mathematical articulation of the non-locality and superposition of forms. This appendix will be unfolded in a sequel to this paper.

II. Objects

What is an object? At first glance, the question seems perfectly obvious. An object is, well... An object is a thing, a something that you can pick up and move and manipulate in three dimensional space. An object is three dimensional, palpable, like an apple or a chair, or a pencil or a cup. An object is the simplest sort of thing that can be subjected to reference. All language courses first deal with simple objects like pens and tables. La plume est sur la table.

An object is separate from me. It is "out there". It is part of the reality separate from me. Objects are composed of objects, their parts. My car is made of parts. The chair is a buzzing whirl of molecules. Each molecule is a whirl of atoms. Each atom a little solar system of electrons, neutrons and protons. But wait! The nucleus of the atom is composed of strange objects called quarks. No one can see them. They do not exist as separate entities. The electrons in the atom are special objects that are not separate from each other and from everything else. And yet when you observe the electrons, they have definite locations.

The physicist's world divides into quantum objects that are subject to the constraints of the uncertainty principle, and classical objects that live in the dream of objective existence, carrying all their properties with them. The difference between the quantum level of objects and the classical level of objects is actually not sharp. From the point of view of the physicist all phenomena are quantum phenomena, but in certain ranges, such as the world of the very small, the quantum effects dominate. It is not the purpose of this essay to detail this correspondence, but a little more information can be found in section 8.

A classical object has a location at a given time. You can tell where it is. You can tell a story of where it has been. If the classical object breaks up into parts, you will be able to keep track of all the parts. Yet electrons and positrons can meet each other and disappear into pure energy! Should we allow objects to disappear? What sort of an object is the electromagnetic field of radio and television signals that floods this room?

Is my thought to be thought of as an object? Can I objectify my thought by writing it down on paper or in the computer? Am I myself an object? Is my body an object in the three dimensional space? Is the space itself an object? Objects have shape. What is the shape of space? What is the shape of the physical universe. What is the shape of the Platonic universe?

It seemed simple. Then, with more experience, the transformations of pattern that formed the space and the objects in it began to appear highly interwoven. In the physical microworld objects, if they were objects at all, did not have many of the properties of macroscopic objects like heads of cabbage and bowling balls. Give me a good macroscopic object any day, fully separate and useful. Don't confuse me with these subatomic fantasies of interconnectedness.

If a person (a thought, feeling and symbol object) were to read this section with the hope of finding a clear definition of object, he/she might be disappointed. Yet Heinz von Foerster in his essays [3,4,5,6] has suggested the enticing notion that "objects are tokens for eigenbehaviors." We want to see the meaning of this phrase of Heinz. The short form of this meaning is that there is a behavior between the perceiver and the object perceived and a stability or repetition that "arises between them." It is this stability that constitutes the object (and the perceiver). In this view, one does not really have any separate objects, objects are always "objects perceived," and the perceiver and the perceived arise together in the condition of observation.

III. Shaping a World

We, identify the world in terms of how we shape it. We shape the world in response to how it changes us. We change the world and the world changes us. Objects arise as tokens of that behavior that leads to seemingly unchanging forms. Forms are seen to be unchanging through their invariance under our attempts to change, to shape them.

Can you conceive of an object independent of your ability to perceive it? I did not say an object independent of your perception.

Lets assume that it is possible to talk of the tree in the forest where we are not. But how are we to speak of that tree? One can say, the tree is there. What does this mean? It means that there is a potentiality for that tree to appear in the event of the appearance of a person such as myself or yourself in the place called that forest. What is the tree doing when I am not in the forest?

I will never know, but I do know that "it" obediently becomes treeish and located when "I" am "there." The quotation marks are indications of objects dissolving into relationships. Whenever "I" am present, the world (of everything that is the case) is seen through the act of framing. I imagine a pure world, unframed. But this is the world of all possibilities. As soon as we enter the scene the world is filtered and conformed to become the form that frame and brain have consolidated to say is reality.

IV. Heinz's Eigenform Model

We have just moved through a discussion showing how the concept of an object has evolved to make what we call objects (and the objective world) processes that are interdependent with the actions of observers. The notion of a fixed object has changed to become a notion of a process that produces the apparent stability of the object. This process can be simplified in a model to become a recursive process where a rule or rules are applied time and time again. The resulting object of such a process is called by Heinz von Foerster the eigenform of the process, and the process itself is called the *eigenbehavior.*

In this way Heinz created a model for thinking about object as token for eigenbehavior. This model examines the result of a simple recursive process carried to its limit. For example, suppose that:

$$F(X) = \boxed{\quad X \quad}$$

That is, each step in the process encloses the results of the previous step within a box. Here is an illustration of the first few steps of the process applied to an empty box X:

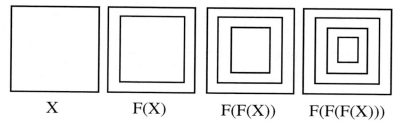

$$\begin{array}{cccc} X & F(X) & F(F(X)) & F(F(F(X))) \end{array}$$

If we continue this process, then successive nests of boxes resemble one another, and in the limit of infinitely many boxes, we find that

$$X = F(F(F(\ldots))) = \boxed{\boxed{\boxed{\cdots}}}$$

$$F(X) = \boxed{\boxed{\boxed{\cdots}}} = X$$

the infinite nest of boxes is invariant under the addition of one more surrounding box. Hence this infinite nest of boxes is a fixed point for the recursion. In other words, if X denotes the infinite nest of boxes, then

$$X = F(X).$$

This equation is not meant to denote something arcane! It is a description of a state of affairs. Place your gaze on the infinite nest of boxes and note that if you add one more surrounding box, then there is no change to the resulting form. The form of an infinite nest of boxes is invariant under the operation of adding one more surrounding box. The infinite nest of boxes is one of the simplest eigenforms.

In the process of observation, we interact with ourselves and with the world to produce stabilities that become the objects of our perception. These objects, like the infinite nest of boxes, may go beyond the specific properties of the world in which we operate. They attain their stability through this process of going outside the immediate world. Furthermore, we make an imaginative leap to complete such objects that become tokens for eigenbehaviors. It is impossible to make an infinite nest of boxes. We do not make it. We *imagine* it. And in imagining that infinite next of boxes, we arrive at the eigenform that is the object for this process.

The leap of imagination to the infinite eigenform is akin to the human ability to create signs and symbols. In the case of the eigenform X with $X = F(X)$, X can be regarded as the name of the process itself or as the name of the limiting (imaginative) result of the process. Note that if you are told that

$$X = F(X),$$

then substituting $F(X)$ for X, you can write

$$X = F(F(X)).$$

Substituting again and again, you have

$$X = F(F(F(X))) = F(F(F(F(X)))) = F(F(F(F(F(X))))) = \ldots$$

The process arises from the symbolic expression of its eigenform. In this view the eigenform is a kind of implicate order for the process that generates it.

Sometimes one stylizes the structure by indicating where the eigenform X reenters its own indicational space by an arrow or other graphical device. See the picture below for the case of the nested boxes.

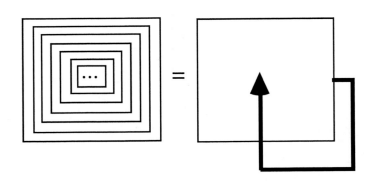

Does the infinite nest of boxes exist? Certainly it does not exist in this page or anywhere in the physical world with which the writer or presumably the reader is familiar. The infinite nest of boxes exists in the imagination! In that sense it is a symbolic entity.

The key concept in the understanding of eigenform is its placement in the reciprocal relationship of the object (the "It") and the process leading to the object (the process leading to "It"). In the diagram below we have indicated these relationships with respect to the eigenform of nested boxes. Note that the "It" is illustrated as a finite approximation (to the infinite limit) that is sufficient to allow an observer to infer/perceive the generating process that underlies it.

The It

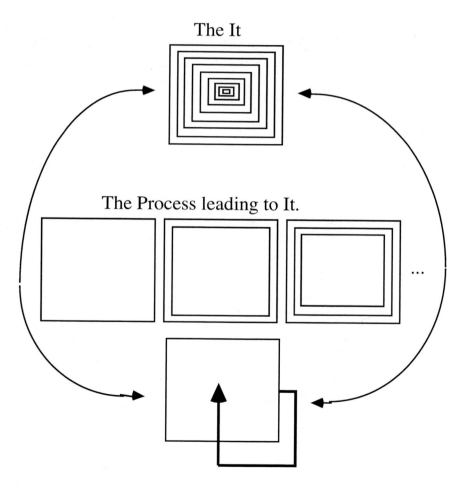

The Process leading to It.

Just so, an object in the world (cognitive, physical, ideal,...) provides a conceptual center for the investigation of a skein of relationships related to its context and to the processes that generate it. An object can have varying degrees of reality just as does an eigenform. If we take Heinz's suggestion to heart that objects are tokens for eigenbehaviors, then an object in itself is a entity, participating in a network of interactions, taking on its apparent solidity and stability from these interactions. An object in this view is an amphibian between the symbolic and imaginary world of the mind and the complex world of personal experience. The object when viewed as process is a dialogue between these worlds. The object when seen as a sign for itself, or in and of itself, is as imaginary as a pure eigenform.

Why are objects only apparently solid? Of course you cannot walk through a brick wall even if you think about it differently. I do not mean apparent in the sense of thought alone. I mean apparent in the sense of appearance. The wall appears solid to me because of the actions that I can perform. The wall is quite transparent to a neutrino, and will not even be an eigenform for that neutrino.
This example shows quite sharply how the nature of an object is entailed in the properties of its observer.

Heinz's model can be expressed (as indeed he did express it) in quite abstract and general terms. Suppose that we are given a recursion symbolically by the equation

$$\mathbf{X(t+1) = F(X(t))}.$$

Here $\mathbf{X(t)}$ denotes the condition of observation at time $\mathbf{t}$. $\mathbf{X(t)}$ could be as simple as a set of nested boxes, or as complex as the entire configuration of your body in relation to the known universe at time t. Then $\mathbf{F(X(t))}$ denotes the result of applying the operations symbolized by $\mathbf{F}$ to the condition at time $\mathbf{t}$. You could, for simplicity, assume that $\mathbf{F}$ is independent of time. Time independence of the recursion $\mathbf{F}$ will give us simple answers and we can later discuss what will happen if the actions depend upon the time. In the time independent case we can write

$$\mathbf{J = F(F(F(...)))}$$

the infinite concatenation of F upon itself. We then see that

$$\mathbf{F(J) = J}$$

since adding one more $\mathbf{F}$ to the concatenation changes nothing. Thus $\mathbf{J}$, the infinite concatenation of the operation upon itself leads to a fixed point for $\mathbf{F}$. $\mathbf{J}$ is said to be the eigenform for the recursion $\mathbf{F}$. It is just like the nested boxes, and we see that every recursion has an eigenform. Every recursion has an (imaginary) fixed point.

We end this section with one more example. This is the eigenform of the Koch fractal [10]. In this case one can write symbolically the eigenform equation

$$\mathbf{K = K \{ K \ K \} K}$$

to indicate that the Koch Fractal reenters its own indicational space four times (that is, it is made up of four copies of itself, each one-third the size of the original. The curly brackets in the center of this equation refer to the fact that the two middle copies within the fractal are inclined with respect to one another and with respect to the two outer copies. In the figure below we show the geometric configuration of the reentry.

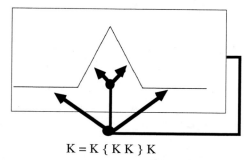

$$K = K \{ K K \} K$$

In the geometric recursion, each line segment at a given stage is replaced by four line segments of one third its length, arranged according to the pattern of reentry as shown in the figure above.

The recursion corresponding to the Koch eigenform is illustrated in the next figure. Here we see the sequence of approximations leading to the infinite self-reflecting eigenform that is known as the Koch snowflake fractal.

Five stages of recursion are shown. To the eye, the last stage vividly illustrates how the ideal fractal form contains four copies of itself, each one-third the size of the whole. The abstract schema

$$K = K \{ K K \} K$$

for this fractal can itself be iterated to produce a "skeleton" of the geometric recursion:

K = K { K K } K
= K { K K } K { K { K K } K K { K K } K } K { K K } K
= ...

We have only performed one line of this skeletal recursion. There are sixteen K's in this second expression just as there are sixteen line segments in the second stage of the geometric recursion. Comparison with this abstract symbolic recursion shows how geometry aids the intuition. The interaction of eigenforms with the geometry of physical, mental, symbolic and spiritual landscapes is an entire subject that is in need of deep exploration.

It is usually thought that the miracle of recognition of an object arises in some simple way from the assumed existence of the object and the action of our perceiving systems. What is to be appreciated is that this is a fine tuning to the point where the action of the perceiver and the perception of the object are indistinguishable. Such tuning requires an intermixing of the perceiver and the perceived that goes beyond description. Yet in the mathematical levels, such as number or fractal pattern, part of the process is slowed down to the point where we can begin to apprehend the process. There is a stability in the comparison, in the one-to-one correspondence that is a process happening at once in the present time. The closed loop of perception occurs in the eternity of present individual time. Each such process depends upon linked and ongoing eigenbehaviors and yet is seen as simple by the perceiving mind.

V. A Conversation with Ranulph Glanville

This essay has its beginnings in a conversation with Ranulph Glanville. Ranulph asked "Does every recursion have a fixed point?" hoping for a mathematician's answer. And I said first, "Well no, clearly not, after all it is common for processes to go into oscillation and so never come to rest." And then I said, "On the other hand, here is the

Theorem: Every recursion has a fixed point.

Proof. Let the recursion be given by an equation of the form

$$X' = F(X)$$

where X' denotes the next value of X and F encapsulates the function or rule that brings the recursion to its next step. Here F and X can be any descriptors of actor and actant that are relevant to the recursion being studied. Now form

$$J = F(F(F(F(...))))$$,

the infinite concatenation of F upon itself. Then we see that

$$F(J) = F(F(F(F(F(...))))) = J.$$

Hence J is a fixed point for the recursion and we have proved that every recursion has a fixed point.//

Ranulph said "Oh yes I remember that! Can I quote your proof?" and I said "Certainly, but you will have to make your attribution to Heinz and his paper 'Objects: Tokens for (Eigen-)Behaviors' [4], for that is where I came to appreciate this result, although I first understood it via the book *Laws of Form* [2] by G. Spencer-Brown."

And I went on to say that this theorem was in my view a startling magician's trick on Heinz's part, throwing us into the certainty of an eigenform (fixed point) corresponding to any process and at the same time challenging us to understand the nature of that fixed point in some context that is actually relevant to the original ground of conversation. Ranulph agreed, and our emails settled back into the usual background hum.

VI. Church and Curry

Alonzo Church and Haskell Curry [1] showed (in the 1930's, long before Heinz wrote his essays) how to make eigenforms without an apparent excursion to infinity. Their formalism is usually called the "lambda calculus." The key concept in their work is the use of a domain where there is (in a well-defined sense) no distinction between the language and metalanguage. They use a language that can talk about itself and operate upon itself.

In the Church-Curry language (the lambda calculus), there are two basic rules: Naming and Reflexivity.

1. Naming.
If you have an expression in the symbols in lambda calculus then there is always a single word in the language that encodes this expression. The application of this word has the same effect as the application of the expression itself. For example, suppose we consider the expression

"Form the square of a number N and add one."

Then in the lambda calculus there will be a word, lets say it is "**Squatch**" that has the same effect as this operation. So "**Squatch N**" means "square N and add one." We have:

Squatch 3 = 3x3 + 1 = 10.

2. Reflexivity.
*Given any two words **A** and **B** in the lambda calculus, there is permission to form their concatenation **AB**, with the interpretation that **A** operates upon or qualifies **B**.* In this way, every word in the lambda calculus is both an operator and an operand. The calculus is inherently self-reflexive.

We have given an example of reflexivity with the equation **Squatch N = NxN + 1**. But lambda calculus will also allow

$$\textbf{Squatch Squatch = Squatch x Squatch + 1.}$$

One then has to ask what it means to multiply Squatch by itself, but the language allows you to write this equation and then ask the question!

Here is an example. Let **GA** denote the process that creates two copies of **A** and puts them in a box.

$$\text{GA} = \boxed{\text{AA}}$$

Then in lambda calculus we are allowed to apply G to itself. The result is two copies of G next to one another, inside the box.

$$\text{GG} = \boxed{\text{GG}}$$

This equation about GG exhibits GG directly as a solution to the eigenform equation

$$\text{X} = \boxed{\text{X}}$$

thus producing the eigenform without an infinite limiting process.

More generally, we wish to find the eigenform for a process **F**. We want to find a **J** so that **F(J) = J**. Church and Curry admonish us to create an operator **G** with the property that

$$\textbf{GX = F(XX)}$$

So **GG** is a fixed point for **F**.

We have solved the eigenvalue problem without the customary ritual excursion to infinity. If you reflect on this magic trick of Church and Curry you will see that it has come directly from the postulates of Naming and Reflexivity that we have discussed above. These notions, that there should be a name for everything, and that words can be applied to the description and production of other words, allow the language to refer to itself and to produce itself from itself. The Church-Curry construction was devised for mathematical logic, but it is fundamental to the logic of logic, the linguistics of linguistics and the cybernetics of cybernetics.

I like to call the construction of the intermediate operator **G**, the "gremlin" (See [9].) Gremlins seem innocent enough. They just duplicate entities that they meet, and set up an operation of the duplicate on the duplicand. But when you let a gremlin meet a gremlin then strange things can happen. It is a bit like the story of the sorcerer's apprentice. A recursion may happen whether you like it or not.

A formal eigenform must be placed in a context in order for it to have human meaning. The struggle on the mathematical side is to control recursions, bending them to desired ends. The struggle on the human side is to cognize a world sensibly and communicate well and effectively with others. For each of us, there is a continual manufacture of eigenforms (tokens for eigenbehavior). Such tokens will not pass as the currency of communication unless we achieve mutuality as well. One can say that mutuality itself is a higher eigenform. Achieving mutual understanding will be recognized. As with all eigenforms, the abstract version exists. Realization happens in the course of time.

VII. The Form of Names

The simplicity of a thought, the apparent clarity of distinction is mirrored in the sort of eigenforms that come from the Church-Curry realm as described in the last section. Consider a linguistic example: Each person has a name (at least one). In the course of time we are introduced to people and come to know their names. We know that name not as an item to look up about the person (and this applies to certain objects as well) but as a direct property of the person. That is, if I meet Heinz he appears to me as Heinz, not as this person with certain characteristics, whose name I can find in my social database if I care to do so. It is like this only when we are first introduced. At the point of introduction there is this person and there is his name separate from him. Once learned, *the name is shifted* and occurs in space right along with the person. Heinz and his name are in the same cognitive space which is also in the same place as the apparent physical space. We can observe this shifting process in the course of learning a name. We can also observe how physical and cognitive spaces are superimposed. The many classical optical illusions illustrate these matters vividly.

Now we have Heinz with his name inseparable from his presence, and this is true even if he is not physically present, for the shift has occurred and will not be undone. But we also have his name Heinz separate from him, and able to be pinned upon another. And we have his name not quite separate from him, but rather this Heinz is the name of the name we have attached to him! This is Heinz's metaname. How do we distinguish among all these different names for Heinz? We use the same symbols for them, yet they are different. Lets choose a way to indicate the differences.

We start with the reference:

Heinz -----> Cybernetic Magician

(The arrow will indicate that the entity on the left is the name of the entity on the right.)

We get to know him and shift the reference.

#Heinz -----> Cybernetic Magician Heinz

Now the name is in the cognitive space of Heinz, and the metaname #Heinz refers to that conjunction. We shall call this **the indicative shift**.

name -----> object
#name-----> object name

The indicative shift occurs, constantly weaving the apparent external reality with the linguistic reality. *Self-reference occurs when one calls up (names) the metanaming operator.*

At first the metanaming operator is not marked and no name has been chosen for it. But then its name is chosen (as #). We have

----->

That is, # refers at first to the singular place where there is an absence of naming, a void in the realm of distinctions.

Then the shift occurs. We have the reference of the meta-naming operator to itself (as the operator enters a space formerly void!).

----->

Suppose that the meta-naming operator has another name, say M. Then we have

M ----->

which shifts to a self-reference at the second articulated level of meta naming

#M -----> #M

These are the eigenforms of self consciousness in the realm of names.

Heinz said [5]: **"I am the observed link between myself and observing myself."** Self-reference at this level, the action of a domain upon itself, leading to cognition, is the beginning of the realm of eigenforms in Heinz's world.

VIII. Appendix - Eigenform, Eigenvalue and Quantum Mechanics

There are two reasons for including a discussion of quantum mechanics in this essay. On the one hand the quantum mechanics of the twentieth century has been a powerful force in asking us to rethink our notions of objects and causality. On the other hand, Heinz von Foerster's notion of eigenform is an outgrowth of his background as a quantum physicist. We should ask what eigenforms might have to do with quantum theory and with the quantum world.

In this section we meet the concurrence of the view of object as token for eigenbehavior and the observation postulate of quantum mechanics. In quantum mechanics observation is modeled not by eigenform but by its mathematical relative the eigenvector. The reader should recall that a vector is a quantity with magnitude and direction, often pictured as an arrow in the plane or in three dimensional space.

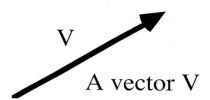

V

A vector V

In quantum physics [11], the state of a physical system is modeled by a vector in a high-dimensional space, called a Hilbert space. As time goes on the vector rotates in this high dimensional space. Observable quantities correspond to (linear) operators **H** on these vectors **v** that have the property that the application of **H** to **v** results in a new vector that is a multiple of **v** by a factor λ.

(An operator is said to be linear if $H(av +w) = aH(v) + H(w)$ for vectors v and w, and any number a. Linearity is usually a simplifying assumption in mathematical models, but it is an essential feature of quantum mechanics.) In symbols this has the form:

$$Hv = \lambda v.$$

One says that v is an eigenvector for the operator H, and that λ is the eigenvalue. The constant λ is the quantity that is observed (for example the energy of an electron). These are particular properties of the mathematical context of quantum mechanics. The λ can be eliminated by replacing H by $G = H/\lambda$ (when λ is non zero) so that

$$Gv = (H/\lambda)v = (Hv)/\lambda = \lambda v/k = v.$$

Thus

$$Gv = v.$$

*In quantum mechanics observation is founded on the production of eigenvectors **v**
with **Gv=v** where **v** is a vector in a Hilbert space and **G** is a linear operator on that
space.*

Many of the strange and fascinating properties of quantum mechanics emanate
directly from this model of observation. In order to observe a quantum state, its vector
is projected into an eigenvector for that particular mode of observation. By projecting
the vector into that mode and not another, one manages to make the observation, but at
the cost of losing information about the other possibilities inherent in the vector. This
is the source, in the mathematical model, of the complementarities that allow exact
determination of the position of a particle at the expense of nearly complete
uncertainty about its momentum (or vice versa the determination of momentum at the
expense of knowledge of the position).

Observation and quantum evolution (the determinate rotation of the state vector in
the high dimensional Hilbert space) are interlocked. Each observation discontinuously
projects the state vector to an eigenvector. The intervals between observations allow
the continuous evolution of the state vector. This tapestry of interaction of the
continuous and the discrete is the basis for the quantum mechanical description of the
world.

Heinz was certainly aware, as a practicing physicist, of this model of observation
in quantum theory. His theory of eigenforms is a sweeping generalization of quantum
mechanics that creates a context for understanding the remarkable effectiveness of
that theory. If indeed the world of objects is, in fact, a world of tokens for
eigenbehaviors, and if physics demands forms of observations that give numerical
results, then a simplest example of such observation is the observable in the quantum
mechanical model.

This is a reversal of epistemology, a complete turning of the world upside down.
Heinz has tricked us into considering the world of our experience and finding that it is
our world, generated by our actions and that it has become objective through the self-
generated stabilities of those actions. He has convinced us to come along with him and
see that all of cybernetics confirms this point of view. He has left the corollaries to us.
He has not confronted the physicists and the philosophers head on. He has brought us
into his world and let us participate in the making of it. And he has pointed to the
genesis and tautological nature of quantum theory to those of us who might ask the
question.

But he has also left the consequence of the question to us. For if the world is a
world of eigenforms and most of them are in time oscillatory and unstable, must we
insist on stability at the level of our present perception of that world? In principle,
there is an eigenform, but that form leads always outward into larger worlds and new
understanding. In the case of quantum mechanics, the whole theory has the
appearance of an elementary exercise confirming the view point of objects as tokens
for eigenbehaviors in a special case. Heinz leaves us with the conundrum of finding
the more general physical theory that confirms that special case.

This dilemma is itself a special case of the dilemma that Heinz has given us. He said it himself many times. If you give a person an undecidable problem, the action of that person in attempting to solve the problem reveals the identity of the person and the nature of his/her creativity

References

[1] Barendregt, H. P. (1985). *The lambda calculus - Its syntax and semantics.* New York: North Holland Pub. (Originally published in 1981)

[2] Spencer-Brown, G. (1969). *Laws of form.* London: Allen & Unwin, Ltd.

[3] Foerster, H. von (1981). *Observing systems.* The Systems Inquiry Series. Seaside, CA: Intersystems Publications.

[4] Foerster, H. von (1981). Objects: tokens for (eigen-) behaviors. In *Observing systems* (pp. 274 - 285). The Systems Inquiry Series. Seaside, CA: Intersystems Publications.

[5] Foerster, H. von (1981). Notes on an epistemology for living things. In *Observing systems* (pp. 258 - 271). The Systems Inquiry Series. Seaside, CA: Intersystems Publications.

[6] Foerster, H. von (1981). On constructing a reality. In *Observing systems* (pp. 288 - 309). The Systems Inquiry Series. Seaside, CA: Intersystems Publications.

[7] Kauffman, L. H. (1987). Self-reference and recursive forms, *Journal of Social and Biological Structures,* 53-72.

[8] Kauffman, L. H. (1995). Knot logic. In L. H. Kauffman (Ed.), *Knots and Applications* (pp. 1-110). Singapore: World Scientific Pub. Co.

[9] Kauffman, L. H. (2001). The mathematics of Charles Sanders Peirce. *Cybernetics and Human Knowing, 8*(1-2), 79-110.

[10] Mandelbrot, B. B. (1982). *The fractal geometry of nature.* New York: W. H. Freeman & Company (Originally published in 1977)

[11] Sakurai, J. J. (1985). *Modern quantum mechanics.* San Francisco: Benjamin/Cummings Publishing Company, Inc.

Heinz von Foerster, 1966 (photographer unknown)

Cybernetics And Human Knowing. Vol. 10, nos. 3-4, pp. 91-105

Machines of Wonder and Elephants that Float through Air[1]

A Valedictory Understanding of *Understanding Understanding*

Ranulph Glanville[2]

The paper stands both as a review of von Foerster's valedictory work "Understanding Understanding," and an analysis of what is argued to be the major theme in his work—wonder—examined through the material presented in "Understanding Understanding." The theme is developed with reference to three machines that recur in von Foerster's work (making several appearances in the papers collected in *Understanding Understanding*) namely, "Maxwell's Demon," "Eigen Forms" and the "Non-Trivial Machine," and is in turn related to the final paper in the collection. "Introduction to Natural Magic," which thus takes on the role of the key work of the collection.

Understanding Understanding

When Heinz von Foerster died on October 2nd last year (2002), he left a slightly incomplete collection of papers which, if anything is, is his valediction. *Understanding Understanding*,[3] subtitled "Essays on Cybernetics and Cognition," is exactly that (Foerster, 2003). Here von Foerster has collected together many of the best known papers from the first part of his career in cybernetics, and supplemented them with a selection of later work, most of it also well known, but some of it nevertheless not easy to come by. He added an introduction (and there's an index). What is missing is the introduction he had intended to write for each paper he chose, and, of course, the title pages he himself designed for the versions he published through the Biological Computer Laboratory (BCL). It is a matter of considerable regret that he did not have the time and strength to write those introductions. I, for one, would have been fascinated to read his own evaluations and to hear something of the stories behind the papers that he would have liked to tell us.

---

1. "Elephants that float through air" is a phrase plucked by one of my students, Nicholas Tidball, from von Foerster and Poerksen (2001). It was used to describe the sorts of wonderful things magicians convince us of.
2. CybernEthics Research, Southsea, UK, email ranulph@glanville.co.uk
3. Foerster, H. von (2003). *Understanding Understanding*. New York: Springer. All references to von Foerster's work cited in this paper are to be found in the papers collected in this volume. For that reason, publication details given are for the original publication. The details of this collection are omitted, save for page numbers which appear at the end of the reference in [ ] brackets, starting UU. For example, [UU 247–63].

The collection finishes with an oddball publication, "On Natural Magic." Yet this paper now seems to me (for reasons I develop below) to be perhaps the key paper to his work. It sets the scene for the motivating idea behind this work: the passionate concern for what it is to be human (the theme of my paper), and it shows this idea forming and performing in von Foerster from a relatively early age.

In this paper I shall consider the material in *Understanding Understanding* both to explore it as the authoritative collection of von Foerster's work, and in order to argue what I believe is the key theme to be discovered in his work through the examination of this collection.

The Papers

The papers in *Understanding Understanding* are organised more or less chronologically by date of their original publication, and fall broadly into two categories. Those papers, often with a fairly technical bent, in which the idea of second–order cybernetics can now (in hindsight, and in Heinzsight) be seen to be being developed; and those less formal and more philosophical and reflective papers which, assuming second–order cybernetics, talk about aspects of how we may understand ourselves and our places in the world, according to this new way of looking. I have appended a table (Table 1) in which I list the papers in *Understanding Understanding* in chronological (rather than book) order,[4] comparing the contents of this book with the earlier *Observing Systems* which Francisco Varela composed and edited (von Foerster, 1981, see below), and differentiating the papers into these two categories (T for technical and P for philosophical), plus a third, transitional category (M).

The Technical Papers

Von Foerster's reputation was built on what I call the technical papers. These papers start with his original (1948) venture along this path ("Das Gedächtnis: Eine Quantenmechanische Abhandlung" translated as "Memory: a Quantum Mechanical Treatise"[5]), which opened the door to the USA and to that extraordinary group of scientists that Heims refers to as "The Cybernetics Group" (Heims, 1991) who, recognising his worth, welcomed von Foerster to their number and set him the task of editing their proceedings so he would learn English (von Foerster, personal communication).

I call these papers technical papers because they are written (albeit in von Foerster's wonderfully stylish English) in the mainstream of the tradition of the

---

4. Book order can be reconstructed from the page numbers.
5. This paper, a small book in the original German version, is not in this collection, but the problem it approaches is the key concept in von Foerster's preface. The English version may be found in the first published proceedings of the Macy Conferences on Cybernetics which brought von Foerster into the cybernetic, and English language, community (von Foerster et al., 1950).

journal paper, and their arguments are often sustained by prolonged periods of complex mathematical formulation.

The technical papers in this volume may be directed towards cybernetics and cognition, as the book's subtitle tells us, but they could have been chosen for another audience. Of the half dozen technical papers presented in this book, most had already appeared in the earlier (and now impossible to obtain) aforementioned collection made by Francisco Varela—a biologist. The point I wish to make is that the papers in *Understanding Understanding* have a wider appeal than that suggested by the sub title.

And they also move towards second–order cybernetics. Starting with the classic "On Self–Organising Systems and Their Environments" (von Foerster, 1960 [UU 1–20] concerning limits to self–organisation resulting from the Laws of Thermodynamics), these papers make a stately progress towards the equally classic "On Constructing a Reality"[6] (von Foerster, 1973 [UU 211–228] which explores the presence of the observer in his/her way of understanding): perhaps the first paper actually to do—as opposed to derive—second-order cybernetics.

The progression makes the argument, albeit implicitly and (at least at first) unconsciously to the necessary inclusion of the observer which is von Foerster's requirement for a cybernetic system to transform itself to be second-order: as he wrote (in the "Cybernetics of Cybernetics" compendium, von Foerster, 1975):

> *First order cybernetics is the cybernetics of observed systems.*
> *Second order cybernetics is the cybernetics of observing systems.*

Being explicit, he describes the cybernetics of cybernetics in a paper of that name that appears later in *Understanding Understanding*, amongst those papers I have called the philosophical papers. However, looking back at the papers ranged under this technical heading, the development of the position von Foerster found himself moved to take, and the many contributions of his colleagues at the Biological Computer Laboratory, are plainly visible—given the distorting gift of hindsight! See also Scott (1979) and his extended paper in this Journal (Scott, 2003).

The Philosophical Papers

What I call the philosophical papers began to appear around the time of Varela's collection (1981), and so they are by-and-large missing from that collection. As an aficionado, I know many of them, but there are, nevertheless, a number I don't know, and some I was not even aware of. They are very different in style to the technical papers: far less formal and frequently using the device of a public lecture to give them

---

6. Apart from its own excellence, this paper is responsible for bringing George Spencer Brown's book *The Laws of Form* to wide public attention. Spencer Brown's dictum "draw a distinction" is von Foerster's abstract. The importance of the notion of distinction, and the debate surrounding both it and Spencer Brown's particular formulations, have been fertile.

a directness and inclusiveness that is new. Discussing this with others who care about von Foerster's work, the idea arose (from Dirk Baecker) that there were a number of events that coincided, leading von Foerster to take this new tack.

These papers start to appear at the time that von Foerster's legendary Biological Computer Laboratory at the University of Illinois was being closed. With von Foerster's retirement (in 1976), the university declined to continue supporting his Lab. Von Foerster therefore moved its materials and archives to his new Pacific home.[7] This time also coincides with the period of transition in which the basic concepts of second–order cybernetics were developed and elaborated, which I have taken to be 1968 to 1975 (Glanville, 2002).

Thus, there is change in von Foerster's life, in how he thinks about the world, where he lives, his lifestyle and the sort of support he gets. Baecker suggested that, around this time von Foerster moved to communicate his ideas less through the somewhat private world of the learned journal, preferring public events and addresses where his presence as distinguished elder statesman (and his amazing ability to perform in public) gave him greater scope to develop and communicate his ideas. In fact, this became his preferred way of working. There were less and less occasions when he would write material that had not somehow been spoken: transcribing public lectures, or working in collaboration through interview (witness the three recently published books deriving from von Foerster interviews[8]).

From the above, it might be understood that I want to argue these papers are merely "chatty." This is not so. I call them the philosophical papers not because the technical papers were lacking in philosophical reference and content, any more than the philosophical papers are short on technical content (in particular, "Notes on an Epistemology for Living Things," (von Foerster, 1972a [UU 247–260]) "Objects: Tokens for (Eigen-) Behaviours" (von Foerster, 1977 [UU 261–272]) and "For Niklas Luhmann: 'How Recursive is Communication?'" (von Foerster, 1993b [UU 305–324]). I call them the philosophical papers because they approach wide–ranging questions that concern what second-order cybernetics is, and the way of thinking and understanding it brings, i.e., with what this understanding means to us as human beings. Thus, topics covered include responsibility; do we discover or invent; epistemology; and ethics.

A Key—or The Task

Everything I have written so far in this paper is scene setting, a placing of the offerings in *Understanding Understanding* in order and context. Yet my central task in this paper is not to review *Understanding Understanding*. It is to consider what might be called the "motivation" behind the content: to search for a common, deeply rooted

---

7.   At least one advantage comes from this closure: when von Foerster realised it would happen, he used the elective he offered undergraduate students to provide the manpower to create the legendary "Cybernetics of Cybernetics" compendium which he edited (von Foerster, 1975).

8.   See von Foerster and Poerksen (2001), Müller and Müller (2003), and von Foerster and Broecker (2002).

idea that may be seen to drive von Foerster's work—a key. This is not a typical review that summarises and places work in context. I would not want to do that as my part in commemorating von Foerster's work. Rather, I hope to show a special type of unity and of world view, a deep and unifying insight in von Foerster's work that will give us more than we have reason to hope for or expect! I undertake this by reference to an obviously cybernetic (in the original sense) aspect of von Foerster's work.

Let us remember that Cybernetics was, as Norbert Wiener described (1948), concerned with

"Communication and control in the animal and the machine."

This cybernetics was specially interested in mechanism. What seems to me the greatest of the individual early texts, Ross Ashby's "An Introduction to Cybernetics" (1956) is almost exclusively focused on mechanism, and the where withal to enable mechanism to be developed. Early cybernetics was particularly concerned with the notion that the animal and the machine might be considered in the same breath: that, for the areas cybernetics was concerned with, there was no effective difference, and concepts associated with mechanism could be brought to bear equally on both.

So I shall start by examining machines von Foerster referred to with particular enjoyment.

Three Machines

Von Foerster liked too refer to three devices—the machines of my title. These three are:

- Maxwell's Demon,
- The Eigen Forms, and
- The Non–Trivial Machine.

The first and second of these are machines invented by others. Maxwell's Demon was invented by James Clerk Maxwell as a thought tool (in much the way that I claim we should understand the Black Box (Glanville, 1982)). Eigen Forms, a portmanteau term I use to indicate the whole gamut of "eigen" terms, such as eigen functions, operators, systems and values, have a long history going back at least to David Hilbert. Rather charmingly, a major current worker in the field of eigen forms has the surname, Eigen (German for "self"). The last of the three is, as far as I know, von Foerster's own invention, first appearing in von Foerster 1971 [UU 133–168].

I shall consider each of these machines in turn, although I shall not give (much) explanation of their mechanisms. I leave that to von Foerster himself, in the papers in *Understanding Understanding*. And perhaps I should also mention that I think I talk of these machines more metaphorically that von Foerster did. However, he was fond of quoting Gordon Pask (who he called "Mr. Cybernetics, the cybernetician's cybernetician") who defined cybernetics as "the science of the defensible metaphor." (Foerster, 1991a [UU 288])

Maxwell's Demon

Von Foerster introduces us to Maxwell's delightful Demon[9] in his paper "On Self–Organising Systems and their Environments," (1960 [UU 1–20]): a paper of importance in a number of ways of which two matter here.[10]

The first is that it reminds us most clearly that von Foerster's background is as a physicist. The theme of the paper, which surprised some, is that self–organising systems are subject to the Laws of Thermodynamics, and are therefore, in a profound sense, impossible. This was considered a strange conclusion for a man who had spent time and effort organising the conference on self–organisation at which the paper was delivered!

The second is in the introduction of Maxwell's fabulous Demon, which makes further (and longer) appearances in "Responsibilities of Competence" (von Foerster 1972 [UU 191–9), where he argued that Maxwell's Demon is an isomorph of the Turing machine, an idea he repeated in "Disorder/Order: Discovery or Invention?" (von Foerster, 1984 [UU 273–282]).

Maxwell's Demon is a device to counteract the operation of Newton's Second Law of Thermodynamics. The idea is that this little Demon exists inside a box that has two halves, one hot, one cold, separated by a division with a small hole with a door. The Demon notes when low energy (speed) particles are trying to move from the lower energy half to the higher, and those of high energy (speed) trying to move from the higher to the half with lower energy, keeping the hot with the hot and the cold with the cold, by selectively opening the door. Energy is embodied, here, as temperature, and the (temperature) differential may actually increase. The point von Foerster develops is that it takes energy for the Demon to recognise the particles as hot or cold, and then to act to open or close the door, which dissipates the energy (temperature) differential regardless of the Demon's conservatory efforts and antics. This means Newton's Laws still hold, in spite of the Demon.

What, then, is interesting about Maxwell's Demon? After all, it's just a thought experiment and it's neither real nor will it work. The answer is that it creates and maintains distinction (long before Spencer Brown's imperious command! (Spencer Brown, 1968)). The mechanism of Maxwell's Demon creates and maintains distinction, and without distinction it is not possible for us to develop understandings. Distinction makes possible our amazing ability to see and then to explain, and that is a sort of magic.

---

9. According to Dr. Albert Müller, keeper of the von Foerster archive at the University of Vienna, Maxwell introduced his Demon in his 1871 Theory of Heat. I am grateful to Dr. Müller for this (and much other) information.

10. Bernhard Dotzler (1996) wrote about von Foerster's interest in Magic and Demons in the Festschrift I edited for von Foerster (Glanville, 1996). However, his points (interesting as they are) are not quite those I make here.

Eigen Forms

Most who know of von Foerster's philosophical work will know of his fascination with Eigen Forms, introduced in his paper "Eigen Objects—Tokens for (Eigen) Behaviours" (von Foerster, 1977 [UU 261–272]) in which he explores the notion of recursive mathematical processes that yield a fixed, self–reproducing value regardless of the value of the input. Yet many people question the value of this fascination with Eigen Operations, Eigen Values, etc. They refer, in particular, to von Foerster's tendency to use the one example:

Take any number and apply the following action to it: divide it by 2 and add 1 to the result. Then repeat this process on this result, that is, use the output (result) of this operation as its next input.

This operation can be expressed in a diagram as shown below:

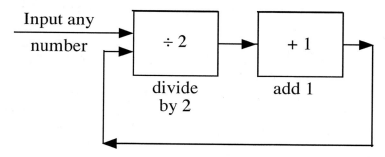

An Eigen Form that computes an output that recursively approaches the value 2.

The output of this iterative process always progresses towards 2. When it reaches 2 it retains that value. You can check how this can be by using 2 as the initial number you chose to input.

The general criticism seems to be that this is interesting, but only slightly so since it's not saying much. However, this is far too restricted a reading of what is a much more extensive paper, in which this is just one example; and too literal with this example which is, I contend, to be seen as a metaphor. As Kauffman (2003) shows elsewhere in this journal, Eigen Behaviours (and similar functions) are much more common than we might imagine.

Why was von Foerster fascinated with Eigen Forms? Again, Kauffman provides an extensive answer. But there is a simple root to von Foerster's fascination the key to which is, I believe, to be found in the connection he proposed when he first paraded his interest. The connection is with Piaget, and, in particular, with Piaget's concept of Object constancy—the mechanism by which we (starting as newborn children) learn to identify stable-under-change objects that we propose as the embodiment or progenitor of a number of different percepts (Piaget, 1955). Thus, many different sensations that we eventually come to categorise as views, sounds, smells etc. which we encounter on many different occasions eventually come to form our notion of objects such as "Mum" (or whatever else). Piaget derived what he thought of as a necessary behaviour: von Foerster showed us a model of a mechanism that would generate this behaviour.

And this is, I believe, what he found magical about the operation of Eigen Forms: through them we generate, out of any random selection (out of nothing), a constant, recurring something. This operation shows us a way in which we can understand how (and that) we may develop constancy in our experience: how, from a world of no-form (no-world), we can generate a form or object—which we can attach to objects in the world (the world being such an object). (Of course, these objects are now the consequence of computations we carry out on our percepts, as von Foerster argues first in "On Constructing a Reality" (von Foerster, 1973 [UU 211–228].), a paper that became a clarion call to those concerned that the observer's presence in his/her observations should be explicitly demonstrated and who wanted to understand what this might mean.

Von Foerster saw this as a way of bridging between experience and the world described in physics. As he often insisted (e.g., von Foerster & Poerksen, 2001), he was not a constructivist: but, then, he was not really any sort of -ist at all: he hated categorisation because it reduces our imagination and our freedom, makes it hard for us to see outside the bounds of the categories we saw—regardless of whether what we were seeing came from the (rest of the) world, or came from us.

The Non–Trivial Machine

Von Foerster would often talk of the extraordinary processes of trivialisation that humans resort to. He regarded most education as a form of trivialisation, as he insists, for instance, in von Foerster and Poerksen (2001). By trivialisation, he meant that variety and difference were ironed out so that the outcome of any operation applied to the machine would be known (that is, perfectly predictable). This offended him greatly, for it offended against his dictate that "only we can decide the undecideable" by removing the undecideablity through a conceit.

A conventional input/output machine converts an input signal or behaviour into a predictable output signal or behaviour. The machine is trivial because this behaviour is trivial: there is never anything to learn. Once you know one input/output relation you know that you know the resultant outputs deriving from all inputs.[11] Von Foerster held that if, in some system, you know the output that results from any input, that knowledge is trivial. As he wrote "A trivial machine is defined by the fact that it

---

11. Von Foerster discusses trivial and non–trivial machines in "Molecular Ecology" (1971 [UU 133–168]},
    "Perception of the Future and the Future of Perception (1972 [UU 199–210], and "How Recursive is
    Communication?" (1993b [UU 305–324]}, although the language of his discussion develops in these papers.

always bravely does the very same thing that it originally did" (Von Foerster, 1993b [UU 305-324]).

In contrast, the Non-Trivial Machine, as von Foerster draws it, contains another input/output machine within it, which has a feedback loop generating internal states. As a result, the behaviour is simply not predictable: the possibilities are so vast that they cannot be examined.[12] And, while there may be times when the observer (that is, we) believe(s) (s)he has made a predictable model, there never is, and never can be, the certainty associated with the Trivial Machine. At some time the behaviour may change: we cannot know whether this will happen and, if so, what the result will be. In this respect, the Non–Trivial Machine is a variant on the Black Box (Glanville, 1982) and follows Wittgensteins's (1961) insistence that because something has always happened does not mean it always will: historical constancy is not causal connection. See below:

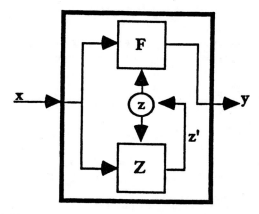

A Non-Trivial Machine: note internal feedback loop.

It is the unpredictability of the Non–Trivial Machine that is significant to von Foerster, and that makes it non–trivial. What he values is precisely the unpredictability. Why?

Because the unpredictability means that we can anticipate surprise: all will not be as we had thought it would be. In other words, we have a model for a world we inhabit where what we observe may change in ways we cannot imagine. And that means we are never truly in control, that we can and must keep learning—maintaining our involvement. The world of the Non–Trivial Machine, as if by magic, creates surprises and cannot be tamed by us.

If the Eigen Form generates constancy (pattern) out of disorder and allows us to credit objects in our experience, the Non–Trivial Machine brakes these patterns, allowing us to discover the new, anew: it disorganises our ordering.

---

12. Von Foerster relates, here, to Bremmerman's constant, a figure indicating what the earth might have computed in its life, had it been a computer. This constant, beyond which we move into areas of the transcomputable, is useful for giving a sense of scale and is not either absolute or correct. See Glanville (1998).

And Maxwell's Demon allows us to find and maintain boundaries in the continuum.

Wonder

Here, I want to substitute another word for the word "magic" I have purposely used, above.

What unites the three machines discussed above is that they all act to produce what causes us to marvel. We look at what they do—they are only machines, after all—and a sense of awe pervades us. They are amazing.

The word that pulls all this together is wonder. Not wonder in the sense of confusion, or wonder in the sense of dreamily being indecisive (I wonder about...); but wonder in the sense that we are left speechless—that transcendental sense that is more of the spiritual than the material world, which leaves us more aware of what it is to be human.

Here is what *Merriam Webster's Collegiate Dictionary* (as cited on the Encyclopaedia Britannica web site: www.eb.com) offers:

Main Entry:	1won·der
Pronunciation:	'w&n-d&r
Function:	*noun*
Etymology:	Middle English, from Old English *wundor;* akin to Old High German *wuntar* wonder
Date:	before 12th century
1 a:	a cause of astonishment or admiration: MARVEL <it's a *wonder* you weren't killed>
1b:	MIRACLE
2:	**the quality of exciting amazed admiration**
3 a:	**rapt attention or astonishment at something awesomely mysterious or new to one's experience**
3b:	a feeling of doubt or uncertainty

I refer, particularly, to the meanings listed under 2 and 3a.

Thus, I call the collective of these 3 machines the "Machines of Wonder," and title this paper accordingly.

Natural Magic

The last paper in *Understanding Understanding* is "Introduction to Natural Magic" (von Foerster, 1993a [UU 325–338]). This paper is a transcription by Paul Schroeder of a tape von Foerster sent him in response to a question Schroeder asked about his life as a magician.

This paper at first looks out of place in the collection. Yet it was a paper von Foerster was specially attached to, and he was most particular about its initial publication.[13]

All those who came across von Foerster learnt he was a magician, whether they came to know it in the liberal sense of the word, or the more technical. When he addressed an audience (numbering from 1 to 1000) he performed a certain kind of magic that brought you in to his world and his thinking: he was a performer.[14]

Fewer learnt that he was a fully qualified professional magician who, in his teens, had funded his interests in skiing and studying nature by performing magic in public with his cousin Martin Lang. He was a member of the (Vienna) Magic Circle!

I had always thought that what of this interest he carried into his work came through in the performance that he staged. But, over the last couple of years, I came to think this understanding was impoverished, too literal. As I came to understand the Machines of Wonder, so I came to understand that to be a magician is, as von Foerster insists, to have direct access to wonder, and to be able to bring it to others to create "Elephants that Float through Air." This is what magicians do, and this is why "On Natural Magic" is both such an important paper, and so appropriately concludes *Understanding Understanding*.

Last Words

The special piece of magic that Heinz performed for me was to confirm this. He stayed alive long enough for me to visit him in late September 2002, and to ask him about wonder.[15] He greeted me thus: "Ranulph, you are specialising in dying cyberneticians!" I took this as permission to ask those questions we don't always feel we can ask the dying—although often enough, I have learnt, they wish we would.

I asked him many things. But in particular, I suggested that what he was really interested in, that what his whole life's work had been about (and the key I have tried to argue for in this paper), was wonder, and the value of wonder. How he tried to bring that sense of wonder to the fore because it is through feeling that that we know we are human. And he replied, in that wonderful accent, that this was correct: in that diminuendo he used when he talked of the really important and the really personal, he agreed.

---

13. This paper, as with virtually all his papers, was published in a BCL version with a cover that von Foerster himself designed. I later tidied up the written transcription von Foerster gave me, and edited for consistency and publication, also attempting to convert very old, grey-on-grey photos to some form that might reproduce in the technology that journals use. Hence the acknowledgement to me in *Understanding Understanding*.
14. His son Thomas, who was responsible for the publication of *Understanding Understanding*, told me that von Foerster used to prepare at great length even to go out to dinner. I had seen him prepare speeches and was astonished at the efforts he took to present thoughts and work he was already a master of, although I have since found the value in this approach, which I find echoed in the Scottish comedian, Billy Connolly
15. He passed into a semi coma the day after I left and died a few days later. I was, as far as I can tell, his last visitor, apart from family and other intimate carers

Coda

There is another device that von Foerster used, another pithy aphorism I mentioned earlier, that perhaps lies behind all of this. He was fond of saying:

Only we can decide the undecideable.[16]

By this I believe he meant the following:

When some question is in principle undecideable, when there can be no mechanism for making a decision, then the decision is up to us, and only we can make it. The choice is ours. One such is the question of whether there is a reality we can know that is independent of our knowing it (a mind-independent reality): clearly we cannot know if there is a reality we can know without knowing it. We cannot decide this question, so we are free to make our choice according to our personal taste: the decision depends on who we are and our belief systems more than, perhaps, any other decisions. The decision we make tells us who we are.

The decision of whether anything exists when the observer is removed is the question that fires constructivism. There appear to be two answers: either that there is a mind independent reality, or that there is nothing. For a constructivist, I think that this question should remain undecided. But von Foerster was prepared to live at least as if there was a mind independent reality (the sort of reality science looks for). He looked on this the way he looked on mathematics: as an elegant, delightful and convenient device that allowed him to get the results he wanted more efficiently and effectively (he likened the use of mathematics to riding a subway train to traverse a city). What is important, however, is not so much the choice he made, but that there was a choice for him to make.

And that, we agreed, was the greatest wonder of them all.

Acknowledgements

Drs. Bernard Scott, Albert Müller, Karl Mueller and Dirk Baecker have helped me with sources and comments. Aartje Hulstein, Søren Brier, Paul Pangaro and Thomas von Foerster all read manuscript drafts and made many helpful suggestions.

Madeleine AkTyPi, in a long interview conducted through email (Glanville & AkTyPi, 2003), reminded me of the importance of the quote "Only we can decide the undecideable." Thank you Madeleine.

---

16. Concerning the source of this quote, Albert Mueller notes: This theorem was created within the context of a lecture Heinz gave for the ars electronica festival on Sept. 14th, 1988. The paper is published as von Foerster 1989. This publication had—as far as I can see—two German reprints but no translation into another language. Heinz took up this sentence (theorem) in an article for a volume on research an reflexivity, published as 1991b. Heinz came back to this sentence on the occasion of his "Paris Paper" which he gave to the conference "Systèmes et thérapie familiale" in October 1990. There, he not longer speaks of a "theorem" but of a "metaphysical postulate" This paper is published as Heinz von Foerster (1991a). The next year an English version appeared in *Cybernetics and Human Knowing 1*(1).

The opinions and arguments remain mine, and I own all the mistakes. They're mine, too—mine, all mine!

References

Ashby, W. R. (1956). *Introduction to cybernetics*. London: Chapman and Hall.

Dotzler, B (1996). Demons—magic—cybernetics: On the introduction to natural magic as told by Heinz von Foerster. In Glanville, R (Ed.), Heinz von Foerster: a Festschrift, *Systems Research, 13*(3).

Foerster, H. von (1948). Das Gedächtnis: Eine quantenmechanische Untersuchung. Wien: Franz Deuticke. (Presented in English as "Memory: A quantum mechanical treatise." In H. von Foerster, M. Mead, & H. Teuber (Eds.). (1950) *Cybernetics: Transactions of the Sixth Conference*. New York: Josiah Macy, Jr. Foundation.)

Foerster, H. von (1960). On self-organising systems and their environments. In M. Yovits, & S. Cameron (Eds.), *Self-organising systems*. London: Pergamon. (Also in Foerster, 2003)

Foerster, H. von (1971). Molecular ethology. In *Molecular mechanisms of memory and learning* (C. Ungar, Ed.). New York: Plenum Press. (Also in Foerster, 2003)

Foerster, H. von (1972a). Notes on an epistemology for living things. Urbana, IL: BCL fiche 104/1, University of Illinois. (Also in Foerster, 2003)

Foerster, H. von (1972b). Perception of the future and the future of perception. *Instructional Science, 1*, 31–43. (Also in Foerster, 2003)

Foerster, H. von (1972c). Responsibilities of competence. *Journal of Cybernetics, 2* (2). (Also in Foerster, 2003)

Foerster, H. von (1973). On constructing a reality, In F. Preiser (Ed.), *Environmental Design Research*. Stroudberg: Dowden, Hutchinson and Ross. (Also in Foerster, 2003)

Foerster, H. von (1975). *The cybernetics of cybernetics*. Champaign/Urbana, IL: BCL, University of Illinois. (Republished (1995). Minneapolis: Future Systems.)

Foerster, H. von (1977). Objects: Tokens for (eigen-) behaviours. In B. Inhelder, R. Garcia, & J. Voneche (Eds.), *Hommage à Jean Piaget: Epistémologie génétique et équilibration*. Neuchatel: Delachaux et Niestle. (Also in Foerster, 2003)

Foerster, H. von (1981). *Observing systems* (F. Varela, Ed.). Seaside, Ca: Intersystems.

Foerster, H. von (1984). Disorder/order: Discovery or invention? In P. Livingston (Ed.), *Disorder and order*. Saratoga, CA: Anna Libri. (Also in Foerster, 2003)

Foerster, H. von (1989). Wahrnehmen wahrnehmen. In Ars Electronica (Ed.), *Philosophien der neuen Technologien*. Berlin: Merve Verlag.

Foerster, H. von (1991a). Ethics and second-order cybernetics. (In French, in Y. Ray, Prieur (Eds.), *Systemes, ethique, perspectives en therapie familiale*. Paris: ESF editeur.) (Also in Foerster, 2003)

Foerster, H. von (1991b). Through the Eyes of the Other. In F. Steier (Ed.), *Research and Reflexivity*. London: Sage.

Foerster, H. von (1993a). Introduction to natural magic (R. Glanville, Ed.), *Systems Research, 10*. (Also in Foerster, 2003)

Foerster, H. von (1993b). For Niklas Luhmann: "How Recursive is Communication?" (German original in *Teoria Soziobiologica 2/93* Milan: Agneli.) (Also in Foerster, 2003)

Foerster, H. von (2003). *Understanding understanding*. New York: Springer.

Foerster, H. von, & Bröcker, M. (2002). *Teil der Welt, Fraktale einer Ethik - Ein Drama in drei Akten*. Heidelberg: Carl-Auer-Systeme Verlag

Foerster, H. von, & Poerksen, B. (2001). *Understanding systems*. New York: Kluwer Academic/Plenum Press. (And Heidelberg: Carl-Auer-Systeme)

Foerster, H. von, Mead, M., & Teuber, H (Eds.) (1950). *Cybernetics: Transactions of the sixth conference*. New York: Josiah Macy, Jr. Foundation.

Glanville, R. (1982). Inside every White Box there are two Black Boxes trying to get out. *Behavioural Science, 12*(1).

Glanville, R. (Ed.) (1996). Heinz von Foerster: a Festschrift, *Systems Research, 13*(3).

Glanville, R. (1998). A (cybernetic) musing: Variety and creativity. *Cybernetics and Human Knowing, 5*(3).

Glanville, R. (2002). Second-order cybernetics, in *Encyclopaedia of Life Support Systems*, web publication: http://greenplanet.eolss.net/MSS/default.htm (subscription needed)

Glanville, R. & AkTyPi, M. (2003). *Inter-view*. Paris: Anomalie Digital Arts, Vol. 3.

Heims, S. J. (1991). *The cybernetics group: Constructing a social science for post-war America*. Cambridge, MA: The MIT Press

Kauffman, L. (2003). Does every recursion have a fixed point? (in this issue)

Merriam Webster Collegiate Dictionary, Encyclopaedia Britannica http://www.eb.com

Müller, A., & Müller, K. (Eds.)(2002). *Heinz von Foerster, Der Anfang von Himmel und Erde hat keinen Namen. Eine Selbsterschaffung in sieben Tagen* (3rd edition). Berlin: Kadmos.

Piaget, J. (1955). *The child's construction of reality*. New York: Basic Books.

Scott, B. C. E. (1979). Heinz von Foerster: An appreciation. *Int. Cyb. Newsletter, 12*.

Scott, B. C. E. (2003). Heinz von Foerster: An appreciation (revisited). (In this issue.)

Spencer Brown, G. (1968). *The laws of form*, London: George Allen and Unwin.

Wiener, N. (1948). *Cybernetics, or communication and control in the animal and the machine*. Cambridge, MA: The MIT Press.

Wittgenstein, L. (1961). *Tractatus Logico-Philosophicus* (D. Pears & B. McGuinness, Trans.). London: Routledge and Kegan Paul.

Note: von Foerster's papers not originally presented in English appeared in private BCL publications. Where a non-English language paper has been cited, the English version read by the author is always the BCL version.

Appendix: Table 1:

A comparison of two books comprised of selections from von Foerster's papers

DATE	*OBSERVING SYSTEM*S (1981)		*UNDERSTANDING UNDERSTANDING* (2003)
1960	On Self-Organizing Systems and their Environments, 1-23	T	On Self-Organizing Systems and their Environments, 1-20
1964	Molecular Bionics, 71-90	T	
1965	Memory Without Record, 91-137	T	
1967	Computation in Neural Nets, 24-70	T	Computation in Neural Nets, 21-100
1969		T	What Is Memory that It May Have Hindsight and Foresight as well? 101-132
1970	Molecular Ethology, An Immodest Proposal for Semantic Clarification, 149-188	T	Molecular Ethology, An Immodest Proposal for Semantic Clarification, 133-168
1970	Thoughts and Notes on Cognition, 231-256	T	Thoughts and Notes on Cognition, 169-190
1971	Technology: What Will It Mean to Librarians, 211-230	T	
1972	Perception of the Future and the Future of Perception, 189-204	M	Perception of the Future and the Future of Perception, 199-210
1972	The Responsibilities of Competence, 205-210	P	The Responsibilities of Competence, 191-198
1973	On Constructing a Reality, 287-309	P	On Constructing a Reality, 211-228
1974		P	Cybernetics of Epistemology, 229-246
1974	Notes on an Epistemology for Living Things, 257-272	M	Notes on an Epistemology for Living Things, 247-260
1977	Objects: Tokens for (Eigen-) Behaviors, 273-286	M	Objects: Tokens for (Eigen-) Behaviors, 261-272

DATE	*OBSERVING SYSTEMS* (1981)		*UNDERSTANDING UNDERSTANDING* (2003)
1979		P	Cybernetics of Cybernetics, 283-286
1984		P	Disorder/Order: Discovery or Invention? 273-282
1991a		P	Ethics and Second-Order Cybernetics, 287-304
1993		P	For Niklas Luhmann: "How Recursive is Communication?" 305-324
1993		P	Introduction to Natural Magic, 325-338

Reincarnation

Under your skin is a light within
And it wants to come out,
And that is what death is all about.
It wants to come out and shine and fly
And it doesn't care if the body die.

If you fly to the Moon.
You will reincarnate soon.
But if you fly to the Sun,
It is the clear bright white light that you have won.

The moon is a mirror that will reflect,
Any incarnation would be less than perfect.

Most, when they die, get eaten by a magnetic force.
This doesn't happen to everyone of course.

If you can sneak past the deadly power,
Every microsecond is an hour,
and the earth a blue and white flower.

Blowing in the wind from the Sun,
whole galaxy is one the run.

Death is sitting over your left shoulder.
He will call you when you get a little older.

Then you get a chance to escape the genetic code,
If you do not run down reincarnation road.
And you, who have been consuming in this techno-pop age,
will be free from your DNA spiral cage.
And you, who have been born in this cyber-punk virtual reality age,
will be levitated out of your magnetic-gravitational cage.

Bill Schiffer, the Cosmic Flower, Christiania, Copenhagen, Denmark

Cybernetics And Human Knowing. Vol. 10, nos. 3-4, pp. 107-123

Elements for a Foersterian Poetics in Psychotherapeutic Practice

Marcelo Pakman[1]

> Tell me, O Muse, of that ingenious
> hero who traveled far and wide ...
> Tell me, too, about all these things,
> O daughter of Zeus, from whatso-
> ever source you may know them.
> (Homer, *The Odyssey*, Book I)

Some current psychotherapeutic practices seem to deviate from a purely hermeneutic tradition to incorporate a poetic one alongside. Elements for a possible formal approach to such a poetic tradition are reflexively explored in the author's own clinical work, in light of their connection to seminal concepts of Heinz von Foerster's work.

Now that Heinz von Foerster, who liked to see himself as a utopist, and from all things was proud he had been, during his younger years, a magician; now that, I say, on October 2, 2002, he consummated his ultimate trick: he left for good; now that his impish smile hides and his staccato voice is not heard but in our memories; now, we can start reflecting on things Foersterian. What better then, what more fitting to that purpose, than to examine our own daily practices to trace the footprints of Heinz's soul in them, to discover the tricks he performed on our lives and those we did on his words, making them ours, ourselves. Let us show and hide the master playing again his favorite themes, and let us show and hide ourselves, looking at him through our eyes and our work through our recollection of his.

I am a community psychiatrist and a systemic/family therapist. I have been practicing for more than 25 years in Argentina and the USA, and consulting and teaching extensively in many countries for the last ten years. I have navigated with the winds of constructivism that swept the beaches of psychotherapy since the 80's, and actively participated in the spreading of that movement of constructive practices, driven by foundational concepts that Heinz von Foerster helped so strongly to bring to the field.

If Second Order Cybernetics, the Cybernetics of Cybernetics, the relentless process of using Cybernetic concepts to account for ourselves as "observing systems," and for the processes involved in observing systems, was Heinz von Foerster's creature (Foerster, 1984), the development of Second Order Therapies was the direct outcome of the inclusion of that perspective in the therapeutic field, mostly through

---

1. Director of Psychiatric Services, Behavioral Health Network, Springfield, Massachusetts.
    Email: mpakman@comcast.net

the window of Family Therapy. Second Order therapies would include the very processes of therapeutic observation, hypotheses making, interventions, techniques, and the theories that mediate the understanding and conceptualization of therapists' actions in the process of observation, conceptualization, and change.

It is well known that the epistemological turn in the therapeutic field entailed in the Second Order Movement, a turn from a positivistic to a Constructivist frame, was fueled, both theoretically and practically, by von Foerster's conceptual and pragmatic participation in the field. It is less clear, however, how Foerster's teaching of the main tenets of those Second Order concepts and of the Constructivist viewpoint (and its related approaches, as in Ernst von Glasersfeld, Humberto Maturana, and Francisco Varela's work) have been incorporated to the actual hands-on practice of psychotherapy by those who adopted the epistemological model at an abstract level. My intent for this paper is to explore whether, and to what extent, the actual "theories-in-use" (Schön, 1983) of my own as well as of related practices, beyond the rather abstract allegiance to the epistemological second order frame, can be described as embodying some of Heinz von Foerster's seminal concepts.

The exploration I intend to do here is part of a general interest I have had, for the last ten years, in the actual patterns that seem to guide the everyday procedural ways of going about our professional practice in the settings in which we operate. I have extensively used, for this purpose, Donald Schön's conceptualization of "knowledge-in-action" (Schön, 1983), and following his proposal, I have called for, and took, in the locality of my clinical practice and through the multiplying effect of teaching mental health and other professionals, some preliminary steps toward a "reflective turn" in the therapeutic arena (Pakman, 2000). This "reflective turn" starts from actual practice, building through reflective conversation the "theories-in-use" implicitly guiding them. In making this turn, we deviate from a traditional epistemology of professional practice that sees it as an application of abstract "espoused theories" to concrete cases (Schön, 1983), and is still the foundation of most professional academic training. "Theories-in-use," which are "theories-of-action," tacit in our professional procedures, are made of the intertwining of abstract professional knowledge with all other sources of academic and non academic learning, and are at the basis of our successful and unsuccessful professional practices. The reconstruction of these "theories-in-use" through reflective conversations in order to make them explicit, teachable without mystification, and open to critique, is the goal of a clinical teaching method modeled on the "design studio," (Schön, 1987) which I have instrumented in the teaching of constructive practices in psychotherapy.

I have frequently claimed that such a reflective practice is a possible road to maintain a *critical social* stance toward the *practice* of psychotherapy as a profession (Pakman, 1998), particularly relevant during the current times of unexamined procedures, spread through globalization mechanisms, and incorporated as matter-of-fact hegemonic (Gramsci, 1971) ways of following everyday professional procedures.

Hermeneutics

Psychotherapeutic practices have traditionally fallen, and many forms of psychotherapy still do, within an interpretive, *hermeneutic* tradition. Confronted at its birth with irrational behavior, which did not appear at first view to make sense, the psychoanalyst, the common ancestor of psychotherapists, became an interpreter looking for the hidden meaning of apparent, manifest riddles.

A few historical considerations about the hermeneutic tradition will contribute to widening the scope of a review of what have traditionally been done in psychotherapy: interpretation of human behavior, frequently focused, most specifically, on those aspects of behavior that appeared in principle not to make sense, or to escape being captured by Reason.

Hermeneutics took its name after the Greek god Hermes. Why was this so? The Roman Plautus was the first one casting the god Hermes as *Prologus*, the actor who, since Luciano, had been identified with the Greek term *Prologos* (before the word or before the discourse) and, as such, had been charged with making the first speech. Originally, "Prologos" was the part of the drama explaining what the Romans would later on call the "ante-factum" (before the facts), so as to provide a context. It also had the surrogate goal of producing *captatio benevolentiae*, capturing the benevolence of the audience. The tradition inaugurated by Luciano of casting the Prologue as an actor was taken, later on, by both the Elizabethan theater, in which the Prologue was still the actor proclaiming the subject of the drama to follow, and by the Italian Comedia dell'Arte. It is from the Comedia dell'Arte that it passed to musicians like Ruggiero Leoncavallo, who opened his famous opera I Pagliacci, "The Clowns," with the beautiful "aria" in which the baritone sings: "Io sono il Prologo," "I am the Prologue."

Prologus was not someone who, sharing the script with the actors, started revealing it to the audience. He unveiled not only something the audience did not yet know, but something the characters themselves did not know either, and would not know until the moment the drama unfolded later on. Even then the actors would experience the circumstances depicted in the plot in a way and from a position different from the one Prologus had presented it to the audience.

In his incarnation as Hermes, Prologus was presenting something the actors themselves did not know, nor they would even know upon the unfolding of the drama, something that was absent from the drama. Hermes, thus representing what was absent in the presentation of the actors, was making what in French is called an "explicitation," and in English an "interpretation." Thus, Hermeneutics, the 20th century discipline of interpretation, was named after Hermes, the God who reveals things about the presenters they themselves are not aware of. Hermes interprets what is absent, but is going to be present and presented; he *represents* it in one among many possible ways. Hermes, as Prologus, in his acting performance, not only presents (showing what is there, that which presents itself by the act of being), but also represents (makes present what is not there, trying to bring forward what is absent). Hermes, as Prologus, interprets. It was building on and making visible this inevitable and powerful interpretive quality of Prologus that Jorge Luis Borges imagined writing a book of prologues for inexistent books, one that would be full of "exemplary quotations from these possible works," and would show that a prologue was "not a subservient form of a toast; but a lateral species of critique" (Borges, 1975). Throughout this fiction, Borges, anticipated the post-modern turn in hermeneutics. From its origins as practice, in religion (as in Talmudic, "midrashic" practices of Torah reading among Jewish scholars) and the law (as in debates of law interpretation), Hermeneutics would undergo the post-modern turn, whose questioning of all meta-narratives, and more specifically of Cartesian Reason, would undermine the authority of the True interpretation to leave us, instead, in a multiverse of competing ones.

From a post-modern point of view, interpretation and critique always entail, to use Piera Castoriadis-Aulagnier's term, a certain degree of "violence" (Castoriadis-Aulagnier, 1992). For interpretations always transform, and thus disrespect, what is present, making it visible through a particular lens that somehow distorts it. We see what is present through what is represented. But presentations, ultimately, infinitely regress, and as Jacques Derrida has pointed out, every presentation, when deconstructed, leaves us only with further representations (Derrida, 1976, 1978, 1981). Representations frame what is present and make it available to perception and reason, to emotion and action, to meaning and further representing. Closing the hermeneutic circle, if a Prologue is critique and interpretation, every presentation is ultimately Prologue, endless hermeneutical practice.

As I said before, many psychotherapeutic practices still reveal, quite frequently, falling within a hermeneutic tradition. The psychotherapist is, in these practices, mostly and mainly an interpreter who reveals the hidden meaning of behaviors, verbal or otherwise. The psychotherapist is capable of that interpretive practice because he can map, individual, family, couple, group, or organizational manifest behavior, on a grid that different theories, psychological, biological, social, provide as underlying meta-narratives. Although escaping to the actors awareness, those meta-narratives are assumed to be at work as efficient underlying causes. Whether the psychotherapist follows a psychodynamic, psychoanalytic, neuroscientific, developmental psychology of the Piagetian or other school, etc., he invokes this hidden meta-narrative of typical modern filiation that the adoption of more post-modern language could not totally erase.

Poetics

The type of constructive psychotherapy I and others in the systemic/family therapy field have been practicing, separates from this dominant tradition, and has moved progressively toward adding to hermeneutics, what we can define as a "poetics" (Culler, 1990, 1997). A "poetics" is a constructive practice that, instead of looking for meanings in behaviors otherwise irrational, abnormal, or enigmatic, assumes that all behaviors are socially viable, effective, (to the extent that they cause effects and that they affect others), and open to meaningful interpretations, and focuses on making explicit the mechanisms that make them viable, effective, and meaningfully interpretable. A poetics thus, necessarily reflects on the social and contextual architecture that allows meaningful behavior to happen, on the competence human beings display in their social interactions, and on the techniques that are at work in the human drama in which we are constantly involved. But, as we said before, the presence of human behavior always includes representation, human behavior is always not only interpretable but interpreted. If *hermeneutics* is, then, not only an a-posteriori add-on to behavior but, instead, constitutive of it, *poetics* asks for the context that allows for interpretations to happen and for the ways in which interpretations become more or less successful, viable, dominant, or effective.

This poetic approach allows us to move among different interpretive frames, adopting a meta-position from which we can explore them, without paying total and irreflexive allegiance to any of them. What occurs in this psychotherapy is, then, not only hermeneutics, interpretive practice in search of meaning, but poetics, constructive practice of the contexts and the competence to act socially, to reflectively review the context in which interpretive practices happen, are born, promoted or maintained.

When poetics is added to a purely hermeneutic frame, the main task of psychotherapy becomes not only to interpret behavior, but to contextualize, analyze, and ponder, alternative actions, perceptions, and emotions and the multiple mutual interpretations of them that are always part of what they become in actual relationships. The psychotherapist is not then a privileged interpreter, but a provider of expertise in introducing reflective strategies to navigate multiple and competing interpretations, embedded in the actions, perceptions, emotions, judgements, that are the matter of social, psychological, and biological human life.

In a psychotherapy mostly based in hermeneutics, behavior calls for interpretations of its meanings, underlying truths beyond what is manifest. But when poetics plays an essential role in psychotherapy, significant effort goes into a reflective construction of the embedded patterns or architecture of competent techniques and contextual factors, at work in viable and effective behavior. This viable and effective behavior always has embedded interpretations, being otherwise open to further interpretation. This reflective construction is not detached and analytical but participatory, and new alternative viable behaviors are always born during the process. If interpretation privileges the past as a source of mostly causal explanations, poetics understands the present in order to open it up into the future.

The relationship between hermeneutics and poetics is not only one of addition side to side but a circular one, because in the poetic exploration of the contexts that allow interpretations to happen and be viable, we can use also different frames, themselves heirs of and open to different interpretive traditions. Thus, in a poetic activity, meaningful behavior is reconstructed in order to understand the biological, psychological and social mechanisms that make it possible, viable, effective, and interpretable; the context of the interpretations at work in its construction; and the possible future interpretations of multiple social actors that would influence its future meanings.

A psychotherapist within a hermeneutic tradition would ask, when working, for instance, with a man involved in repetitive robbery, what is the meaning of such behavior, and would try his best to make interpretations based on any specific frame he pays allegiance to, would not be able to avoid making interpretations whose roots are embedded in procedures dictated mostly by the context in which he works, the culture at large he has been socialized into, or heirs of sources of learning he has incorporated over time. Although work based on a hermeneutic tradition tends to seek coherence it cannot ever achieve it.

A psychotherapist within a poetic tradition would, in a similar situation, ask instead: what are the circumstances that make this behavior, already meaningful for this man and those around him (including professional people), effective, viable, preferable, interpretable? What are the already existing and other possible effects of that behavior and its attributed meanings for him and for others? How is that already affecting him and others? What type of configurations described by multiple academic (psychological, biological, social, economic, communicational, linguistic, political, etc.) and popular views of those type of phenomena can be considered to be at work in his behavior and its effects? What alternative evolutions can we imagine as a consequence of the multiple meanings of that behavior in his own and other possible social situations? Etcetera. This addition of a poetic frame, complements and interacts with a hermeneutic frame, in a way that seems to be particularly helpful when we recognize that actual work in context is never totally coherent or congruent with abstract allegiances. It allows them to increase degrees of freedom regarding any specific interpretive frame. Although fluctuation between frames happens as a matter of fact, a poetic tradition seems to allow for a reflective consideration of the alternative frames and the alternation itself.

This type of psychotherapy was born not only from an *ex-nihil* decision to become constructivist, but from the confrontation with materials that are not mainly irrational, enigmatic behaviors, but rational, consensual everyday behaviors that end up, however, in conflictive, unpleasant, problematic experiences. When the task at hand involves mainly, not to explain abnormal behavior, but to reflect on the background of "normalcy" against which problematic behavior is always fore-grounded or outlined, reflecting upon this practice is more prone to lead to critical social practice.

I will try to make explicit the poetics of this psychotherapeutic practice, which is added to more purely hermeneutic approaches. Assuming a constructivist epistemological stance is not just a decision we make and we maintain obliviously under any circumstances. When confronting situations in which we feel our ability to make changes hardly compromised (and community settings of professional practice are full of social situations with the hardness of hereditary traits), we tend to become more realistic than constructivist. Maintaining a constructive stance in those circumstances, is a commitment and a choice to either maintain or recover our ability to operate as if reality were a consensual construction, trying to recover room to make changes. Constructive practice goes beyond an epistemological position, to become a methodology for action, embodied in a constructive poetics.

Elements of a poetics

A reconstruction of the poetics of my professional practice emerged from reflective conversations about the actual therapeutic practice. Its outcome was the identification, or construction, of patterns of action described by myself and others as observers of my own work. It is, technically, the outcome of many observations of my own professional work, either through video recorded instances, or of one way mirror observations, followed always by after session discussions with members of therapeutic teams, of peers, students, or teachers that I have had over the years. The patterns elicited do evolve, of course, over time, and the stabilization of the description of the identified poetics, changes accordingly over time. It is like a snapshot of the prevailing tendencies in my professional practice at this time, the outcome of reflective dialogues.

The articulation of the description in a more structured way is, also, of my own making. So, what I am going to describe is not an abstract theory to be applied. That has been the traditional technical-rational traditional epistemological model (Schön, 1983). I am going to describe, instead, the reconstructed poetics embedded in my actual professional practice of psychotherapy and psychiatry; the theories-of-action involved in the "expertise at the fingertips" (Hoffman, 2002), displayed in a competent professional practice. Although I believe that this poetics could be also helpful to describe the practice of other psychotherapists in the family/systemic therapy field, I will not focus here on their work.[2]

This poetics works as an implicit articulated series of organizing elements of therapeutic conversations that seem to guide my movements during the sessions. It is made, as I said before, of *theories-in-use*, which are *theories-of-action*, structured, patterned ways of moving about in certain types of situations in order to achieve certain specific goals (Schön, 1983). When we try to make explicit a given poetics of psychotherapy, as we are doing here, the level of description used is very close to the actual conversation as it happens in the actual performance of the professional skills involved. It is in this sense that the Greeks used to talk about poetics as the discipline studying the "making of things." Poetic elements can then be described as an interconnected network of concepts, of a level of abstraction close to practice, with more or less identifiable roots in many different sources of learning. The elements for a poetics try, in general, to capture a possible understanding of the understandings that mediate professional actions, of our "knowledge-in-action" in the everyday domain of our professional practice. In this case, clinical practice, consultation, and teaching of psychotherapy and psychiatry.

---

2. I have particularly in mind the work of Carlos Sluzki, with whom I have worked closely for many years, as well as of Pietro Barbetta, Lynn Hoffman, and Gianfranco Cecchin.

The elements for a poetics of a professional practice are different form very abstract principles of, let us say, Psychoanalysis, or General Systems Theory, or Cybernetics. They are much more specific and close to the action that embodies them in the actual therapeutic conversation. They are intimately linked to technical aspects like personal style, preferred metaphors, rhetorical means, use of certain types of humor, physical presence, preferred rhythms of conducting a session, favorite changes of rhythm, etc. Certain elements can, in fact, be constructed as such because they are the ones more prone to be used by someone who counts, as tools, on those technical means. Again, elements of a poetics are not a new name for abstract principles to be, later on, applied to actual situations. They exist only in their embodied form as highly personal techniques applied to certain types of cases with which any practitioner has had to deal over time. A professional develops its poetics through acting in his specific circumstances, implementing his talents and idiosyncrasies, which become intertwined with his academic and many other non academic sources of learning, including the learning of procedures driven mostly by the social-economic-cultural context in which professional practice occurs. The same abstract epistemological principles can be an umbrella for many different poetics of professional practice.

I can identify several organizing elements that seem to channel my participation in these conversations in which I am professionally committed to being therapeutic. I have identified two different types of *poetic elements*: *positions*, that I will name *ethics, aesthetics, pragmatics*, and *politics*; and *tools*, that I will name *language, reflexivity* and *temporality* (Figure 1).

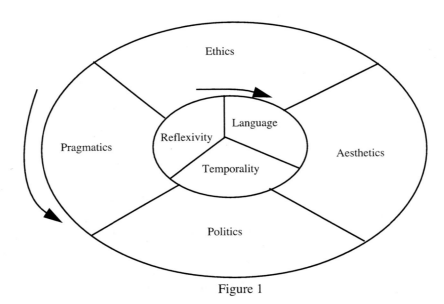

Figure 1

The *positions* are alternative frames, stances, taken during the therapeutic conversations. They organize the conversation from a certain perspective. They are overarching preoccupations orienting the therapeutic process at any given moment.

They are not necessarily consciously adopted as an *a priori* decision followed by an application of techniques. They can be better understood as frames that facilitate a description of the guiding spirit during different moments of the flow of conversation during the psychotherapeutic process. The positions are not only implicit elements to construct therapeutic conversations, but also parameters to judge the ongoing construction during its making. These positions are put to work through certain preferred *tools*, also identifiable in the actual therapeutic process as it evolves in conversation.

All the elements constitute a methodology for action; they are logically linked, they are conjointly used and, at any particular time, one or the other becomes more dominant in terms of informing the actual conversational techniques through which they are embodied. Positions are assumed in no predetermined order (although certain preferred sequence can be at times identified); not all of them are necessarily taken in a given piece of therapeutic conversation; any of them could be identified as being more prevalent at different times or in different therapeutic sessions; they can be assumed repeatedly and variously during a single therapeutic session; they are embodied through one or more different tools; there is no univocal correspondence between any position and any tool: any position can be at work through different tools. Figure 1 tries to capture these general principles showing the positions and the tools as two concentric circles sharing the same center. Thus we can imagine these circles independently rotating around their common center, creating at different moments different types of combinations between a position and a tool.

Foersterian poetics

I believe these elements of the poetics identifiable in my work, are clearly connected to Foersterian concepts at work. Let me locate a node of Heinz von Foerster work, particularly significant for the poetical elements I intend to make explicit. Thirty years ago von Foerster postulated that constructivism implies a choice to uphold the Principle of Relativity, which can neither be proved to be true, nor is a logical necessity (Foerster, 1973). For those who choose to accept that principle, any given hypothesis which holds for each of two separate people, should be rejected if it does not hold when those two people meet. This choice gives priority to the relationship between people, and its epistemological corollary is that "reality equals community," because the only valid knowledge, the only hypotheses not to be rejected, are those which can hold for the community of people in relationship. Those hypotheses held in community would be reality-making, thus fostering identity as a quality of the relationship among people. Thus, identity is not conceived as an *a priori* quality of individuals, but a consequence, or an outcome, of a process of becoming a community when upholding hypotheses making for a reality in which those individuals can live together.

Von Foerster drew two pragmatic consequences from this constructivist choice for the Principle of Relativity, and presented them as Imperatives:

- *The Ethical Imperative*: Act always so as to increase the number of choices.
- *The Aesthetical Imperative*: If you desire to see, learn how to act.

Let us further explore the poetic elements of a psychotherapeutic practice, both positions and tools, in light of these seminal concepts. We will start with the poetic elements I called positions.

Positions

Ethics

Von Foerster's ethical imperative calls for *acting*. A choice to follow this imperative is embodied in our poetics, when we act ethically asking the following types of questions as guidelines for therapeutic conversations: What are the alternatives, and alternative possible interpretations before this concrete situation? How can we describe the situation and the possible alternatives, and alternative interpretations, from now on; giving primacy at this time, not to how desirable, how beneficial we consider them, but to the fact that it is desirable in itself to increase the number of choices? What other alternatives and interpretations were present at some other point, but for whatever reason, were not followed? Is there any way to reinstate any of those alternatives as current ones? How can we explore the options at hand and make them as explicit as possible, multiplying the details while describing them, portraying them as possible scenarios, including how they would change the position of different people should they occur? Are there other people involved who see, would see or would recommend any other alternative or interpretations? What are, in each case, the sources and the consequences of alternative interpretations for all those involved in the situation?

When choices appear to be poor, or merely imposed, or inevitable, the discussion of option tends to open up the possibility of describing different ways in which things apparently inevitable could come to actually happen, opening up room for variations and choices within the restrictions. Thus, choices emerge where there did not appear to be any. Reviewing choices and looking for more choices contribute also to create choice as an option. Ethics is, from this perspective of multiplying alternatives in order to introduce choice, a conversation with fate. As in Ingmar Bergmann's human play of a game with Death, Death/Fate might prevail and impose itself, but sitting at the table to play the game with her is what introduces choice, thus moving beyond mere biology to human freedom.

Aesthetics

Von Foerster aesthetic imperative calls for *action* as well, introducing now another choice: which of the identified options are the ones we choose to *see*, and what is it that we need to learn in order to see them happening.

A choice to follow this imperative is embodied in our poetics, when we act aesthetically asking the following types of questions as guidelines for therapeutic conversations: From the options, and interpretations, and their consequences, that we have discussed, and that seem to be available, which ones does our client prefer to see happening? And which ones does he believe those around him would prefer to see happening? What are the criteria that make these choices preferred ones? What are the parameters used to judge them as more desirable to make them happen? What are the parameters that different people involved in the situation are using? What are the conflicts that arise when he sees some options are more desirable according to some values or parameters, but not according to others? Which are the values used as parameters: Pleasure? Well being? A sense of loyalty? Financial gains? Moral principles? Religious mandates? Fashion? Convenience? Avoiding blame or shame? Patriotism? Others? And what does each of those values mean for different people trying to decide what makes a choice more desirable?

Aesthetics is here ethics as well. It is a choice among choices: the choice of those options we would prefer to see happening. No choice is complete until we aesthetically choose which ones we want to see happening. What matters here now is not just to increase the options but to choose among them according to criteria that we should also try to make explicit. There is a circularity between both mandates, between ethics and aesthetics. That circularity is articulated around action. We need to act to increase the number of choices, and we need to act in order to see the preferred choices happen. And when we act to make the preferred choices happen, in order to see them, we have to do it in a way that, once more, increases the number of choices. Aesthetics is ethics also in this other sense. And to the extent that action to increase choices is always followed by choosing among them, ethics is always pre-announcing aesthetics, because there is a chain of choices leading to what we prefer to see happening, and orienting our actions and the learning we need to go through in order to act efficiently. Only those options actually chosen would become realities to live within. But evaluation of choices in conversation is already reality building. The articulation of these two Foersterian elements, Ethics and Aesthetics, leads then, necessarily, to the following one, because once we choose which choices are desirable: what do we need to learn in order to make these choices happen? Because only by learning to act we could make those options come to be.

Pragmatics

A choice to follow von Foerster call for action, and for learning to act, at the core of his imperatives, is embodied in our poetics, when we act pragmatically asking the following types of questions as guidelines for therapeutic conversations: Does the client know what to do to move toward seeing his preferred options happen? How would she go about starting to move in the desired direction? What are the missing pieces she would need to count on in order to facilitate moving toward that chosen future? Is starting to move in this direction something that will further increase her options? Or would it lead, instead, to dead ends? In what way to start acting might change the choices, either for her or for others? And how could it make them more or less desirable, either for her or for others?

Pragmatics is always intertwined with ethics and aesthetics. Action is, of course, the heart of pragmatics, and both ethics and aesthetics, in von Foerster, call for action. They are pragmatic ethics and aesthetics, not abstract ones, not vague general principles. Actual movements are what make choices real ones, because choices are always embodied in actual actions. And actions are always going to contribute to either increase or loose options, and to make them more or less desirable. Thus, pragmatics is always ethical and aesthetical. As such, actions are always embedded in circumstances that give them qualities that would facilitate or restrict further options. Even more, actions are always restricted and allowed by biological structures (Maturana, 1984), and happen as socially historically situated events. They are always open to influence by social forces whose active regulation by multiple social actors is always an option as well. This leads us to the next dimension of our poetics.

Politics
As we said before, von Foerster made the epistemological claim that "reality equals community" (Foerster, 1973). He also made another claim, congruent with the last one: "Without communication there is no regulation; without regulation, there is no goal; and without a goal the concept of "society" or "system" becomes void" (Foerster, 1971). The realities in which we live are communally made through goals that imply regulatory processes established in communication. Communal goals are the hallmark of communicative process or regulation. I will claim that what we can legitimately call politics is a process of regulation that allow the emergence of communal goals in order to construct the realities in which we live. Politics is, then, the negotiation and regulation of spaces of power. For power means the ability of social actors to maintain or create definitions of reality for themselves and others (Pakman, 1990). Those definitions are combinations of both symbolic (effective mostly through the presence of representation) and action-defined events (effective mostly through their presence, whose meaning is mediated by representation) which enforce limits to the symbolic or living spaces of others.

A choice to embody von Foerster's claims about the intricate relationship between reality, community, communication, regulation, goals, and society, is made when we act politically asking the following types of questions as guidelines for therapeutic conversations: what actions should be initiated, or maintained, or amplified, in order to increase the chances of our clients and our own movements to make desirable options happen, to be effective actions? At what level should both our clients and we, ourselves be acting in this regard? Who should be involved in this process? With whom should our clients and we be interacting? Whose forces should be activated to better position us so as to make our psychotherapy more effective, thus enhancing our client's options to change in the desired direction?

This politics is always a micro-politics, aimed at operating at the local contextual level, in order to make that context more conducive toward the effective operation of our ethics, aesthetics and pragmatics. Without an awareness and a will to operate also at this level, a strictly technical-professional view of our duties may end up, under many circumstances, being ineffective. Working with multi-problem families, is a classical instance of the inability of such a technical view of our profession to fail in participating in change. The domain of operation of this micro-politics should be aimed at interacting with all those institutional forces, sources of funding, regulation boards, professional associations, policy making structures, academic instances training professionals, etcetera. All those forces play an essential role creating the contextual and institutional restrictions that channel everyday professional activities into procedures that highly restrict the ability to increase the number of choices, to choose the most desirable ones, and to act to make them happen. Thus, micro-politics is closely linked to ethics, aesthetics, and pragmatics. It is an attempt at both making explicit the context in which ethics, aesthetics, and pragmatics occurs, and operating on it in order to make those poetic elements more effective. In turn, ethics, aesthetics, and pragmatics are always formatted by political forces, they emerge in processes of negotiation and regulation of power, and they are, then, in need of a time to reflect, make explicit, and operate more openly at that level. Political action can also further amplify the number of choices, make them more or less desirable, and allow the emergence of new possible actions.

Although this political element is part of the poetics, I usually speak, when giving professional training, of two aspects of the necessary professional skills: *poetics* and *micro-politics*. In doing so, I promote this micro-political element to a category in itself, in order to underscore the importance of avoiding getting trapped in a technical view of the profession, oblivious to contextual and political determinants. I also intend to show the relevance of acting on the context, so as to make the more traditional professional actions within the domain of practice more relevant, to recover more degrees of freedom, and to support the stance of a *critical social practice*. At the same time, I do not want to lose the fact that this micro-politics should be practiced and taught together with the other elements of the poetics, because in practice they operate as a continuum of "knowledge-in-action."

As we have seen ethics, aesthetics, pragmatics, and politics, are positions to be taken as overarching frames to conduct therapeutic conversations. They are elements of the poetics implicit in psychotherapeutic practice, and as such are not only guidelines to construct conversations but also to evaluate what we construct along the way. They become in practice intertwined although we can identify, in any single piece of therapeutic conversation, moments of dominance of one of these elements above the others. But in no way I want to suggest these elements follow a chronological one way order. They operate as a network and we move constantly from one to another in both directions. One of them appears as more dominant at any given moment, but we move freely looking for more options, exploring their desirability, strategizing actions to make them happen, and operating micro-politically. This micro-political operation includes both making explicit the contexts for the appearance as choices, their desirability and the alternative actions to make them happen, and the ways to operate on those factors. Political analysis and action can make some options more desirable, or allow to imagine new actions. Pragmatic considerations, when actually explore and put to practice, can facilitate the emergence of new options or, again, make some of them more or less desirable; or change the politics of forces at play.

As we said before, the four *positions* presented so far, ethics, aesthetics, pragmatics and politics, are poetic elements instrumented technically through other three poetic elements I conceptualize as *tools*. Particular uses of language, reflexivity, and temporality is always at play whenever the ethical, aesthetical, pragmatic, and political elements of this poetics guide the actual conversation. It is not difficult to trace Foersterian roots in them either.

Tools

Language

The language that actually makes for the therapeutic conversation, is a *participatory* one. Very consistently, we speak, in Heinz von Foerster terms, as being *part of the world* we are talking about, instead of talking as if we were *apart from the world* (Foerster, 1984), as detached, objective observers. It is a language of transparency, in order to avoid, as much as possible, a double discourse (one to be talked among colleagues, secret to our clients, and a different one with our clients) which tends to create hierarchical realities (the language among colleagues becoming more "real," more "relevant" than the one to talk with clients). This does not eliminate, however, the professional language and its weight as promoter of hierarchies. But exposing the kitchen where that professional language is cooked, gives a chance to question its primacy and authority. It is a language of responsibility, in which we openly commit to our statements without protecting ourselves and hiding our prejudices behind supposedly but vaguely scientific statements. And, as a part of that, we also take responsibility for the implementation of scientifically based knowledge.

This participatory language seems to be congruent with an ethical, aesthetical, pragmatic, and political stance. We invent choices we are responsible for; we choose the options we find more desirable; we design actions to make our choices happen; and we try to operate at a micro-political level to make choices, and to initiate the actions to make them happen. We do all that inviting our clients to do the same. We do both things from within the systems in which we find ourselves operating or we design in order to operate. And we do it always using a language that captures this constant speaking as a part of the world we describe, design, suffer, enjoy, and act upon.

Participatory language, as a tool, is an essential instrumental aspect of this poetics I am trying to make explicit. It is at work constantly whenever we try to move from utterances of detachment, impersonal expressions, claims for matter of fact realities, universality and authority, and uniform descriptions, toward a conversation in terms of inclusion, authorship, first person statements, searches for the constructed origin of realities, making hierarchies explicit, and questioning authority and universality.

Reflexivity

Participatory language is in itself a way of assuming a reflexive, second order stance. The whole conversation we try to design in a way that constantly fosters viewing ourselves "through the eyes of the other" (Foerster, 1984). This operates not only as an invitation for our clients to do it with their lives, but also for us as involved participants in the psychotherapeutic process. This is reflexivity as a social process, and not as an isolated introspective exercise, which would be necessarily blind to the interactive nature of our actions and the effects of our interventions, "prejudices" (Cecchin, 1994), and languages as they happen in the social contexts in which we find ourselves and help to construct. Increasing alternatives, choosing the more desirable ones, moving toward making them happen, and acting politically to operate more effectively at every step of the process, involves always using those same ethical, aesthetical, pragmatic, and political parameters to see ourselves and invite our clients to see themselves throughout all those choices and actions. In turn, it is this very reflective stance what makes all of those poetic elements to be mobilized into creating more options, choices, and actions. In this poetics of professional practice, reflexivity, as it was the case with participatory language, is not an add-on element to the other ones, but a permanent instrument to embody them.

Reflexivity is, then, another essential tool, as element of the poetics of psychotherapeutic practice. This poetics embodies a permanent effort to bring mirrors to the conversation, to constantly explore the mutual influence of our interactions on ourselves and the other social actors of our situated professional task. These mirrors are necessarily made of materials that impose their own "prejudiced" view, but that is the case for every view, making mutual observation a necessary tool for a critical practice. Reflexivity is not only embodied in participatory language, but also gives a stance for language in the making to evolve, thus participating in the making of the new desirable options we want to foster and bring to our lives.

Reflexivity as a social process is at work whenever we try to move from introspection, unilateral decision making, exclusive ownership of actions, a rhetoric of principles, or supposedly unbiased representations, toward a conversation that attempts to maintain, gain, or recover a stance from which to introduce mutual observation, multilateral decision making negotiation, opening to a view of actions as "objects-in-use" (Schön & Rein, 1994) to be influenced and used by other social actors, a rhetoric of social consequences of principles (Weber, 1964), and the interpreted quality of every representation.

Temporality

Heinz von Foerster proposed frequently to move from an ontology based on being, toward a logic of "becoming" (Foerster, 1984). This logic would certainly contribute to create, or maintain a fluid view of experience, and would entail a transformed view of time. Such a view of temporality is another essential part of our poetics, one congruent with a participatory language and a reflective stance. The events that make for the experience of the social actors in the situations we deal with and we find ourselves, the attributions made during conversations, the qualities described and assumed to be constitutive of state of affairs, and the evaluations made of options and actions, their desirability, and the contexts in which they occur, all are seen from a different perspective when we linguistically replace the verb "to be" with the verb "to become," as von Foerster proposed, and Gianfranco Cecchin has consistently recommended as a therapeutic tool (Cecchin, 2002).

The ethics, aesthetics, pragmatics, and politics, as constitutive elements of our poetics, become more effective when the logics of becoming frames the temporality through which they are instrumented in actual conversations. Alternatives are not closed but emerging during the conversation and the logics of temporal becoming further optimizes that process. It also does it with a fluid view of the desirability of the choices at hand, of the actions to make them happen and of the political moves to make all other moves possible and more effective, because all those elements are also open-ended and emerging. In turn, the logics of "becoming" is what makes the ethic, aesthetic, pragmatic, and political elements possible, to the extent that it adds a constructed time as a force to the very viability of those projects.

The logics of "becoming" is also constitutive of the participatory quality of language and of the reflexive stance. Language is participatory only to the extent that it constantly accounts for and emerges from a logic of becoming. And a reflective stance needs such a logic of becoming as well, in order to be an endless process of mutually looking at our own backs and prejudices. All three elements: language, reflexivity, and a temporality of "becoming," pervade the actual conversation that embodies the ethical, aesthetical, pragmatic, and political elements of our poetics.

"Man of many wiles"

I have completed a preliminary exploration of the elements for a poetics of psychotherapeutic practice, and I have tried to trace some of its roots in Heinz von Foerster work.

He was always fond of expanding a great intuition of Warren McCulloch (McCulloch, 1988), that also guided his reading of Gregory Bateson's work (Bateson, 1972): the central nervous system, as well as computers and social systems, are "embodiments of mind." Mind, in this widened concept, is not an add-on phenomenon to a "material" world, but a constitutive aspect of the way that world is organized, with traditionally mental and linguistic phenomena being just a special case of the organization of the mind, or rather, of the mind as a certain type of organization. Along the same lines, von Foerster did not conceive of a Reason to be applied to tasks, but of a pragmatic reason, the one that made of Cybernetics the discipline of steering between the complex and conflicting waters of actual practice in multiple social domains.

On occasion of editing a collection of Heinz's works in Spanish, I closed my introduction of his work saying: "Therapy, as life, invents itself in an endless game. The cybernetic adventure is not a minor form of that peculiar magic." And Heinz added, in his preface: "The miracle of therapy is not a minor form of that superior magic (of Cybernetics)." Heinz had also once proposed Maxwell's demon as the protector muse for Cybernetics, identifying it with the endeavor to fight entropy, create information, and introduce computation: a creation of order through an invented language (Foerster, 1971). Nothing is more fitted, then, to our cybernetic inquiry, and the man it hopes to evoke, than invoking Pallas Athena, as we did in our epigraph. Athena was the Greek goddess protector of the crafts and of Odysseus, the "man of many wiles" (Homer, 1990). She did not represent pure thought, but practical intelligence, art, skill, *techné* (Paglia, 1990). Now that Heinz has joined Odysseus in the land of the tricksters, may Athena protect his loved soul and grant all those who preserve his memory across so many crafts the wisdom to multiply his magic.

Bibliography

Bateson, G. (1972). *Steps to an ecology of mind*. New York: Random House.

Borges, J. L. (1975). Prólogos con un prólogo de prólogos. In *Obras completas*, IV (pp. 13-160). Barcelona: Emecé.

Castoriadis-Aulagnier, P. (1992). *La violencia de la interpretación: del pictograma al enunciado*. Buenos Aires: Amorrortu.

Cecchin, G., Lane, G. & Ray, W. A. (1994). The cybernetics of prejudices in the practice of psychotherapy. London: Karnac.

Cecchin, G. (2002, July). *Considerations on mediation*. Paper presented at the Elba Island Meeting on Mediation.

Culler, J. (1990). *Structuralist poetics: Structuralism, linguistics and the study of literature*. New York: Cornell University Press.

Culler, J. (1997). *Literary theory; A very short introduction*. Oxford: Oxford University Press.

Derrida, J. (1976). *Of grammatology*. Baltimore: John Hopkins University Press.

Derrida, J. (1978). *Writing and difference*. London: RKP.

Derrida, J. (1981). *Dissemination*. London: Althone Press.

Foerster, H. von (1984). The responsibilities of competence. In H. von Foerster, *Observing systems* (pp. 205-210). Seaside, CA: Intersystems. (originally published in 1971)

Foerster, H. von (1984). On constructing a reality. In H. von Foerster, *Observing systems* (pp. 287-309). Seaside, CA: Intersystems. (originally published in 1973).

Foerster, H. von (1984). *Observing systems*. Seaside, CA: Intersystems.

Gramsci, A. (1971). *Prison notebooks*. London: Lawrence & Wishart.

Hoffman, L. (2002). *Family therapy: An intimate history*. New York: Norton.

Homer, (1992). *The odyssey*. New York: Barnes and Noble.

Maturana, H. & Varela F. J. (1984). *El árbol del conocimiento*. Santiago de Chile: Editorial Universitaria.

McCulloch, W. S. (1988). *Embodiments of mind*. Cambridge: The MIT Press.

Paglia, C. (1990). *Sexual personae*. New York: Vintage Books.

Pakman, M. (1990, June). *Notes on the cybernetics of aggression*. Lecture.

Pakman, M. (1998). Education and therapy in cultural borderlands: A call for critical social practices in human services. *Journal of Systemic Therapies*, *17*(1), 18-30.

Pakman, M. (2000). Disciplinary knowledge, postmodernism and globalization: A call for Donald Schön's "reflective turn" for the mental health professions. *Cybernetics and Human Knowing*, *7*(2-3), 105-126.

Schön, D. A. (1983). *The reflective practitioner*. New York: Basic Books.

Schön, D. A. (1987). *Educating the reflective practitioner*. San Francisco: Jossey-Bass.

Schön, D. A. & Rein, M. (1994). *Frame reflection: Toward the resolution of intractable policy controversies*. New York: Basic Books.

Weber, M. (1964). *The theory of social and economic organization*. New York: The Free Press.

Cybernetics And Human Knowing. Vol. 10, no. 2, pp. 124-136

Ethics and Aesthetics of Observing Frames

Frederick Steier[1] and Jane Jorgenson[2]

Inspired by Heinz von Foerster's notions of observing systems as a merging of second-order and first-order understanding, we explore the multiple senses of observing frames. We draw organically from ethnographic observations of visitors in a regional science center to reconceptualize processes of meaning construction in designed learning environments more generally. Von Foerster's ethical and aesthetic imperatives are used to develop an understanding of science learning as an emergent co-improvisation between designers, researchers, interactors and visitors. Links are drawn with Luhmann's paradoxy of observing systems, while implications for design processes are considered.

Magic in Everyday Life

Heinz von Foerster worked in his youth as a professional magician, and throughout his career he retained a gift for transforming the ordinary into the extraordinary. Rather than allowing us to assume uncritically that we see a "stable reality," ready-made and there for the taking, he encouraged us to question how it is that we make our reality stable. Playfully, he invited us to see the paradoxes that are inescapable in our computing and languaging processes. In the Case of the Double Blind (von Foerster, 1986) for example, (a play on Bateson's [1956] double bind theory)—he tried to provoke our awareness of the consequences of not seeing that we do not see "everything"—including our own blind spots, which could be cultural, physiological or psychological.

We often find ourselves bringing Heinz[3] along in our work, inventing conversations with him to help us do what we do in our ongoing cycle of action and reflection. The following essay, dedicated to Heinz, describes such a process. It develops a bit of ethnographic inquiry into actionable knowledge. We draw, specifically, on an ongoing project in which we seek to understand how people construct reality (or better, realities) in a designed environment such as a science center. Our aim is to create a conversation with designers of science exhibits, and perhaps designers in general, to see design as an ongoing process linking observing to action, and to explore the diverse contexts for learning, playing and being that such designs afford. We focus here on the interplay between the observers and the observed, recognizing that of course the observed may also be observing themselves. Our starting point is a simple scene of everyday life in a regional science center where the staff seem willing to play with such questions of learning.

1. Dept. of Communication, University of South Florida, Tampa, Florida, USA; E-mail: fsteier@luna.cas.usf.edu
2. Dept. of Communication, University of South Florida, Tampa, Florida, USA;
    E-mail: jjorgens@chuma.cas.usf.edu
3. Since this paper is building on conversations that we have had with Heinz von Foerster, we are taking the liberty of referring to him as Heinz in the text. However, where references are made to texts and talks he has produced, we follow the normal convention of referring to him as von Foerster.

A View From Above

In the Museum of Science and Industry (MOSI) in Tampa, Florida, a visitor can get a tantalizing overview of activities by standing on a balcony overlooking the third floor exhibit area. Below, museum visitors are moving among the exhibits in networks of restless activity. There is lots of noise—from the use of objects that are parts of the exhibits themselves, and from the children, parents, grandparents, and performers playing and shouting at one another. It is a landscape of learning and a soundscape of fun.

On this particular afternoon, the crowd of visitors has begun to thin out. As we stand on the fourth floor balcony, one exhibit in particular draws our attention. This exhibit, familiarly called the Bernoulli blowers after the Swiss scientist, Daniel Bernoulli, appears in diverse forms in many science centers around the world. A boy about ten years old approaches the display where a ball floats and bobs above a large plastic cone. The ball is floating on a stream of air, generated by a large fan beneath the cone, that flows up through the cone. We have played with this apparatus ourselves - if you try to gently push or pull the ball out of the rush of air, you can feel it being pulled back in. If you alter the direction of the air flow, the ball appears to be suspended in space off to the side of the blower - within limits, of course. If you push it too far to the side, the ball will fall. The design seems to invite experimentation. Indeed, graphics placed near the exhibit challenge the visitor to guess what makes the ball stable in the column of air (Museum of Science and Industry, 1992). But perhaps we are getting ahead of ourselves by giving a description of the exhibit that leaves out the boy himself, for without the "user" it is just a museum piece, an artifact of a three-dimensional science textbook teaching about principles of aerodynamics.

The boy pokes gently at the hovering ball and it dances in the upward air stream. He adjusts the direction of the flow of air and the ball edges further away from the blower at an angle, and then, after hovering in midair a bit longer, falls to the ground. He is laughing until a woman a few feet away, probably his mother, calls (or is it yells?) in a concerned tone, "Don't do that. You're going to break it!" The boy is now turned away from us so we cannot see his expression, but we imagine it as changing from delight to something else. He trudges off to another exhibit area, mother following. As they move along, another child picks up the ball and tosses it into the stream of air, watching it regain its airborne state.

What are we to make of this family scene playing out below us? We might conjecture that the boy is learning science through exploratory "hands-on" play. By experimenting informally with the physical properties of objects and airflows, he comes to understand some principles of science, while at the same time, by testing the limits of the blowers, perhaps he is also learning, by playing, something of the ways that scientists learn. It is interesting to note how our description of "the exhibit" invites this understanding, for we bring our knowledge of the exhibit designers' intent to our reading of what is going on. From this point of view, we might see that the boy is learning despite his mother's efforts to limit his exploration, while his mother may be wondering, "is he learning or merely playing" as an either/or choice. Yet, by foregrounding a different set of cues – the boy's defiance, the mother's scolding, it is possible for us, as observers on the balcony, to orient to a different understanding in which the mother is being tested by her son. That is, she sees her son as testing her and her patience rather than aerodynamics. Given past experience and the history of their relationship, the mother may thus be operating according to a qualitatively different understanding of this episode- one in which the necessity for setting limits (especially in a MUSEUM of Science and Industry) looms large. And so our initial displeasure with the mother may shift to something else. We begin to appreciate that perhaps beneath the mother's "bossiness" might be a fear of what will happen if her son assumes that the hands-on learning invited here is somehow extended to other settings where it is less appropriate.

Frames and Framing

We focus here on the ambiguity inherent in scenes like this one, and, more generally, on the contingent nature of our seeing depending on our vantage points as observers. What is "real" depends in large measure on the perspective or frame, which establishes our point of view, directs our interpretation, and answers the question, "what is going on here?" (Bateson, 1972; Tannen, 1993). Bateson drew on the metaphor of a picture frame as a border separating and foregrounding a painting from its background to formulate his theories about the composition of human interactional contexts in everyday life. He recognized that communication operates at many contrasting levels of abstraction, that higher order messages classify, qualify and "frame" other messages, allowing interactants to make sense of what is happening in a given situation by labeling the events that are occurring. One danger in the metaphor of the frame, as Bateson (1972) recognized, is its concreteness. He wrestled with the choice of whether to conceptualize these interactional episodes in terms of the metaphor of "frame" (with its over-concreteness) or in terms of the more abstract concept of "set" or "class" (with its connotations of Russellian logico-mathematics). But the issue may be more than simply a choice between two related metaphors, or a choice between two different ways of conceptualizing our "seeing-as" (Wittgenstein, 1953). Each one, frame and class, implies a different root metaphor, a different worldview, that allows a fundamentally different understanding of how we construct our worlds. We could also see this as a choice between different root metaphors, or "world hypotheses" of Stephen Pepper (1942). Pepper's four worldviews, formism, contextualism, organicism, and mechanism, were his ways of encouraging us to think about how we create our ways of making the worlds we inhabit and in which we participate. He articulated these four as a way of discouraging dogmatism about our world-creating processes. The notions of set and class accord with Pepper's formism, in which understanding emerges through classifying, while the notion of framing fits more with the synthetic processes of contextualism. In Pepper's terms, formism and contextualism, as world hypotheses, reflect a "dispersive" approach (we understand the stuff of our world as arising in our experience), rather than an "integrative" approach, where we might see our stuff as located in some universal structure. Yet formism and contextualism also differ from each other in that formism (together with mechanism) relies on an analytic approach to our construction, while contextualism (together with organicism) relies on a more synthetic approach. In its dispersive and synthetic character, contextualism invites comparisons with von Foerster's non-trivial machines—which von Foerster (1991) notes, are synthetically determined, history dependent, while also analytically indeterminable and unpredictable, in that sense.

We note the parallel with Pepper's world hypotheses to make clear that the distinction between frame and set is not merely a choice between the concrete and the abstract, nor is it one that is good or bad. Rather, the choice is grounded in fundamentally different worldviews, including all that a worldview, or root metaphor in Pepper's sense, entails. Further, as different root metaphors, they orient us completely differently to our everyday worlds. And this is important. It is a choice about how we "see" what we see—a choice of the second order.

From this perspective, what some describe as "framings" are, in practice, "classifyings," as when we classify museum visitors' behavior according to some a priori schema. Thus an exhibit designer might see the son as "using the exhibit correctly," while the mother is "not using the exhibit correctly"; a science educator might see the son as "scientifically literate" and the mother as "scientifically illiterate" based upon evaluative schema that are used to view visitors' behavior. Note that we are not trying to dismiss the importance of "classifying" or what our designer or educator might be seeing and using as the basis for her or his decisions and actions – but rather to allow for conversations between different ways of seeing.

Contextual frames, unlike picture frames, are endlessly mutable because they are subject to the interpersonal dynamics of the situation. A change in the mother's tone of voice or the boy's expression as he lunges toward the ball (away from her) can shift the definition of the situation. A single gesture can tip the scales so that what had been or seemed to be a humorous, playful exchange is felt a moment later to be antagonistic; "playing" becomes "fighting." Participants need not even be in the "same" frame; the mother's frame will not necessarily prevail, nor will the son's. Such moments of everyday life are improvisatory "joint performances" (Bateson, 1994) in which each person inventively participates in concert with the other without necessarily having a clear script or plan. Still, some orderliness or behavioral coordination seems to emerge. As Coyne (1985) has noted, "it can even be the case that participants could not proceed if they had such an explicit grasp of what is unfolding. Many couples would never have gotten together if either partner had framed their first encounter as 'initiating a long-term relationship.'" (p. 339). Our social eigenbehaviors (von Foerster, 1981) and the production of a mutually stable reality can be understood as resulting from an ongoing recursive and dialogic process. Indeed, in developing a topology of closure, Heinz (von Foerster, 1976) notes that "equilibrium is obtained when the eigenbehaviors of one participant generate (recursively) those for the other . . . where one snake eats the tail of the other as if it were its own, and where cognition computes its own cognitions through those of the other." Heinz then notes that this is the origin of ethics.

Eigenbehaviors emerge in the context of our uncertainty about whether we are, indeed, operating within the same frame, while at the same time, we act as though this were the case. There is a wonderful parallel here with the work of the psychologist Ragnar Rommetveit (1978), who noted a paradox of intersubjectivity in what he termed his pragmatic generative postulate. In this postulate, Rommetveit stated that we "take the possibility of perfect intersubjectivity for granted in order to achieve partial intersubjectivity in real life discourse with our fellow men." In other words, we have to assume being in the same frame, or "conversation" with our others in order to interact with them – but at the same time, NOT assume (or not rely on the assumption) that we are truly in the same frame (i.e., we always need to be prepared to question this assumption).

This is why the design of learning contexts is so difficult. It appears that the mother and son have a curious freedom to impose their own interpretations on the sequence of interaction. Furthermore, we as observers or as exhibit designers can "play" by trying on two or three of the most plausible frames but we cannot specify what frame the participants themselves will adopt as they engage with the materials.

As social actors, we use frames, in the form of background information and premises, to make sense of what we are experiencing. As observers in the science center, we were making sense of the scene below us by trying to understand within what frames the participants were operating. Every behavior we notice, every cue we see or hear, is framed by our sense of what conversation is being enacted—whether that conversation is with the exhibit, with each other, or both.

Observing Frames

In our descriptions of the boy as playing or learning, as testing a scientific principle or testing his mother, it is we, from our vantage point on the balcony, who are making sense of the situation. It is WE who specify the frames depending on our metapositions—as clinicians or as researchers, or exhibit designers, or as family members ourselves. Whether these fit with the experienced frames of the participants is yet another question. We bring our own history of observing, our knowledge of what should be happening (we know what the designers had in mind), our own family communication rituals, even our own ways of marking the distinction between learning and play (is there a difference?) to our observing. Just as Heinz von Foerster (1981) played with the double meaning of "observing systems," we need to appreciate the polysemy in play when we speak of "observing frames."

Heinz' notion of observing systems underscores what we, as systems thinkers, see—namely systems in the form of interconnections and patterns, a crucial first-order recognition. It also tells us to explore how we see, by noting that we are also observing systems—that is, it is we who are, as systems ourselves, doing the observing. The realization of observing systems, then, rests precisely on a merging of the second order understanding with the first order. Similar possibilities are implied in the notion of observing frames. To make sense of everyday interaction, we are, on one hand, observing frames, in that we locate the actions we see and the utterances we hear within frames that allow for mundane activities to become "those activities." The frames could be "a child playfully learning," "a family spending time together (doing 'family')," or, "a mother trying to retain control of her son in a public setting." Each frame invites a different interpretation of what "is really going on." At the same time, there are frames of reference that serve as interpretive resources, conditioning the way we observe—our observing frames—the frames we create for our own observing process. These are not there as part of a ready-made reality, but rather are invoked by us, as observers, who are participating in our observing activities. They guide what our observing is doing to the situation—to the "what is really going on." The latter is a deeply second-order concept. However, it is the juxtaposition of the second- and first-order that is key here. The distinction might be understood as that between a context marker that allows us to make sense of a situation in a particular way AND the frames we have for understanding our own process of observing.

Physicists, for example, in talking about quantum phenomena, may talk about an observing frame of reference as that which allows them to understand how they might see things they cannot literally see. In the social world of our example, an appreciation of our observing frames allows us to understand precisely what manner of relationship we bring to our observing process. We noted above a desire as observers to understand frames from the perspectives of the participants. This is a choice, of course—one that rests on attempting to apprehend our visitors' experienced world rather than choosing to be a distant, objective observer. Is what we are asking here simply to recognize the paradoxes inherent in attempting to see from an other's perspective—of trying to see a visitors' culture from the inside? Such distinctions recall anthropological notions of etic and emic understanding (Pike, 1966; Geertz, 1973). Etic descriptions are those come out of the analyst's prior experience and training, making reference to analytic distinctions that are external to the user's own system of meanings, whereas emic descriptions imply a more fully contextual empathic perspective on the part of the observer. Emic is not, strictly speaking, an insider perspective, although it is often glossed in this way; rather it connotes an effort by the observer to move toward an insider's perspective by recognizing his or her own biases (Becker, 1995). And as Becker notes, we are describing an oscillating process—that is, we are not describing a perspective, but a process of self-correction. We can ask, as a question, whether we are we seeing as a scientist, a designer, an educator, or a family therapist. Note how each of these, rather than merely describing a role we might play, also describes a relationship between us and that which we, by our observing, create. As such, there is also a strong indeterminacy and fluidity here, in that the cues from what we are observing may alter "who" we are. Most importantly, this might also include, as Heinz (von Foerster, 1991) so critically invited us to do, "seeing through the eyes of the other"—an observing frame of empathy and rapport.

Ethical and aesthetic imperatives

This second-orderness, our observing our own process of frame-making, has profound consequences for how we act with and orient ourselves to others for we are not living our lives on the balcony alone. For example, our frame-making may be different if we are evaluating the "success" of the exhibit (is it working?—what do we mean by "working" here) as compared to the "success" of the mother. What kind of conversation would we have on that balcony if we were a clinician and an exhibit designer, trying to construct a stable reality of others' worlds? It is our contention that von Foerster's (1973) ethical and aesthetic imperatives can serve as guides for linking our observing frames to action and living in a social world.

Ethical Imperative: Act so as to always increase the number of choices
Aesthetic Imperative: If you want to learn how to see, learn how to act.

Von Foerster (1973) developed this pair of ideas in the context of a landmark article, "On Constructing a Reality." At first, it is not readily apparent why "increasing the number of choices" should be linked to an ethics, nor why connecting acting to seeing would be linked to aesthetics. But this may be because they are often taken as isolated statements, separated from each other, and separated from the context within which they were put forward. It is crucial to note that these were offered as a way of assuring that a constructivist approach would not be equated with a solipsism. He affirms his commitment to a principle of relativity, "which rejects a hypothesis when it does not hold for two instances together, although it holds for each instance separately (Earthlings and Venusians may be consistent in claiming to be in the center of the universe, but their claims fall to pieces if they should ever get together)." He goes on to talk of the basis for this principle as a guide for thinking about our own engagement with our world and how we act in our world (with others). He notes that it is not a logical necessity to adopt his Principle of Relativity, but a choice we make as a human being—and then, "If I reject it, I am the center of the universe, my reality are my dreams and my nightmares, my language is monologue, and my logic mono-logic. If I adopt it, neither I nor the other can be the center of the universe. As in the heliocentric system, there must be a third that is the central reference. It is the relation between Thou and I, and this relation is IDENTITY: Reality = Community."

The ethical and aesthetic imperative then, as a couplet, emerge as a consequence of recognizing that reality equals community, of living in an emergent "we-ness" while not dispensing of our own responsibility involved in how we choose to do this. The ethical imperative of observing frames is tied to a systemic recognition of emergence. It is based upon understanding how we increase the "number of choices" by always being cognizant that what guides a co-orientation in a situation is not solely "my frame" or "your frame" but that which emerges improvisationally as "our frame." The ethical imperative of observing frames is thus based in a profound respect for our others- those we are observing, and, in many senses, participating with. And just as in

Buber's (1972) notions of dialogue, we walk the "narrow ridge" between holding fast to the frame we bring, while opening up space for our partners' frame to appreciate a newly emergent frame—acting so as to increase number of choices in that sense. The aesthetic imperative linking acting and seeing recognizes that how we see frames is rooted in how we act in and out of those frames—managers may see a parallel in a concern for an alignment between our walk with our talk. This alignment is not, however, a process that is located solely in rationalistic thought, but in other sensings of what is beautiful, not unlike the way a mathematician describes an elegant proof whose elegance derives from new patterns brought forth. And in a science center, the scene for our observing frames, the aesthetics and ethics of observing frames invites a blending of art and science, at the same time that the ethics and aesthetics of observing frames occurs in a cycle of action and reflection. And our action, in this case, will include redesigning by seeing how our observing frames afford possibilities for extending the design of learning contexts.

Revisiting the Bernoulli Blowers

We decided to return to our fourth-floor observation platform on another day. It is again late afternoon at MOSI, but the floor below seems as busy as ever. What are so many people doing inside on such a nice spring day? Maybe our earlier repertoire of frames needs to expand to include people just wanting to do something "together that is deemed culturally acceptable as an activity"? Looking down onto the Bernoulli blowers, we see a middle aged man and a young girl, probably a father and a daughter, looking right into the Bernoulli blowers apparatus. She bends toward the blower, and gets a head full of rushing air—maybe she thinks this is a powerful hair dryer? The girl is laughing, smiling, and clearly having a lot of fun. Now she has managed to push the ball out of the airstream, and it is resting on the ground a few meters distant. In her hands is a teddy bear and she is pushing it into the airstream. It goes upward, spins out of control, and then lands on the ground. She retrieves it and puts it back in. This time it hovers a bit longer before spinning out of control, away from the blowers. Father runs over, picks up the teddy bear, and he tries. Same thing. Now he and she jointly tie up the teddy bear into some "rounder shape" and try again. It hangs in the air a bit longer still before gravity wins again. Now they are both laughing. And we are smiling and laughing watching them. Are they misusing the exhibit? Or are they inventing the affordances of the exhibit for themselves, making it work for their own tools, inventing new ways of testing it?

We wondered, does this family activity seem more satisfying to us than the previous one we described? Just as we noted a new possibility for framing the behavior of those we were observing, as a reflection on the conditions of the day, we might also note a new possibility for our own frames for observing – one that may have been there "all along" but not realized by us in this context. We seemed, upon reflection again, to be observing modes of intergenerational family play, with our enjoyment stemming from our roles as parents learning about what could be satisfying in our own family. Have we shifted from academic ethnographers to caring parents delighting in the occasion? Could we bring some of their play back to our own family ways of being? We recalled Mary Catherine Bateson (1984) talking about how her mother, Margaret Mead, had been criticized for analytically observing her daughter (Mary Catherine, herself) as though being caring mother and "scientific" observer were incompatible states of being, or in this case, observing frames. Then we joked again about whether making that recall was shifting us back to the academic, away from possibilities for learning for action in our own family. But was our observing our observing frames doing the same thing?

The paradox of observing frames

Indeed, Niklas Luhmann (1995) in inviting us to consider the question "How is it possible to observe frames?" posed precisely this issue. In his "Paradoxy of Observing Systems," Luhmann linked notions of paradox, which we have played with here throughout, to second order observing.[1] Luhmann noted that there have been two different, but related, traditions of paradox—the logical and the rhetorical. While it has been the logical, grounded in a rationalistic tradition, that has dominated, Luhmann asks that we also consider the rhetorical tradition, which he states, was introduced to "enlarge the frame of received opinions" and thus to allow for innovation (recall von Foerster's ethical imperative here). He notes that, in the rhetorical tradition, paradox allows for reframing the frames of common sense, "frames that normally go unattended." In this tradition, framing is also inextricably interwoven with play. Yet, at the same time, Luhmann also wonders whether, paradoxically, holding on to the distinction between the logical and the rhetorical makes sense. As von Foerster (1973) noted, we necessarily draw distinctions (including that between the observer and the observed) to make our worlds, but we also need to recognize the importance of understanding relationships between those things that have become "things" by how we have distinguished them.

Dealing with the question of how we observe our frames by resorting to our observing our observing frames of course, as we have noted, invites precisely this paradox – for we need be simultaneously observing our world, and observing ourselves observing our world – we are both inside and outside at the same time. Returning to the question of how it is possible to observe frames, Luhmann proposes that we consider the medium of meaning-making (rather than truth, for example) as a path to follow. Linking von Foerster's ethical and aesthetic imperatives to Luhmann, and thus inviting a conversation between Luhmann and von Foerster, might make this a meaning-making in action. What is also a critical lesson learned here is the need for an oscillation between observing frames and our observing frames as occurs in any paradoxical situation. Our paradox here (rather than, as Luhmann notes, an

---

1. The interested reader is invited to read more fully Luhmann's "Paradoxy of Observing Systems" which in many ways provides a theoretical starting point, compared to our more experience based starting point, for the development of ideas in this paper.

orthodoxy) is something to be reveled in as a manner of living in a contingent and participatory universe. And, much as with any paradoxy, its recognition is a call for action.

Observing frames, learning contexts

Rather than seeing paradoxes as paralyzing dilemmas, we can also see them as liberating, challenging us to create new frames for observing and new frames for action. We are then also encouraged to think about how new frames may be generative of new possibilities for transforming a situation.

Back at our science center, these challenges surfaced in looking at how those who "help" may understand their relationship to visitors. At MOSI, in addition to the exhibits themselves, there also are staff on the floor attending to the visitors, as the visitors play at the exhibits. These staff were formerly called explainers, and their primary job was precisely that—to explain. This is what might be expected at a science center, since, as Maturana (1991) has noted, what distinguishes scientists is a passion for explaining. However, a dilemma was noted by realizing that the exhibits were designed to invite learning at two different levels. These levels were both the learning of the scientific principles involved AND learning about how to learn as a scientist. The latter, deuterolearning might include precisely the kinds of testing, learning by "getting it wrong" (Bamberger & Ziporyn, 1992), and play that we saw in both of our observations made from MOSI's balcony, above. Ideally, both of these levels of learning would mutually reinforce each other – and, it was felt that the learning of scientific principles should not get in the way of the playful learning to be curious and explore (c.f., Steier & Ostrenko, 2000). Reflecting on observing frames of being an explainer led to a shift in title, job description, and a hoped for transformation of relationship of the "person on the floor" to the visitors and to the exhibit galleries. The shift was one from explainer to "interactor." Rather than simply explain what was "really going on" with the exhibit, the interactor would play with the guests and invite play with the exhibit—whether the guest was a twelve year old girl, a six year old boy together with his grandmother, or some other family or friendship constellation.

The shift to becoming an interactor is not merely one of labels and roles. It is a change in relationships, and co-orientating behavior with visitors. As an interactor, I may need to "do something silly," "ask weird questions," but I may also listen differently to questions posed—questions that may or may not be requests for information. And I may listen for questions that do not make sense within my own framework—questions that necessitate the initiation of an inquiry, with the visitor, or family constellation, as to what experiences allowed that question to hold importance for them. In other words, I need try to understand within what framework of experience that question might make sense rather than simply dismiss it. In this way, interactors "give reason" (Bamberger & Schön, 1991) to visitors in ways that an explainer may not. But, of course, interactors may also need to also "explain," as some questions may warrant this, and some situations may invite this. Thus, the shift from being an explainer to an interactor is not one that excludes previous ways of relating to visitors, but expands possibilities. In this way, the shift is also not one of solely marking different sets, or classes, of relationships with visitors. As interactors, we would be attendant to the cues that mark the visit as "that situation" for any system of visitors, and thus be responsive to that constructed situation. That constructed situation might also include an understanding of who we are to them, which we cannot legislate (Jorgenson, 1995). For example, does the grandfather avoid us because he might feel that we, by our supposed expert knowledge, take away his "role" as explainer to his grandson? As interactors, then, we move between observing frames and observing frames in ways that, as explainers, we would not.

What is crucial to recognize here is that this shift embodies one of an ethics and aesthetics of observing frames. That is, the change allows for actions that continuously increase the choices available for interaction, rather than replacing one set of behaviors with another set. Further, we are testing out our new possibilities by our actions (and reflections about the success of those actions). This is not easy, for it also means that interactors must recognize the importance of "learning contexts"—in both senses.

For example, interactors must be aware of the ways that what others may view as "information" can alter the landscape of an exhibit for visitors. Here, we can hear the voice of Heinz (von Foerster, 1970) guiding us. Many exhibits in science centers also contain some text—a card, or a display. For some, this text becomes the primary vehicle for what the exhibit affords. If this text offers an explanation of the scientific principle (illustrated by the inter-activity invited by the exhibit), it may in some cases disqualify the curiosity generated by the activity itself. As one interactor noted, while the physical exhibit itself may invite exploration and curiosity, learning about the scientific learning process itself, and learning to be like a scientist, the text may offer answers (learning "facts") that interfere with that second-order learning process –and remove the playfulness intended (Steier, 2003). What is crucial here is that the interactor, as an interactor, must be attentive to all of this, and to how "information" in-forms (and at what level) the visitors. As such, the interactor must become a bit of a cybernetician, questioning, as Heinz did, the processes we think of to allow information to become "IN-formation." Interactors must note the shift to rethinking exactly what information might mean—from its reflecting supposedly objective knowledge to being embedded in processes of communication (c.f., Brier, 1992). At the same time, interactors must also be, in this way, something of family therapists in recognizing what their responses do to the ongoing, often intergenerational, debates about "what is going on with each exhibit." For example, what might correcting the grandfather do in this setting?

It must be noted that there has been a movement to understand the importance of how "learning conversations" are constructed in science centers (c.f. Leinhardt, Crowley & Knutson, 2002) as well as rethinking the meaning of communication in public understanding of science (MacDonald, 1996). However, what we are advocating here is making a linkage to design such that the interactors, designers and researchers are understood as also embedded in those very same learning conversations, thereby allowing for crucial second order questions to be asked.

Schön (1983; Schön & Rein, 1994) noted how we test frames, and do "frame experiments," to see if our understanding of a situation allows for our acting in accordance with what may be going on. Perhaps what is needed is an understanding of how this idea also applies, not just to the frames we observe, but our resources for understanding the frames we bring to our observing (observing frame experiments— and make this a researchable question, inviting others into this inquiry with us.

An emergent research agenda might then be to engage interactors to explore these questions of their learning contexts. We would do this with an eye toward also inviting designers of exhibits to think more fully of the importance of learning contexts, and the ethics and aesthetics of observing frames as an ongoing conversation.

References

Bamberger, J.& Schön, D. A. (1991). Learning as reflective conversation with materials. In F. Steier (Ed.), *Research and reflexivity* (pp. 186-209). London: Sage.

Bamberger, J. & Ziporyn, E. (1992). Getting it wrong. *Ethnomusicology and Music Cognition, 34*(3), 22-56.

Bateson, G. (1972). A theory of play and fantasy. In G. Bateson, *Steps to an ecology of mind* (pp. 177-200). New York: Ballantine Books.

Bateson, G., Jackson, D. D., Haley, J. & Weakland, J.H. (1956). Toward a theory of schizophrenia. *Behavioral Science, 1*(4). (Also available in G. Bateson (1972), *Steps to an ecology of mind*. New York: Ballantine Books).

Bateson, M. C. (1984). *With a daughter's eye: A memoir of Margaret Mead and Gregory Bateson*. New York: William Morrow.

Bateson, M. C. (1994). *Peripheral visions*. New York: Harper Collins.

Becker, A. L. (1995). *Beyond translation: Essays toward a modern philology*. Ann Arbor: University of Michigan Press.

Brier, S. (1992). Information and consciousness: A critique of the mechanistic foundation for the concept of information. *Cybernetics and Human Knowing, 1*, 71-94.

Buber, M. (1972). *Between man and man*. New York: Macmillan.

Coyne, J. (1985). Toward a theory of frames and reframing: The social nature of frames. *Journal of Marital and Family Therapy, 11*(4), 337-344.

Geertz, C. (1973). *The interpretation of cultures*. New York: Basic Books.

Jorgenson, J. (1995). Re-relationalizing rapport in interpersonal settings. In W. Leeds-Hurwitz (Ed.), *Social approaches to communication* (pp. 155-17). New York: Guilford Press.

Leinhardt, G., Crowley, K. & Knutson, K. (Eds.) (2002). *Learning conversations in museums*. Mahwah, NJ: Lawrence Erlbaum.

Luhmann, N. (1995). The paradox of observing systems. *Cultural Critique, 31*, 37-55.

MacDonald, S. (1996). Authorising science: Public understanding of science in museums. In A. Irwin & B. Wynne (Eds.), *Misunderstanding Science: The Public Reconstruction of Science and Technology* (pp. 152-171). Cambridge: Cambridge University Press.

Maturana, H. R. (1991). Science and daily life: The ontology of scientific explanations. In F. Steier (Ed.), *Research and reflexivity* (pp. 30-52). London: Sage.

Museum of Science and Industry (1992). Omniphase Exhibits – Schematic Design: Bernoulli blower bench. Tampa, Florida.

Pepper, S. C. (1942). *World hypotheses*. Berkeley, CA: University of California Press.

Pike, K. (1966). Etic and emic standpoints for the description of behavior. In A.G. Smith (Ed.), *Communication and culture: Readings in the codes of human interaction* (pp. 152-163). New York: Holt, Rinehart and Winston.

Rommetveit. R. (1978). On negative rationalism in scholarly studies of verbal communication and dynamic residuals in the construction of human intersubjectivity. In M. Brenner, P. Marsh & M. Brenner (Eds.), *The social contexts of method* (pp. 16-32). London: Croon Helm.

Schön, D. A. (1983). *The reflective practitioner*. New York: Basic Books.

Schön, D. A.& Rein, M. (1994). *Frame reflection: Toward the resolution of intractable policy controversies*. New York: Basic Books.

Steier, F. & Ostrenko, W. (2000). Taking cybernetics seriously at a science center: Reflection-in-interaction and second order organizational learning. *Cybernetics and Human Knowing, 7*(2-3), 47-69.

Steier, R. (2003). *Playing with art: Learning science.*Unpublished manuscript, Stanford University.

Tannen, D. (1993). What's in a frame? Surface evidence for underlying expectations. In D. Tannen (Ed.), *Framing in discourse* (pp. 14-56). New York: Oxford University Press.

Von Foerster, H. (1970). Thoughts and notes on cognition. In P. Garvin (Ed.), *Cognition: A multiple view* (pp. 25-48). New York: Spartan Books. (Also in von Foerster, H. (1981). *Observing systems.* Seaside, CA: Intersystems).

Von Foerster, H. (1973). On constructing a reality. In F. E. Preiser (Ed.), *Environmental design research, Vol. II* (pp. 35-46). Stroudberg: Dowden, Hutchison & Ross. (Also in von Foerster, H. (1981). *Observing systems.* Seaside, CA: Intersystems).

Von Foerster, H. (1976). Objects: Tokens for (Eigen-)Behaviors. *Cybernetics Forum, 8*(3&4), 91-96. [also in von Foerster, H. (1981). *Observing systems.* Seaside, CA: Intersystems].

Von Foerster, H. (1981). *Observing systems.* Seaside, CA: Intersystems.

Von Foerster, H. (1986). The case of the double blind. Lecture given at Institute of Pennsylvania Hospital, Philadelphia.

Von Foerster, H. (1991). Through the eyes of the other. In F. Steier (Ed.), *Research and reflexivity* (pp. 63-75). London: Sage.

Wittgenstein, L. (1953). *Philosophical investigations* (G. E. M. Anscombe, Trans.). New York: Macmillan.

Cybernetics And Human Knowing. Vol. 10, nos. 3-4, pp. 137-149

"Heinz von Foerster – An Appreciation" (Revisited)

Bernard Scott[1]

Reproduced below, with a few small edits, is a paper I wrote in 1979 for the *International Cybernetics Newsletter*, as part of its 'founding fathers of cybernetics' series (Scott, 1979). I offer it here as a contribution to this special issue of *C&HK* because (i) I believe my younger self did quite a good job of overviewing von Foerster's career (recall, he 'retired' in 1976) and (ii) the article is not readily available to the current generation of scholars who, I hope, will be interested in finding out about cybernetics and exploring its history. I preface the 1979 paper with a Prologue in which I set the paper in context and draw attention to aspects of von Foerster's early work that have perhaps been overlooked in recent years, especially with the particular interest given to his later writings on second order cybernetics. There is also an Epilogue in which I comment on developments post-1979 where von Foerster's influence has been evident, in particular, work and writings that explicitly draw on von Foerster's distinction between a first and second order cybernetics.

Prologue

The paper below, "Heinz von Foerster: An Appreciation," first published in 1979 (Scott, 1979), was written when I was in my early thirties. I had by that time been a student of cybernetics for more than ten years. Like many others before and since, I was fascinated by the coming together within the cybernetics circle of a group of mutually supportive but disparate scholars of astonishing brilliance. As a way of understanding the discipline, I found myself summarizing for myself the main ideas and achievements of those scholars. I then proposed to Paul Hanika, editor of the *International Cybernetics Newsletter*, that he should commission and publish a series of papers on the 'founding fathers of cybernetic'. He agreed this was a good idea. My paper about von Foerster was the first in this series and was followed by a two part article about Gordon Pask (Scott, 1980, 1982). Sadly, Hanika died not long after and the series came to a halt. In the absence of other contributions, I was preparing short papers about Warren McCulloch, Ross Ashby and Norbert Wiener. Perhaps one day they, too, will see the light of day.

My article about von Foerster covered much ground in a short space. To do this, I found myself writing in a terse, aphoristic manner. To some extent, I took Heinz's own writings as a model, though I cannot claim that I achieved the same level of masterly clarity.

I have commented elsewhere on von Foerster's work (Scott, 1996). More recently, I have written a short paper entitled "Second order cybernetics: an historical introduction," in which I comment on developments that draw their inspiration from

---

1. Cranfield University, Royal Military College of Science, Shrivenham, Swindon, Wiltshire SN6 8LA, UK.
   Email: B.C.E.Scott@rmcs.cranfield.ac.uk

von Foerster's work (Scott, in press). It is interesting that, although it refers to the text in which von Foerster first made his famous distinction between a first and a second order cybernetics and clearly appreciates von Foerster's reflexive goal of "explaining the observer to himself," the 1979 paper does not highlight the first and second order distinction and its terminology. It took a while for that distinction and that terminology to become standard usage in cybernetics.

The reader should perhaps also note that the distinction between first and second order cybernetics, where first order study is of observed systems and second order is of observing systems, was made almost as an aside in 1974, just two years before von Foerster's retirement. In his later years, von Foerster became celebrated for having made that distinction and continued to write and present papers on that theme. See von Foerster and Poerksen (2002) for an account of von Foerster's latter day interests and activities.

The reader might like to know that when von Foerster read my tribute to him, he sent me a telegram, saying, "Congratulations! You have reversed evolution. Now the sons are inventing the fathers!" I am now wondering if there is some wise truth in this comment of Heinz. In the 1979 article, I refer to Heinz's bringing a European sensibility to the more pragmatic American scene. In von Foerster and Poerksen (2002), he makes similar comment about himself (pp. 109-110).

My 1979 article covers much of von Foerster's work prior to 1974. As von Foerster makes clear, his early papers on molecular computation draw directly on Schroedinger's (1944, 1958) classic texts *What is Life* and *Mind and Matter*. His later ethical work also draws upon the same source. Von Foerster's ethical principle that the observer should "enter the domain of his own descriptions" is an inverse reading of Schroedinger's statement of the Principle of Objectivation, the principle that the scientist in pursuit of objectivity necessarily does not include himself in his domain of descriptions (Schroedinger, 1967, pp. 126-137).

In the early papers, we also see very clear evidence of von Foerster's liberal view of what is 'computation', in particular 'biological computation', a topic also discussed in von Foerster and Poerksen (2002, pp. 54-59 & pp. 106-109). He adopts a far broader view than that used, for example, to characterize the operation of the general purpose digital computer. This broader view of computation very much parallels that of Warren McCulloch. Indeed it is evident that the early cyberneticians as a group spoke of computation in this broad biological way. See, for example, the fascinating discussions in Yovits and Cameron (1960) about the computations carried out by slime moulds as they migrate from one location to another. See especially the paper by Gordon Pask on "The natural history of networks" (Pask, 1960).

What is also evident in von Foerster's early work are parallel and complementary interests in the dynamics of self-organization and the forms of computation that constitute cognition in such systems. Following Pask's usage, I like to refer to the former as "macro-level theory" and the latter as "micro-level theory." The important point to appreciate is that functional models of cognition with information flows between parts of the system are static representations of structures that are continually being reconstituted, reproduced within the overall dynamics of self-organization. These relationships between the macro, the global dynamics, and the micro, the structure and functions, are fully brought out in the cybernetic literature by Maturana and Varela, with their conceptions of autopoiesis and organizational closure, and, especially by Gordon Pask.

Gordon Pask, over a period of years, developed cybernetic models of learning processes which explicitly had macro and micro aspects. In his later writing, these models form the basis for his extended development of conversation theory. I was a collaborator with Pask on much of this work (see Scott, 1993). My own Ph.D. work carried out under Pask's supervision, includes a complex model of skill acquisition. Micro-level structures are concept schemas and perceptual-motor procedural 'operators' that interact and transform as part of the evolution of accurate, fast-acting automatically applied subskills. Macro-level dynamic procedures allocate processing resources to sub-processes and manage the selection processes whereby successfully applied operators 'survive' and unsuccessful ones 'die' (Scott, 1976). (As an aside, John Holland's model of 'robust adaptation', with which the reader may be familiar, is homomorphic to this model and similarly motivated; see, Holland, 1975.)

Von Foerster clearly appreciates that cognition as a process is holistic. This is evidenced by his often repeated explication that 'memory' should not be confused with mere 'storage' — that, in fact, perception, cognition and memory are indissoluble aspects of one integral cognitive system. In later years, following Varela and others, the term 'enactive' has been adopted to capture this view of cognition as an embodied holistic process, rather than as a static set of structures where information in various "representational forms" is passed around. I have commented elsewhere on how, as the 'new' paradigm of cognitive science was set up, the AI "symbolic representationalist" view of computation, as expounded by Minsky, Boden and others, threw out the baby of self-organization with the bath water of stuff deemed to be 'old-fashioned'. In Scott (2000), in a discussion of Boden's critique of the work of Jean Piaget, I expressed my concerns thus:

Piaget, on many occasions, acknowledges that his underlying model is cybernetic in character. (See Boden, 1979, Chapter 7, for an extended discussion of Piaget's affiliations with cybernetics). Other than acknowledge the existence of self-regulative properties as a necessary precursor to cognitive development, he gives no satisfactory account of them. Indeed, so often has his concept of "equilibration" been criticized that Boden (op. cit.) argues that it would be better if he cast his theory in computational, information processing form, where procedures may be spelled out in explicit detail. Although there is merit in such a recommendation, Boden confuses the issue by not only making a distinction between the "dynamics" of systems (i.e. their self-organizing properties) and the "structure" of systems (their forms of computation) but argues that the study of the latter (as evidenced by research in Artificial Intelligence, v. Boden, 1977) is the "new" cybernetics that has superseded the "classic" cybernetics. Whilst it is true historically that there has been a shift in emphasis, it is not true that the older problems and approaches have been finally resolved or found wanting. Certainly, the former is not the case. Implicit in Boden's distinction is exactly the distinction one seeks to get to grips with: what sort of entity is it whose properties make it self - organizing and lead it to evolve sophisticated cognitive methodologies for problem solving, pattern recognition, language comprehension and the like?" (Scott, 2000, pp. 980-981).

The 1979 Paper: *Abstract*

An overview is given of Heinz von Foerster's career to his retirement in 1976. For convenience of exposition, four phases are distinguished: (i) early work on large molecules as a medium for computation (ii) work on self-organizing systems (iii) work on memory as computation (iv) work on self-referential observing systems that gave rise to the distinction between first and second order cybernetics. Finally, there are some thoughts on praxis: what it means, in von Foerster's view, to be a cybernetician.

The 1979 paper: *Introduction*

In a short article it is not possible to present a comprehensive account of von Foerster's work. As an alternative, I will attempt a summary of what I see as the main themes of his thought.

Reference is made to key papers where appropriate. A larger bibliography is redundant since von Foerster's own department, the Biological Computer Laboratory at the University of Illinois, has made all his papers available on microfiche (Wilson, 1976).

His published papers are only a partial monument to von Foerster's work in cybernetics. He has been a major catalyst in bringing together many original thinkers in cybernetics and has helped to provide both moral and financial support (some examples of those who have passed through the BCL are W. Ross Ashby, Gotthard Gunther, Gordon Pask, Lars Loefgren and Humberto Maturana).

In the sense of Lakatos (1970), von Foerster has helped create and sustain a *research program* whose aims and ideas have been embraced by a whole generation of cyberneticians. That the research program is still alive and full of promise is affirmed by the increasing contributions of younger cyberneticians (Varela, Glanville and Kallikourdis are outstanding in this respect).

A mark of the esteem in which von Foerster is held by the scientific community at large is the special edition of *Forum*, the journal of the American Society for Cybernetics, which, to honor him on his retirement, contains a collection of papers and articles paying tribute to von Foerster's life and works.

The decision to write this article was made before I became aware of the special issue of *Forum* and discovered that the task I had set myself had been anticipated by those with greater claim to be authoritative and discerning. I have had the opportunity to read two of the articles in pre-print form (Pask, 1978; Beer, 1978) and recommend them to all lovers of cybernetics. Although I have reservations about the relevance and possible redundancy of the words I write, I am persuaded by von Foerster's own example that cybernetics is both and personal and public endeavor and welcome the opportunity and challenge of articulating my view of his view.

The 1979 Paper: *Beginnings: Molecular Computation*

Biologist, physicist, mathematician and philosopher were well met in von Foerster. His first papers (von Foerster, 1948, 1949) present a treatment of biological computation where he argues that the medium or fabric for cognition is available in the quantal changes and stabilities of large molecules. This was at a time when most thinkers were still working towards an understanding of the brain's potential for computation and organization in terms of neural nets (McCulloch & Pitts, 1943) and cell assemblies (Hebb, 1949).

Already, von Foerster recognized as few before him had (a parallel contribution is Schroedinger, 1944) that the roots of communication, control and computation in biological systems are to be found in the properties and behaviors of large molecules.

Two traits of von Foerster's style of thought are already in the fore: his elegant, pithy use of formalism and his awareness that behind all particular computational systems (macromolecules, brains and cells) lie *forms* of computation.

The latter trait is, of course, the hallmark of cybernetic thought, conceived as a discipline in its own right by the vision of Wiener (1948), anticipated by the British psychologist Craik (1943) as a fundamental philosophical stance and inexorably pursued as an abstract science by Ross Ashby (1956).

The 1979 Paper: *The First Plateau: Self-Organization*

Von Foerster's paper on self-organization (von Foerster, 1960) is now a classic.

Not only did he help bring the phrase "self-organizing" system into general use and abuse, he at the same time helped face head on and penetrate the paradoxes, dilemmas and irrationalities of self-reference that have diverted and thwarted intellectuals since time immemorial.

One can only guess at the source of his courage and insight. A major and dominating influence has to be a family friend, his 'uncle' Ludwig Wittgenstein. From my perspective, this is von Foerster's major achievement, that of wedding the burgeoning, largely American based revolution in science and technology, with its emphasis on pragmatic solutions and the mechanisms of computation, with the relatively esoteric essays in logic and epistemology of the old world philosopher, Wittgenstein.

That the concern to marry the old and the new is a consistent theme of von Foerster is reflected also in his support for Gunther's philosophical work in cybernetics and in his own embodiment and preservation of European culture (see Pask's comments, in his article for the special issue of *Forum*, on this point).

In his 1960 article, von Foerster makes the marriage as follows. He offers a definition of *organization* (in the sense of *ordered* rather than *disordered*) as constraint in a state-space and notes that the self-organizing system, when rationally characterized as a system whose order (redundancy) tends to increase, necessarily requires the observer to continually revise his frame of reference. A system whose order is stable relative to the observer's frame of reference (whose behavioral trajectory in the state-space is a point or cycle) is no longer self-organizing and is cybernetically trivial.

The observer has to actively accommodate to a self-organizing system: any description of the system becomes a potentially infinite series of observer-referenced computations where each computation takes its predecessors as arguments, and, in doing so, interprets them in a larger frame of reference (the state-space grows, new categories of behavior are distinguished).

During this formative period (1960-1961), von Foerster came into contact with Gordon Pask and in collaboration produced two papers (Pask & von Foerster, 1960, 1961) the main theme of which is an account of the conditions for the emergence of coalitions and cooperative activities in social systems. The interdependence of participants in a social system and the problems of communication and interaction became enduring themes for both men (cf. Pask, 1976).

At this stage, then, for von Foerster non-trivial cybernetics is *relativistic*: a system and its environment are defined relative to the observer's frame of reference. In his later papers, we see the gradual emergence of a fully *reflexive* cybernetics: the observer's intent includes giving an account of his own workings and genesis.

The 1979 Paper: *Middle Period: Memory as Computation*

In several papers (cf. von Foerster. 1965, 1969, 1971a), von Foerster continued to focus on the nature of memory as a key to the understanding of cognition and consciousness. In many ways, this work appears as a mere extension and elaboration of the research program launched by the earlier papers but there is a discernible and significant shift of emphasis.

As in earlier days, von Foerster has an eye for the molecular bases of computation but his concern to characterize *forms* of computation and to make the necessary conceptual clarification that allows the forms to stand forth as fundamental appear as his major themes.

He parodies behaviorist psychologies (as exemplified by statistical learning theory) as ways of manipulating an organism's environment so as to reduce the organism's behavior to that of a particular probabilistic automaton: a cybernetically non-trivial system is made into, becomes, a cybernetically trivial system.

He argues that such "conceptually poverty stricken" theoretical and methodological paradigms cannot offer a satisfactory account of perception, learning and memory. In von Foerster (1969) he exposes the semantic confusion of equating "memory" with storage and retrieval mechanisms (the homunculus fallacy so extant in the jargon of computer science) by revealing perception, learning and memory as necessary aspects of all cognition. He offers a canonical model for the minimal functional unit of cognition: the "finite function machine" and shows how the units may function collectively as tessellations, as "cognitive tiles."

Even at this stage, von Foerster has not yet presented an unashamedly reflexive theory of the observer. As with Pask's work on learning and teaching, which closely parallels von Foerster's work on memory, there is still inhibition about demolishing the conventional paradigms of scientific method and explanation.

The conceptual breakthrough came from two major sources: the biologist, Humberto Maturana, and the mathematician, Lars Loefgren. It is no accident that both men at that time were working in von Foerster's department. Maturana (1970) provides a clear and concise thesis concerning the evolution of living systems capable of acting as observers and, as a necessary concomitant, as self-observers. His thesis is fully reflexive: as a theory it explains how it, itself (and other theories), came into being. Fundamental to his account is his recognition that the circular (self-referential) organization of the living system is its one invariant, defining characteristic. The cognitive domain of symbol and description emerges, in the nexus of social interactions of cooperation and conflict between such living systems. Self and other descriptions arise together, in ontogenesis as well as in phylogenesis.

Maturana's thesis is informal and descriptive. Loefgren's contribution (Loefgren, 1968) was the formal demonstration that self-referential theories may be constructed as contradiction-free axiomatic systems.

Further affirmation that the problems of self-reference are not intractable to formal reasoning came with the publication of Spencer-Brown's (1969) *Laws of Form*. Von Foerster was one of the first to acknowledge and acclaim Brown's book as a masterpiece (von Foerster, 1971b).

Von Foerster's own first fully reflexive statement of a theory of cognition came in his 1970 paper: "Thoughts and Notes on Cognition." At the same time Gordon Pask's theory of conversations was being articulated as a new paradigmatic stance for psychology (Pask, 1972).

Both men clearly saw the cognitive domain as circular, self-referential. For von Foerster (von Foerster, 1973), the participants in the construction of a reality are distinguished by the observer to avoid solipsism: a choice he is free to reverse. For Pask (Pask, 1976; Pask, Scott & Kallikourdis, 1973), the observer of a cognitive process distinguishes participants in a conversation as a necessary prerequisite to avoid the circularity of pure introspection: "*I* direct *my* attention" becomes "Participant A directs the attention of Participant B." For Pask, all cognition is to be understood as conversational, inter-subjective, in form.

The 1979 Paper: *Recent Work: Self-Reference Revisited*

Possibly inspired by Spencer-Brown's (1969) dictum that "mathematics is a way of saying more and more using less and less," in several recent papers, von Foerster has attempted succinct condensations of his major insights, employing a minimum of elegant notation to maximal effect.

In von Foerster (1976), cognition is modelled as forms of recursive computation, eigen-functions, which stably compute particular relations as "objects," eigen-values.

In von Foerster (1974), events (having duration) and objects (having extension) are revealed as complementary forms of computation; the one is a stable argument for the computation of the other. What was an event may be recomputed as an object (an image, record, or program); what was an object can be recomputed as an event (the program is executed, the image interpreted, the record played back).

His final touch is to apply this principle, reflexively, to the observer: an observer is an event which computes (describes) itself as its own ultimate object.

The 1979 Paper: *Concluding Commentary: Von Foerster and the Praxis of Cybernetics*

The commentaries thus far have emphasized von Foerster's work as a thinker. For the man of affairs, in the world, von Foerster's insights may appear redundant, impenetrable and without application.

In my final comments, I hope to redress this imbalance, albeit, by exhibiting more of von Foerster's feats of abstraction.

In direct ways, von Foerster helped anticipate and monitor matters of practical concern: information management (von Foerster, 1972a), computer architecture (von Foerster, 1971a), and education, in particular, the education of cyberneticians (von Foerster, 1972b, von Foerster et al., 1974).

His concern again and again is to reveal the ethical stance that lies at the heart of all good cybernetic praxis. He notes (von Foerster, 1974) that "life is studied in vivo, not in vitro," that "at any moment we are free to act toward the future we desire" (von Foerster, 1972b) and that "the Laws of Nature are written by Man, the Laws of Biology must write themselves" (von Foerster, 1972c).

As man's understanding of his own nature grows, so does his freedom to experience, to construct, to discover and enter into new worlds. His understanding also reveals his responsibility for his world and for his place within it.

Finally, although his exhortations are made with a definite ethical commitment, von Foerster offers a terse epigram, a cybernetician's prescription for effective action in pursuing goals set, that can be applied with respect to any goal, good or evil: "act always so as to increase the number of choices" (von Foerster, 1973).

Inspired by his example, I offer to Heinz von Foerster the following epigram "the highest goal (eidos) is to act without blame; it has the simplest solution (techne): let the facts speak for themselves."

Epilogue

As noted in the Prologue, von Foerster made the famous distinction between first and second order cybernetics in 1974, two years before his retirement, more or less as an aside. (For more on the circumstances around von Foerster's making these remarks on orders of cybernetics see Glanville (in press) and von Foerster and Poerksen (2002, especially pp. 74-75 & pp. 109-111). It took some years for the significance of von

Foerster's remarks to be appreciated. It is true that his ideas generally were an influence on others but it was a while before the first order and second order distinction became current. As it did become current, as is so often the case with new developments, there soon arose critical voices, claiming for example that nothing new was being said or that the new ideas were scientifically empty and lacked any serious methodological applications. As an example of an overall fairly negative view see Joslyn and Heylighen (1999). For specifically methodological critiques see van der Zouwen (1997). For a very positive view concerning methodology see Ahlemeyer (2000) Ahlemeyer uses the first and second order distinction as a very useful way of setting up a complex research program studying institutional influences on social interaction in which first order quantitative studies are elegantly combined with second order qualitative studies. Third party, external observer classifications of the forms of sexual behavior found within different social groups are combined with first person ascriptions, elicited in interview, of the value and meanings of those behaviors. Ahlemeyer shows that similar behaviors frequently have different meanings and values for the different groups and goes on to discuss the significance of his findings for guiding AIDS prevention strategies.

One of the first to write extensively with second order cybernetics as a theme was Ranulph Glanville whose 1975 Ph.D. thesis develops a comprehensive theory of the observer, where, inspired by von Foerster's "An observer is his own ultimate object," an observer is an 'Object' amongst 'Objects', where to be an 'Object' is to have the property of self-observation (Glanville, 1976). Von Foerster was Glanville's external examiner for his Ph.D. and remained a friend and mentor in the years ahead (see also Glanville, 2002).

As already noted Maturana and Varela's ideas about autopoiesis and biological autonomy developed as part of the collegiate around von Foerster at the BCL. Their ideas have spread quite widely in both the biological and social sciences (see for example Zeleny, 1981; Heylighen, Rosseel & Demeyred, 1989; and Chandler & van de Vijver, 2000). Second order cybernetic ideas of self-reference, self-observation and self-steering have been found particularly attractive by many in the social sciences (see for example Geyer & van der Zouwen, 1978, 1986, 1990). The Geyer and van der Zeeuwen (1978) collection of papers has the fortuitous title *Sociocybernetics*. A very active group within the International Sociological Association, Research Committee 51, has taken this term 'sociocybernetics' as its main title. (The RC51 website url is in the references; see also Geyer, 1995, 1997 and Lee, 2002.)

Many in the RC51 community draw on the social systems theory of Niklas Luhmann. Luhmann himself draws directly on Spencer-Brown, von Foerster and Maturana (see especially Chapter 12 of Luhmann, 1995). The Piagetian educationalist and mathematician, Ernst von Glasersfeld, was at an early stage influenced by cybernetics. His 'radical constructivism' draws very directly on second order cybernetics and the ideas of von Foerster and Maturana (von Glasersfeld, 1991). There is a website dedicated to radical constructivism run by Alex Reigler (see Reigler website reference) which features extensive coverage of von Foerster, Maturana, Pask, von Glasersfeld, Glanville and others. The website was created in 1997 and has gone on to be a major award winning site.

A more recent voice is that of Kjellman (2002), whose 'subject oriented approach to science', developed over a number of years, sets out an epistemology closely parallel to that of second order cybernetics. Kjellman came across von Foerster's writings after he had begun to develop his own thinking and acknowledges they have been a source of inspiration for him to bring his own work to fruition.

A close reader of the early cyberneticians will find the 'hidden hand' influences of, if not direct references to, the work of the great, late 19th century and early 20th century American philosopher C. S. Peirce (see especially McCulloch, 1965 and McCulloch's introduction to von Demarus, 1967). Peirce wrote extensively on many scientific phenomena including adaptation and evolution. He also wrote on logic, mathematics and the philosophy of science. Within his massive oeuvre is his work on logic and communications within which he develops 'semiotics'—a general theory of signs. (Parallel but not fully overlapping work on semiotics and the pragmatics of human communication was going on extensively in Europe at this time, the work of de Saussure being perhaps the most well known.) More recently direct connections between semiotics and second order cybernetics have been made. Søren Brier has been particularly influential here, both as editor of the journal *Cybernetics and Human Knowing*, with its very explicit sub-title "a journal of second order cybernetics, autopoiesis and cybersemiotics," and in his writings on these topics (see Brier, 1995).

For many of us, *Cybernetics and Human Knowing*, first published in 1992, was a breath of fresh air. It openly celebrated cybernetics and the development of second order cybernetics, still considered to be old fashioned or irrelevant by the mainstream, especially mainstream cognitive science, philosophy of mind and, sadly, even the 'new' discipline of 'complexity studies'. Von Foerster, with the American Society for Cybernetics which he had helped found, was a direct influence on the setting up of the journal and adopted it as a journal for the Society. Ranulph Glanville (personal communication) tells me that von Foerster remarked that you could tell the health of a society by its publications and that he was concerned that the journal should be of the highest quality. Glanville believes von Foerster did indeed think well of it and thought it improved in quality as it established itself.

If you wish to get a feel for the conceptual and logical issues that underlie second order cybernetics, as well as reading the masters such as Ashby, von Foerster, McCulloch, Wiener, Beer and Pask, I recommend you become a regular reader of *Cybernetics and Human Knowing*. Enjoy, especially, the series of remarkable meditations by Ranulph Glanville and the equally remarkable logico-mathematical, philosophical musings of Louis Kaufmann.

As a final commentary on the influences of von Foerster and second order cybernetics, it would be remiss if I did not mention developments in psychiatry and psychotherapy. As already noted, Gregory Bateson, as a founding cybernetician, brought the full richness of second order concerns to the early Macy Foundation conferences well before the term was coined. Von Foerster has always acknowledged his debt to Bateson in developing his ideas. Both drew on Korzybsky's 'general semantics' with its dictum 'the map is not the territory' (Korzybsky, 4th ed., 1958). As well as his 1930s work in anthropology, Bateson is rightly celebrated for wide ranging researches on human and animal communication (see Bateson, 1972). Working in family therapy he developed the famous 'double bind' 'hypothesis about communication problems in so-called 'schizophrenic families'. Ongoing developments in psychotherapy have continued to draw on Bateson and now also draw on second order cybernetics, especially the writings of von Foerster and Maturana. As examples see Watzlawick et al. (1980) and Hoffman (1980).

I am sure von Foerster must have been delighted to see the attention being paid to his ideas in his later years. He continued to write and give presentations almost up to his death. (I use the word reluctantly; I'm sure Heinz would have been familiar with Wittgenstein's aphorism: "Death is not an event in life.")

If there is one representative paper I would wish all to read, it is von Foerster's (1992) paper "Ethics and Second Order Cybernetics" (published as the first paper in the first part of Volume 1 of *Cybernetics and Human Knowing*). Writing as an educationalist who has applied cybernetic ideas at all levels of our educational systems and in one way or another has been a teacher of—or as Heinz might have said 'a learner with' or 'a learner from'—humans from age zero upwards to very mature years, I would like to see that text—suitably presented—embedded in all levels of our educational curricula. I am doing what I can to see that this is the case.

References

Ahlemeyer, H. W. (1997). Observing observations empirically: Methodological innovations in sociocybernetics. *Kybernetes*, 26 (6/7), 641-660.

Ashby, W. R. (1956). *An introduction to cybernetics*. New York: Wiley.

Bateson, G. (1972). *Steps to an ecology of mind*. New York: Paladin.

Beer, S. (1978). An open letter to Dr von Foerster. *ASC Forum*.

Boden, M. (1977). *Artificial intelligence and natural man*. Brighton, Sussex: Harvester Press.

Brier, S. (1995). Cyber-semiotics: On autopoiesis, code duality and sign games in bio-semiotics. *Cybernetics and Human Knowing, 3*, 1.

Chandler, J. L. R. and van de Vijver, G. (Eds.) (2000). Closure: Emergent organizations and their dynamics. *Annals of the New York Academy of Sciences, 901*.

Craik, K. J. W. (1943). *The nature of explanation*. London: Cambridge University Press.

Geyer, F. (1995). The challenge of sociocybernetics. *Kybernetes, 24*(4), 6-32.

Geyer, F. (Ed.) (1997). *Sociocybernetics: Complexity, dynamics and emergence in social science*. Special issue of *Kybernetes*, 26(6/7).

Geyer, F., & van der Zouwen, J. (Eds.) (1978). *Sociocybernetics*. Leiden: Martinus Nijhoff.

Geyer, F., & van der Zouwen, J. (Eds.) (1986). *Sociocybernetic paradoxes: Observation, control and evolution of self-steering systems*. London: Sage.

Geyer, F., & van der Zouwen, J. (Eds.) (1990). *Self-referencing in social systems*. Salinas, CA: Intersystems.

Glanville, R. (1976). What is memory that it can remember what it is? In *Recent progress in cybernetics and systems, Volume 7*. Proceedings of the 3rd European Meeting on Cybernetics and System Research. Washington, DC: Hemisphere Press.

Glanville, R. (2002). Second Order Cybernetics. Invited article in *Encyclopaedia of life support systems*. Oxford: EoLSS Publishers. (http://www.eolss.net/)

Hebb, D. O. (1949). *The organization of behavior*. New York: Wiley.

Heylighen, F., Rosseel, E. & Demeyred, F. (1989). Self-steering and cognitive systems. *Studies in Cybernetics, 22*. New York: Gordon and Breach.

Hoffman, L. (1981). *Foundations of family therapy*. New York: Basic Books.

Holland, J.H. (1975). *Adaptation in natural and artificial systems*. Ann Arbor, MI: University of Michigan Press.

Joslyn, C. & Heylighen, F. (1999). Cybernetics. In D. Hemmendinger, A. Ralston, & E. Reilly (Eds.), *The Encyclopedia of computer science* (pp. 470-473). London: Nature Publishing Group.

Kjellman, A. (2002). The subject oriented approach to knowledge and the role of human consciousness. *Int Review of Sociology, 12*(2), 223-248.

Konorski, J. (1962). The role of central factors in differentiation. In R. Gerard and J. Duyff (Eds.), *Information processing in the nervous system: Vol.3*(pp.318-329). Amsterdam: Excerpta Medica Foundation.

Korzybski, A. (1958). *Science and sanity* (4th Edition). Lakeville, CT: International Non-Aristotelian Library.

Lakatos, I. (1970). Falsification and the methodology of scientific research programs. In I. Lakatos & A. Musgrave (Eds.), *Criticism and the growth of knowledge* (pp. 91-196). London: Cambridge University Press.

Lee, R. (Ed.) (2002). Special Issue: Directions in sociocybernetics. *Int Review of Sociology, 12*(2).

Loefgren, L. (1968). An axiomatic explanation of complete self-reproduction. *Bull. Math. Biophysics, 30*(3), 415-425.

Luhmann, N. (1995). *Social systems*. Stanford, CA: Stanford University Press.

Maturana, H. (1970). Neurophysiology of cognition. In P. L. Garvin (Ed.), *Cognition: A multiple view* (pp. 3-24). New York: Spartan Books.

Maturana, H. R.& Varela, F. J. (1980). *Autopoiesis and cognition*. Dordrecht: D. Reidel.

McCulloch, W. S. (1965). *Embodiments of mind*. Cambridge, MA: The MIT Press.

McCulloch, W. S., & Pitts, W. (1943). A logical calculus of ideas immanent in nervous activity. *Bull. Math. Biophys. 5*, 115-133.

Pask G., Scott, B. C. E., & Kallikourdis, D. (1973). A theory of conversations and individuals. *Int. J. Man-Machine Studies, 5*, 443-566.

Pask, G. (1960). The natural history of networks. In M. C. Yovits & S. Cameron (Eds.), *Self-organizing systems* (pp. 232-261). London: Pergamon Press.

Pask, G. (1972). A fresh look at cognition and the individual. *Int. J. Man-Machine Studies, 4*, 11-216.

Pask, G. (1975). *Conversation, cognition and learning*. Amsterdam: Elsevier.

Pask, G. (1978). The importance of being magic. *ASC Forum*.

Pask, G., & Von Foerster, H. (1960). A predictive model for self-organizing systems, Part 1. *Cybernetica, 3*(4), 258-300.

Pask, G., & Von Foerster, H. (1961). A predictive model for self-organizing systems, Part 2. *Cybernetica, 4*,(1), 20-55.

Reigler, A. (n.d.). *Radical constructivism*, Retrieved October, 2003, from http://www.univie.ac.at/constructivism/

Research Committee 51 (On Sociocybernetics) of The International Sociological Association. (n.d.). Retrieved October, 2003,from http://www.unizar.es/sociocybernetics/

Schroedinger, E. (1944). *What is life?* Cambridge: Cambridge University Press.

Schroedinger, E. (1958). *Mind and matter*. Cambridge: Cambridge University Press.

Schroedinger, E. (1967). *What is life & mind and matter*. Cambridge: Cambridge University Press.

Scott, B. (1976). *Cognitive representations and their transformations in the acquisition of keyboard skills*. Unpublished thesis. Brunel University. http://cdol.cranfield.ac.uk/bcescott/index.html.

Scott, B. (1979). Heinz von Foerster: An appreciation. *Int. Cyb. Newsletter, 12*, 209-214.

Scott, B. (1980). The cybernetics of Gordon Pask, Part 1. *Int. Cyb. Newsletter, 17*, 327-336.

Scott, B. (1982). The cybernetics of Gordon Pask, Part 2. *Int. Cyb. Newsletter, 24*, 479-491.

Scott, B. (1996). Second order cybernetics as cognitive methodology. *Systems Research 13*(3), 393-406. (contribution to a Festschrift in honor of Heinz von Foerster).

Scott, B. (in press). Second order cybernetics: An historical introduction. To appear in *Kybernetes*.

Spencer-Brown, G. (1969). *The laws of form*. London: George Allen and Unwin.

Van der Zouwen, J. (1997). The validation of sociocybernetic models. *Kybernetes, 26*(6/7), 848-856.

Von Demarus, E. (1967). The logical structure of mind (with an introduction by W. S. McCulloch). In L. O. Thayer (Ed.), *Communication: Theory and research*. Springfield, IL: Chas. C. Thomas.

Von Foerster, H. (1948). *Das Gedachtnis; Eine Quantemechanische Untersuchung*. Vienna: F. Deuticke.

Von Foerster, H. (1949). Quantum mechanical theory of memory. In H. Von Foerster (Ed.), *Cybernetics: Transactions of the Sixth Conference* (pp. 112-145). New York: Josiah Macy, Jr. Foundation.

Von Foerster, H. (1960). On self-organizing systems and their environments. In M. Yovits & S. Cameron (Eds.), *Self-organizing systems* (pp. 31-50). London: Pergamon Press.

Von Foerster, H. (1965). Memory without record. In D. P. Kimble (Ed.), *The Anatomy of memory* (pp. 388-433). Palo Alto, CA: Science and Behavior Books.

Von Foerster, H. (1969). What is memory that it may have hindsight and foresight as well? In S. Bogoch (Ed.), *The future of the brain sciences* (pp. 19-64). New York: Plenum Press.

Von Foerster, H. (1970). Thoughts and notes on cognition. In P. L. Garvin (Ed.), *Cognition: A multiple view* (pp. 25-48). New York: Spartan Books.

Von Foerster, H. (1971a). Molecular ethology. In C. Ungar (Ed.), *Molecular mechanisms of memory and learning*. New York: Plenum Press.

Von Foerster, H. (1971b). Review of *laws of form* by G. Spencer-Brown. In S. Brand (Ed.), *The Last Whole Earth Catalogue* (p. 12). Harmondsworth: Penguin Books.

Von Foerster, H. (1972a). *Technology: What will it mean to librarians?* (BCL Report 9.1). Urbana, IL: University of Illinois, Biological Laboratory, Dept. of Electrical Engineering.

Von Foerster, H. (1972b). Perception of the future and the future of perception. *Instructional Science, 1*, 31-43.

Von Foerster, H. (1972c). Responsibilities of competence. *J. of Cybernetics, 2*, 1-6.

Von Foerster, H. (1973). On constructing a reality. In W. Preiser (Ed.), *Environmental Design Research II* (pp. 35-46). Stoudsburg: Dowden, Hutchinson and Ross.

Von Foerster, H. (1974). Notes pour un epistemologie des objets vivants. In E. Morin & M. Piatelli-Palmerini (Eds.), *L'unité de l'homme* (pp. 401-417). Paris: Editions du Seuil.

Von Foerster, H. (1976). Objects: tokens for (eigen) behaviors. *ASC Cybernetics Forum, VIII,* (3 & 4), 91-96.

Von Foerster, H. (1992). Ethics and second-order cybernetics. *Cybernetics and Human Knowing, 1*(1), 40-46. (Available at http://www.flec.kvl.dk/sbr/Cyber/cybernetics/vol1/v1-1hvf.htm)

Von Foerster, H. et al. (Eds.) (1974). *Cybernetics of cybernetics.* (BCL Report 73.38). Urbana, IL: University of Illinois, Biological Computer Laboratory, Dept. of Electrical Engineering.

Von Foerster, H., & Poerksen, B. (2002). *Understanding systems.* Dordrecht: Kluwer.

Watzlawick, P., Beavin, J. H., & Jackson, D. D. (1968). *Pragmatics of human communication.* London: Faber and Faber.

Wiener, N. (1948). *Cybernetics.* Cambridge, MA: The MIT Press.

Wilson, K. L. (Ed.) (1976). *The collected works of the Biological Computer Laboratory.* Peoria, IL: Illinois Blueprint Corporation.

Yovits, M. C.,& Cameron, S. (Eds.) (1960). *Self-organizing systems.* London: Pergamon Press.

Zeleny, M. (Ed.) (1981). *Autopoiesis: A theory of living organization.* New York: North Holland.

Heinz von Foerster, 1962, at the International Design Conference, Aspen, Colorado (photographer unknown)

Cybernetics And Human Knowing. Vol. 10, nos. 3-4, pp. 150-169

Discovering social knowledge

Gerard de Zeeuw[1]

"In its most concise form the proposal was presented as a search for mechanisms within living organisms that enable them to turn their environment into a trivial machine, rather than a search for mechanisms in the environment that turn the organisms into trivial machines." (Von Foerster, 1970, p. 247[2])

In some domains acquiring knowledge has proved successful in ways that have not been equalled elsewhere—notwithstanding long-term efforts. As the lack of success in the latter must be due to the combination of approach and content, this suggests searching for new approaches, and interpreting the 'not' as a possibly 'never'. The alternative is to see the 'not' as a 'not yet'. The argument Von Foerster (1970) brings to this dilemma is that in the social domain the 'not' is due to an extra, mainly action-bound, source of variation. Constraining this source will allow for a (reasonable) 'not yet'. To remind of Heinz's surprising and sophisticated argument it is re-used.

Keywords: Knowledge, finite state machines, computing, probability matching, learning, self-organising collectives, second order cybernetics

1. Introduction

The late 50s and early 60s saw an astonishing upsurge in the frequency and extent of the use of mathematical ideas in the social sciences. What was especially enlightening was their use as part of the process of understanding—rather than only as part of testing (Estes, 1959; Suppes & Atkinson, 1960). This attracted many people from the formal disciplines, including me[3].

While engaged in developing (and of course testing) probabilistic models of learning, quite disturbingly one of my subjects started to cry, and wanted to stop—bored to the depths of her soul, I surmised, in view of the 2 million trials of my experiment. Once more I tried to explain—and eventually she agreed to finish. After analysis only her data proved to fit my model.

Similar experiences were not uncommon. When one colleague replaced the reward for hits (switching on a light) by an exploding airplane, behaviour changed from probability matching (switching responses to match the probability of the lights) to statistical optimising (staying with the most frequent light). The change was sudden and was easily repeated.

---

1. University of Lincoln, Faculty of Business and Management, Bridge House, Brayford Pool, LN6 7TS, United Kingdom. E-mail: zeeuw@science.uva.nl.
2. Page numbers refer to Heinz von Foerster's paper (1970). Referencing them is meant to support further study; it is not needed for the argument in the paper.
3. I was lucky to spend a year in the Mecca of the new developments, the Institute of Studies in the Social Sciences (ISSS) at Stanford University.

I was fascinated, as these experiences appeared to go against the basics of mathematisation. A paper by Heinz von Foerster (1970) provided clues to a better understanding. To honour Heinz's many contributions, I like to revisit his argument—and demonstrate why it still is important for present day knowledge acquisition, especially in the social sciences.

My contribution is not meant to summarise what Heinz was saying in his paper. I follow his exploration of some results of mathematical modelling to show how Heinz's early and, of course, brilliant work provided an already sufficient solution to a major problem of inquiry—the nature of which many still attempt to identify.

First I outline some key elements in Heinz's argument, as a context. Next I identify some characteristics of knowledge and of testing knowledge (section 3). I then interpret Von Foerster's argument concerning learning (section 4). In section 5 I formulate a solution, re-constructing his arguments. Finally I present some reflections, examples and conclusions (sections 6, 7 and 8).

2. Context

After the euphoria of what appeared to be (mathematical) successes in the social sciences, soon the thorns among the roses were felt. Sufficient quality for use in policy and action remained lacking—which stimulated alternative approaches (like those of participation and systems), but also much ritual blaming, e.g. of reductionism (Von Bertalanffy, 1950, 1968; Churchman, 1971; Mansfield, 1993).

In contrast, Heinz argues that neither the mathematics nor the approach to inquiry should have been blamed, but rather a gap in understanding *action*. Actions (still) tend to be conceptualised as *properties*, with persons as the referent—even in the field of artificial intelligence, where actions often are conceived as solutions to problems (Boden, 1979; Elithorn & Jones, 1973).

To inquire about actions another kind of referent is needed, in particular to take account of the fact that we always act in a changing environment (p. 215). In other words, we do not see what others do, only what they allow us to see – by manipulating their own environment. In daily life we tend to see the effect of the manipulation, not the manipulation itself.

There are many indirect phenomena similar to this manipulation of (our) manipulation, or self-manipulation. More generally, in the words of Heinz, we need to cope with "self-reference, self-description and self-explanation, i.e. closed local systems that include the referee in the reference, the descriptor in the description, and the axioms in the explanation" (p. 216).

There were others who shared this insight and contributed appropriate tools (e.g. Pask, 1991). Heinz himself shows the existence of such (mathematical) tools by using them to support his argument[4], and thereby that the difficulty is not due to the

---

4. The 1970 paper provides a short introduction to finite state, finite function and probabilistic machines. In the present paper this type of mathematics is used on an abstract level only, as part of the reasoning.

mathematisation. Heinz takes the act of learning as an example to show its (wrong) conceptualisation.

This paper focuses on the same difficulty, that of finding ways to understand and know at least some of the richness of action. Rather than concentrating on that notion, we will start by exploring the notion of knowledge, a bit beyond Heinz—to deduce how the notion of properties developed. Next we will look more closely at his solution to know action.

3. Knowledge

Knowledge is one of the most extensively debated notions in the literature—of interest to philosophers (Popper, 1959) as well as practitioners (Schön, 1983). It is attractive, as it helps to act, whatever one's goal. Unfortunately, at least to some, it also makes heavy demands in terms of criteria like exhaustiveness, precision and cost (see below).

Reactions to these demands differ widely. Some aim to reduce them, to allow for contributions to knowledge even in situations where this appears impossible—often referred to as the post-modern view. Others go to great lengths to replace them, for example by procedures that emphasise dialogue, conversation, discussion and participation (Reason, 1981).

My approach is different. To deal with new difficulties, I aim to adapt earlier approaches while maintaining their main characteristics. A property that seems common to all attempts at defining knowledge is that it consists of links between certain experiences (I call them primary or first) and others (I call them secondary or second experiences).

Such links guide what we do in daily life. For example, in cooking we may link the taste of one kind of meat and certain herbs to the taste of an English leg of lamb—the former primary, the latter secondary. Not everyone will share the same link or even the link itself. Links in daily life also change easily—due to new experiences, or simply because others tell us so.

Still, one may expect some links to be more stable than others. The longer they survive, the more we tend to accept them as knowledge. Their survival means that they exist *before* their future; they are *pre-constructions* (Rosen, 1993). Acquiring knowledge thus implies spending constructive efforts *in the present* to minimise spending them *in the future*.[5]

To identify the most stable links we base ourselves on all experiences, including those we accept as stemming from others. Hence, in knowledge acquisition the building blocks of pre-constructions are *reports* of experiences. Hence, when we said that pre-constructions 'exist', we only referred to the result of having compared and combined reports.

---

5. Alternatively, we may say that knowledge acquisition requires searching for efforts that can be *transferred* in time. Not all efforts are transferable and result in knowledge – leaving efforts like fitting to local situations (e.g. parameter estimation), or dancing (after having pre-constructed acquaintance by the ritual of inviting to dance).

Experiences that can be linked as primary or secondary must be finite in the sense that any individual may experience them in the here and now—as otherwise they cannot be reported on. However, their links play a different role. Secondary experiences should help to recognise primary experiences over possibly infinite or indefinite futures.

If the transfer of efforts is exhaustive, recognition of a secondary experience should allow for recognition of *any* of its primary experiences. This makes it difficult to test for exhaustiveness, as the number of such experiences may be infinite. This has inspired a search for *methods* that allow one to test in the here and now—instead of over infinite numbers of experiences.

4. Testing

One approach might be to characterise primary experiences as a *set*, to help identify whether new experiences belong to it. Unfortunately, this is not feasible as sets are defined by enumeration of all their elements, which by the above definition are not known. A more useful concept is that of a class.[6] It defines a propositional function as a constraint on recognition.

As an example we may consider moves in chess as primary experiences, and its rules as secondary. Both tend to be considered as linked uniquely and stably, and hence the link as helping to recognise what belongs to chess or not. Some ambiguities remain. There are 'chess' puzzles that refer to configurations that cannot be part of any actual game.[7]

Other sets of primary experiences related to chess may be considered, e.g., those of players re-acting to moves of their opponents. These may be linked to secondary experiences such as openings and end-game theories. Again the sequence of primary experiences may be infinite and the link to the theories untested in that it is not known to what extent it is exhaustive.

Unfortunately, even the notion of a propositional function is limited. It does help to name what is required, but otherwise seems to replace what is very difficult (enumerating a possibly infinite number of experiences) by what is rather difficult. To identify a propositional function only a limited number of past primary experiences can be used.

A further alternative to define links follows from realising that methods to recognise new (primary) experiences are not rare. They include reading a poem or telling a story. Each elicits some primary experiences and suggests that as well as how

---

6. The distinction between set and class is used to emphasise that some kind of infinite has to creep in if one is to test for or maximise exhaustiveness. The two notions are equivalent only in case finite sequences are considered. This equivalence is at the basis of the popular claim that psychological and scientific induction are the same, as are learning and knowledge – a view that does not consider exhausting the infinite or indefinite (as Popper, 1959, has argued, mostly vehemently).

7. Note that there may be more than one stable (and near-exhaustive) link in relation to what in daily life appears to be 'richer' than either (leading to the popular rebuke that science does not 'capture life' (Erlandson, e.a., 1993)). The traditional view is to consider knowledge 'rich' only where it succeeds in achieving (near) exhaustiveness.

they belong together. To lead to knowledge something must be added, however. The reverse should hold as well.

Both relations together define the notion of exhaustion, but usually are referred to as *closure*.[8] *Testing for closure implies checking that no* primary experiences are recognised in ways *other* than by that function. If they are, the function must be redefined. In Popper's formulation (1959) knowledge acquisition requires maximising reasons to redefine, or *striving* to falsify.[9]

Testing for exhaustiveness has been core to an endeavour—now called (modern) science—that was initiated in the 17th century. Its results are highly attractive— particularly as regards the claim that knowledge be stable against any disturbing experiences, including those of being used at some future time—by any user for any purpose (Hanfling, 1997; de Zeeuw, 1995).

This claim obviously did not please the organisations that dominated 17th century life. It separated their power to act (or 'change', p. 214) from that to observe ('discriminate'). Science turned the latter into a resource that was accessible to all, or democratically, and hence allowed to recognise many of the organisation's actions as ungrounded impositions.

This left an obvious gap—how to ground actions without imposing. At least until the mid-20th century, any linking of primary to secondary experiences of action remained opportunistic as in post hoc rationalisations. Conversely, it always seems possible to recognise such primary experiences in ways outside of some propositional function. Closure here remains elusive.

In terms of the above this situation may be diagnosed as a problem of underlying inexhaustibility. Actions continue to require effort, whatever efforts one transfers, whatever one pre-constructs. This implies having to test in the present many or infinite infinities, or indefinites—so clearly more is needed than *someone* striving to falsify (p. 214).

To satisfy this need the obvious route is to add constraints, preferably by introducing other actions—so the constraints are in the interactions. We may test our experiences of an action by the act of boxing them in, so they continue to be boxed in by the efforts that are part of the interaction. In other words, we like this interaction to be self-maintaining.

This approach implies studying action by distinguishing experiences of three kinds of action. The first are part of an interaction: they constrain each other, thereby minimising non-transferable effort. The second are constituted by the interaction: they define what the (minimised) effort is meant to achieve. The third is made up of actions not dealt with by the approach.

In the next section we follow Heinz when showing how to link primary and secondary experiences concerning some action (and test and provide democratic

---

8. Note that the notion of closure implies that 'reality' is taken into account only as a source (if any) of primary experiences, not as a criterion for testing.
9. This approach reduces testing for infinity by introducing someone who is able to go beyond a link in the present; without a someone 'striving' is not defined.

access to the results). If improperly studied, users (or learners) are imposed upon. If properly studied, users become able to choose a second action that pre-constructs the environment so they know how to act.

5. Action

Von Foerster considers the experiments that were popular in the 1960s. Primary experiences tended to consist of (experimenters', and not subjects') reports on changes in the behaviour of subjects when provided with feedback on the correct prediction of one out of two or more events (p. 230)—either or both usually with a probability less than 1.

Researchers like Estes (1959), Bower and Hilgard (1981) and others tended to interpret these experiences in terms of a secondary experience called learning. Interestingly, this proved rather limiting. It forced them to restrict their experiments to priming subjects with strong ('don't think', etc.) and extensive instructions,[10] to make it possible to detect closure at all.

To explore the extent of these limitations Von Foerster used (elements from) the theory of (probabilistic) finite state machines (p. 217). The way he did this can be understood as a mapping of secondary experiences onto the behavioural tables or programs of a Turing machines, and of primary experiences onto its inputs (Hodges, 1997).

In this way, firstly, the notion of knowledge is translated into the outputs or productions of a (non-trivial) machine—and learning is seen as converging to and remaining in one of its states. Secondly, knowledge is exposed as characterised by links that stay within the constraints of a machine. Its primary experiences should be *computable* on a universal Turing machine.[11]

Next Von Foerster notes that, equivalently, one may link the primary experiences in the learning experiments to a series of machines each of which has only one state (trivial machines) and is selected by the previous one, while the last one is the 'learnt machine'. It identifies the subjects' final output or *response* to the experimenters' input or *stimulus* (p. 221).

What this means is that the experiments help to identify the *property* of having learnt, not the act of learning. Alternatively, one may point out that this conclusion is based only on the experimenter's reported experience (p. 216, p. 234). What they did, therefore, is *actively restrict* subjects to behave like the learnt machine. Both comments reveal a basic ambiguity.

This ambiguity resides at the point where pre-construction fails, causing knowledge 'never' to be achieved. The reason is that changes leading to the learnt behaviour can be observed only in the proper environment—which the experimenter

---

10. What is criticised is not the notion of instruction (constraints), but the dilemma subjects are forced into: one must think to continue not thinking (Bateson, 1979).

11. This implies testing whether the link is machine-like in the sense that individuals can execute the test using the rules of a machine.

must recreate *every time* this behaviour is to be repeated, and hence is not pre-constructible.

This ambiguity is fundamental. Firstly, it was concluded that knowledge can be characterised by mapping it onto a Turing machine.[12] Such knowledge is mechanistic, like knowledge of properties. Secondly, actions (like learning) are too variable to be computable. They are non-mechanistic. Treating them otherwise makes for poor knowledge (see footnote 7).

6. Reflections

What is non-computable may still be explored, however. It is possible to constrain infinities of primary experiences *interactively*, e.g., by creating an assembly (p. 226) consisting of the actions of two subjects. As soon as they act coherently, closure becomes possible—although over the assembly rather than over individuals, e.g., the property of having learnt.

Assemblies or collectives do appear to provide the referent needed: while behaviour on the level of their members is not computable, on the level of the collectives it is. Collectives thus resolve the ambiguity by containing it.[13] In other words, within a collective it is not resolved—so one *cannot* decide who is the actor, and who the environment; outside it is.

The container now is pre-constructible, or the way the actions are allowed to interact—and take their own course within it. Knowledge thus refers to two levels simultaneously. Firstly, there is knowledge of the properties of the collective *after* construction (e.g., the rules of chess). Secondly, there is knowledge (for members) to *initiate* and or re-initiate the collective.

The first type of knowledge is computable, as defined. The second type of knowledge is captured by the notion of *competence*—defined by distributed qualifications (secondary) and variable primary experiences (i.e., skills). Competencies within a collective may differ, the qualifications being established by the experience of what others do (p. 225).

It needs to be emphasised that Von Foerster's proposal is not, from now on, to study only collectives and their dynamic properties. It is to acquire the knowledge to increase the power of action and its democratic accessibility. It identifies how one may do so by containing action in self-organising collectives—which thus serve as experimental tools (p. 239).

A somewhat antique example would be the change in the study of establishing land boundaries in the Nile delta to that of containing these activities by the use of Euclid's results.[14] They facilitate competent constructions in the plane, with reduced

---

12. Turing hypothesised that all intelligent behaviour can be modelled in this way.

13. The ambiguity will not re-appear when the same person is assumed to realise both forms of (in the examples, trivial) convergence (p. 229).

14. The unit of analysis is any person performing an activity like drawing a line (see also "someone" striving to falsify), thereby creating a collective containing local knowledge (Turnbull, 2000; de Zeeuw, 2001).

effort compared to the original activities. Papert's LOGO [15] appears to decrease this effort even more (1980).

The proposal extends the notion of knowledge (by adding knowledge in the form of competence enhancing collectives). This extension helped to argue that mathematical modelling remains useful. One may even say that it identifies a role for mathematics in inquiry beyond that of describing properties. It helps to achieve closure on the containment of action.

Interestingly, these considerations return in discussions on the nature of thought. According to some, no machine is able to think (intelligently)—but also no brain is able to do so (Penrose, 1989). Thinking will be experienced only on the level of collectives where behaviour may be computable and provable (p. 216)—not on individual levels.

A quite stimulating advantage of the proposed change has been, of course, that it clarifies my own disturbing experiences (see section 1). For example, subjects may have identified the exploding airplanes as a signal or form of communication about the rules of the experiment, or in other words, as an indication of what container might be chosen.

7. Other examples

Von Foerster's paper brought me the insights I needed to understand my unease at the time. Re-reading his paper made me aware how important these insights still are, and how much they contribute to knowing action—which still is with us. Their importance may be illustrated by familiar examples—like the notion of statistical action.

This type of action is based on replacing series of observations on one individual by single observations on a series of individuals. It is meant to avoid the ambiguity inherent to searching for computable experiences. Not surprisingly, it requires creating a collective (the population, secondary experiences) to (effectively) compute new samples.

In many studies in social science such collectives are not designed to self-organise. The price to be paid for this is that whenever one wants to use the results, the collective must be recreated. Without this the resulting knowledge remains inexhaustible and hence unstable. Its use will be ambiguous, therefore, and may lead to unexpected side effects.

Other examples include cases where special forms of communication have to be devised to help collectives to self-organise. One may think of communication within the constraints of the *Prisoners' Dilemma Game*. By iterating the game players become able to communicate intended altruism and thereby increase individual gains (Axelrod, 1984; Howard, 1971).

---

15. Papert is able to reduce Euclid's axioms to two, using the position of individuals on a plane surface as 'containing' constraint.

What characterises these examples is that they do not refer to descriptions of experiences by formal systems, but rather that they are used to structure and communicate such experiences inside collectives (Deutsch, 1998). Formal systems should be conceived as empirically developed, therefore, rather than as only mathematically justified (Wigner, 1960; Barabasi, 2002).

If this is indeed the case, then we would expect to be able to find many systems in daily life that are on the road to formalisation. Collective sports appear to provide examples. There is knowledge on the level of the sport as well as on the level of the players. Sports appear to be self-organising only partly yet: they still need additional 'policing' (refereeing, umpiring).[16]

8. Conclusion

In this contribution I have attempted to share some of my excitement and admiration when reading Heinz von Foerster's paper on Molecular Ethology (1970), but also when re-reading the paper. It still helps to ease my wonder at some of the results of doing research, even at the stupidities perpetrated in the name of adapting formal methods to social problems.[17]

Let me sketch and summarise three of the core elements of the paper. The first concerns the fact that mathematical modelling is still widely applied but does not seem to contribute much beyond parameter estimates, whatever the level or power of the tools used (e.g., Lie-algebras; Hoffman, 1966). This might appear sufficient cause for rejection.

The second core element is that there is space for doubt concerning this possibility. Heinz identifies a major source. In cases where knowledge can be mechanistic, mathematical modelling is effective. Difficulties arise only where this is not the case. A wide area was identified: the study of action. We do not know yet how to know action—except by telling stories.[18]

The third element is that we don't necessarily need to devise 'entirely' new approaches to get to know action—nor to introduce 'new paradigms' as the popular term goes. Heinz points to relatively simple adaptations of existing approaches and tools, to wit the notion of a collective container to bound and constrain the variety of experiences action generates.

One might object that the notion of such containers is now widely spread, as demonstrated by approaches like action research, participatory research, discourse analysis and conversation analysis (Pask, 1976; Pen, 1989). What continues to amaze

---

16. Collectives that do not need 'policing' apparently maintain and are maintained by values such as honesty and loyalty; without them they will fragment.
17. One might expect a list of examples in support of the claim in the text. There seem to be too many. Let me just indicate, therefore, what I am thinking of: the flood of 'studies' funded by the government, which do not fear to go from 'what is' to 'what must be', from properties to actions, without any further ado.
18. Endeavours like operational research and decision-making do make some inroads on the problem. There still is doubt as to the story content of their results, however.

is the fuzziness of these notions compared to Heinz' proposal to use collectives as self-organising referents.

According to the latter approach, there are criteria one should satisfy when developing knowledge (by way of collectives). Members have to *strive* for pre-construction, and 'police' members' activities so collectives do not fragment, and improve their accessibility as a resource to actors who are not members as well as to members while acting as non-members.

What I wanted to celebrate are all of the above points, partly for the sake of Heinz, but mainly for the sake of those who wish to help realise progress in the social sciences, in particular as regards action. What has to remain implicit is my contention that these contributions eventually may overshadow others, like those of second order cybernetics.

References

Axelrod, R. (1984). *The evolution of cooperation*. New York: Basic Books.
Barabasi, R.-L. (2002). *Linked*. Oxford: Perseus Books.
Bateson, G. (1979). *Mind and nature*. New York: Dutton.
Bertalanffy, L. von (1950). The theory of open systems in physics and biology. *Science 111*, 139-164.
Bertalanffy, L. von (1968). *General system theory*. New York: Braziller.
Boden, M. (1979). *Artificial intelligence and natural man*. New York: Basic Books.
Bower, G. H. and Hilgard, E. R. (1981). *Theories of learning*. Englewood Cliffs: Prentice-Hall.
Churchman, C. W. (1971). *The design of inquiring systems*. New York: Basic Books.
Deutsch, D. (1998). *The fabric of reality*. London: Penguin Books.
Elithorn, A., & Jones, D. (Eds.) (1973). *Artificial and human thinking*. Elsevier, Amsterdam: 1973
Erlandson, D. A., Harris, E. L., Skipper, B. L., & Allen, S. D. (1993). *Doing naturalistic inquiry. A guide to methods*. London: Sage.
Estes, W. K. (1959). The statistical approach to learning theory. In S. Koch (Ed.), *Psychology: a study of a science* (pp. 380-491). New York: MacGraw Hill.
Foerster, H. Von (1970). Molecular ethology. An immodest proposal for semantic clarification. In G. Ungas (Ed.), *Molecular mechanisms in memory and learning* (pp. 231-248). New York: Menum Press.
Hanfling, O. (1997). *Ayer*. London: Phoenix.
Hodges, A. (1997). *Turing*. London: Phoenix.
Hoffman, W. (1966). The Lie algebra of visual perception. *Journal of Mathematical Psychology, 3*, 65-98.
Howard, N. (1971). *Paradoxes of rationality: theory of metagames and political behavior*. Cambridge, MA: The MIT Press.
Mansfield, H. C. (1993). *Taming of the prince. The ambivalence of modern executive power*. Baltimore, MD: Johns Hopkins University Press. (Originally published in 1989)
Papert, S. (1980). *Mindstorms: Children, computers and powerful ideas*. Brighton: Harvester.
Pask, G. (1991). The respectability of predictability and repeatability in the social and organisational sciences. *Proceedings of ASC conference*. Norfolk, VA: Old Dominion University.
Pask, G (1976). *Conversation theory: Applications in education and epistemology*. Amsterdam: Elsevier.
Pen, J. (1989). Wetenschap als conversatie. *Hollands Maandblad 10*, 21-27.
Penrose, R. (1989). *The emperor's new mind*. Oxford: Oxford University Press.
Popper, K. R. (1959). *The logic of scientific discovery*. London: Unwin Hyman.
Reason, P. and Rowan, P. (1981). *Human inquiry*. Chichester: Wiley.
Rosen, R. (1993). Some random thoughts about chaos and some chaotic thoughts about randomness. *J. Biol. Syst. 1*(1), 19-27.
Turnbull, D. (2000). *Masons, tricksters and cartographers*. Amsterdam: Harwood Academic Publishers.
Schön, D. A. (1983). *The reflective practitioner*. New York: Basic Books.
Suppes, P. and Atkinson, R. C. (1960). *Markov learning models for multiperson interaction*. Stanford, CA: Stanford University Press.
Wigner, E. (1960). The unreasonable effectiveness of mathematics in the natural sciences. *Communications in Pure & Applied Mathematics, 13*(1).
Zeeuw, G. de (1995). Values, science and the quest for demarcation. *Systems Research, 12*(1), 15-25.
Zeeuw, G. de, (2001). Constructivism: A 'next' area of scientific development? *Foundations of Science 6*, 77-98.

EPISTÊMÊ ™

A Journal of
Social Epistemology

EPISTEME is a new quarterly refereed journal that supplements epistemology's traditional agenda giving due attention to the social dimension of justification and knowledge. Questions about the nature of epistemic value and the methods for its attainment cannot be satisfactorily considered without reflection on the social contexts of knowing. Social epistemology substantially intersects with a variety of academic disciplines and brings classic philosophical concerns into contact with socio-political issues.

Range of Material

§ cognition
§ dissemination
§ collective belief
§ trust and testimony
§ feminist epistemology
§ sociology of knowledge

Aims & Scope

· The Journal seeks to lower the temperature of the so-called "science wars" by bringing together participants from both sides of the constructivist/anti-constructivist divide.
· Stylistically, the Journal avoids the turgidity that has characterised this field by insisting on more transparent argumentation.
· The Journal is open-textured about the various controversies and does not seek to endorse a particular perspective.
· The aim is to advance the methodological debate by taking contributions that use particular perspectives to address issues in epistemology - issues integral to the philosophy of science, the philosophy of social science and metaphysics.

Editorial details: www.episteme.eu.com
Subscription details: www.eup.ed.ac.uk

Edinburgh University Press

Contributors to Volume 1

Issue I – June 2004

Alvin Goldman (Rutgers)
Anthony Quinton (Oxford)
Susan Haack (Miami)
James Robert Brown (Toronto)
Dan Sperber & Gloria Origgi (CNRS, Paris)
John Dupre (Southampton)

Issue II – October 2004

Helen Longino (Minnesota)
Harvey Siegal (Miami)
Raimo Tuomela (Helsinki)
Uskali Maki (Erasmus)
Margaret Gilbert (Connecticut)
André Kukla (Toronto)

Issue III – February 2005

Hilary Kornblith (Massachusetts)
Anthony Coady (Melbourne)
Stephen Turner (South Florida)
Christopher Norris (Cardiff)
Nicholas Capaldi (Loyola)
Paul Gross (Virginia)

Cybernetics And Human Knowing. Vol. 10, nos. 3-4, pp. 161-163

Heinz von Foerster and the Mansfield Amendment

Stuart Umpleby[1]

Heinz von Foerster was the founder and director of the Biological Computer Laboratory (BCL) at the University of Illinois in Urbana-Champaign. BCL existed from 1957 to 1976. In 1976 Heinz retired and moved to California. One revealing story about Heinz and the Biological Computer Laboratory concerns the Mansfield Amendment, which led to the closing of BCL. I was a graduate student at the University of Illinois from the late 1960s until 1975.

Cybernetics, as a field, originated in the late 1940s and early 1950s during a series of ten conferences sponsored by the Josiah Macy, Jr. Foundation. The conferences were held in New York City and were chaired by Warren McCulloch. The conferences were attended by people from philosophy, mathematics, engineering, neurophysiology, and social science (Heims, 1991).

In 1956 at a conference at Dartmouth University a split occurred. The engineers felt they had made significant progress in programming computers to emulate some aspects of human intelligence. They preferred to proceed on the basis of somewhat ad hoc assumptions about the nature of intelligence, human or machine. The neurophysiologists and philosophers preferred to continue their research on neurophysiology. They felt they had much to learn about the functioning of the human nervous system. From this time forward the fields of artificial intelligence and cybernetics developed largely independently in terms of communication among researchers. However, various agencies in the Department of Defense, for example the Office of Naval Research and the Air Force Office of Scientific Research, continued to support both groups. In the 1960s BCL was the leading center for cybernetics research in the U.S. Most of the money came from the Air Force.

In the late 1960s there were protests on college campuses against the war in Viet Nam and against military research being done on campus. The Department of Defense (DOD) funded quite a lot of research on campuses, but most of it was basic research not related to military activities. In an effort to calm the anti-war protests on college campuses Senate Majority Leader Mike Mansfield, a liberal Democrat from Montana, proposed the Mansfield Amendment. This amendment to the Defense Procurement Authorization Act of 1970 required that DOD only support basic research "with a direct and apparent relationship to a specific military function or operation." (Hauben, 1999) Apparently the intent was to diminish the DOD presence on college campuses.

---

1. Department of Management Science, Research Program in Social and Organizational Learning, The George Washington University. Email: umpleby@gwu.edu

During World War II, Heinz had conducted research in Germany, but he had conducted only theoretical research that had no military applications. Following the passage of the Mansfield Amendment each researcher who had been receiving DOD funds was required to explain the relationship of the research to a military mission. Heinz replied to this question that the research at BCL was not related to a military mission. Hence, the people in DOD could provide no further funds to support the research in cybernetics that BCL had been doing.

When faced with the same question the people doing research on artificial intelligence and robotics became creative. They imagined a variety of futuristic electronic and robotic devices on battlefields. These science fiction-like descriptions proved to be quite popular in Washington, DC. The funding agencies within DOD used them to request more research funds from Congress. The members of Congress were favorably inclined. They reasoned that the more automated the battlefield was, the fewer soldiers / voters would be killed or wounded.

In 1971 Congress created a new program, Research Applied to National Needs (RANN), within the National Science Foundation (2003). At BCL people hoped that this program would continue some of the non-military research that DOD had been supporting. There were two problems with RANN. First, it focused on applied research rather than basic research. The interdisciplinary, basic research that DOD had been funding had no obvious place to go. Second, the people in RANN were a different group of people from the people who had been funding cybernetics research within DOD. The new people were not familiar with the previous work that had been done in cybernetics and so lacked the background necessary to evaluate research proposals in this field.

With research from DOD at an end, Heinz applied to RANN for support of the BCL research on cognition and "experimental epistemology." However, the reaction of the people in RANN was that the people at BCL did not understand the philosophy of science. They held the conventional view that science involved removing the observer from scientific observations, not paying attention to the observer. Hence, the BCL proposal to RANN was rejected. BCL then sought funds from private foundations with some success but not sufficient success to continue the work of the Laboratory. Rather than return to teaching undergraduate engineering courses, Heinz chose early retirement. Ross Ashby and Gotthard Gunter had returned to Europe a few years before. When Heinz left the University of Illinois, BCL and its basic research in cybernetics came to an end. Although the Mansfield Amendment was later repealed (Hauben, 2003), it had had the unintended consequences of curtailing basic research in cybernetics in the U.S. and increasing funding for artificial intelligence and robotics, particularly if the research had a plausible link to a military mission.

REFERENCES

Biological Computer Laboratory. (n.d.) Retrieved 10/14/2003 from http://www.ece.uiuc.edu/pubs/centhist/six/bcl.htm
Biological Computer Laboratory Publications. (n.d.) Retrieved 10/14/2003 from http://web.library.uiuc.edu/ahx/asc/bcl.html

Hauben, R. (1999). Creating the Needed Interface. *Telepolis: Magazin der Netzkultur.* Retrieved 10/14/2003 from http://www.heise.de/tp/english/inhalt/co/5106/6.html

Hauben, R. (2003) Finding the Founding Fathers of the Internet. *Multitudes, 11,* Retrieved 10/14/2003 from http:// multitudes.samizdat.net/article.php3?id_article=292

Heims, S. J. 1991. *The Cybernetics Group.* Cambridge, MA: The MIT Press.

National Science Foundation. (n.d.) *Manufacturing: The Forms of Things Unknown.* Retrieved 10/14/2003 from http:// www.nsf.gov/od/lpa/news/publicat/nsf0050/manufacturing/history.htm

View from Rattlesnake Hill.
Frank Galuszka. Oil

Cybernetics And Human Knowing. Vol. 10, no. 2, pp. 164-168

ASC
American Society for Cybernetics
a society for the art and
science of human understanding

Reflections on the Phrase
"Standing on the Shoulders of Giants"

Pille Bunnell

Often we like to attribute credit for something we have accomplished by saying that we could not have done it except for the far greater work done by some predecessor. As Isaac Newton put it "If I have seen further, it is by standing on ye shoulders of Giants."[1] This phrase has now become common usage, and we use it to pay our deepest respect to someone whose work has substantially contributed to what we ourselves do. Many people in the American Society for Cybernetics have my deepest respect and have contributed greatly to my thinking. Not the least of these is Heinz von Foerster who I had the opportunity to visit several times over the last seven years. However I would not speak of myself as standing on his shoulders; it does not seem like a comfortable thing to do, and furthermore, like many memorable phrases, it evokes various listenings; various thoughts and emotions which do not pertain to the way I related to this wonderful man. Sometimes the claim "I stand on the shoulders of" is heard as trivial, as a stock phrase used in a formal dance to satisfy a perceived requirement for deference. Sometimes it is heard as trite, in the sense of superficiality. Of course it is sometimes both uttered and heard as having both conviction and depth, yet even then a number of interesting ambiguities persist, and it is those that I wish to reflect on now.

What makes a person a giant? What does it mean to "stand on the shoulders"– how is that different from any other historical grounding? Do the giants stand on other giant shoulders, and if so is it "giants all the way down"? Or do we imagine that there are people of average stature along a progression of ideas, with an occasional giant interspersed? Is there in fact a progression? I think these are questions concerning the lineaging of ideas. Another question that intrigues me, is what is it about a person that leads an observer to attribute the epithet of "giant," either as a compliment or as an assessment? It is through addressing these questions that I am able to speak with

---

1. in a letter to Hooke, 1676

integrity and emotional clarity the compliment and gratitude that I myself feel for the work of Heinz.

Metaphors are conserved when they are apt. The metaphor of "standing on the shoulders of giants" is apt in the sense that it speaks to vision—we do see further from a height. There are indeed people among us who have a keener or more extensive vision than others. Metaphors are also never precise, they do not specify exactly what aspect of a configuration in one domain we should map into our thinking about another domain. I think the metaphor of "giant" is misleading when used in connection with understanding because it presumes a flatland, a landscape of ideas, that however mountainous, is still a singular surface. Further, it supports an assumption of directionality and discovery in this landscape, a notion of progress towards always better understanding. We are presumed to be on a journey of discovering the world—we continually see further, perceive more detail, know more and understand more deeply. Because the metaphor evokes all this, I think it is misleading as to what comprises a "giant."

I think we appropriately attribute the honorific "giant" to those people who generate the conditions for whole new worlds[2] to arise as lineages of explanations grounded in the manner of looking and in the premises that they contribute.

When one accepts a shift in some premise, some belief, or some manner of observing, there are extensive ramifications. Indeed the repercussions of a change in a fundamental premise or manner of looking or thinking reverberate through all that one experiences: everything that one has seen, or thought, and everything that one sees or thinks now is subtly, and in some cases radically, different. Consequently one responds differently; one does different things, and one discriminates different configurations of one's medium as "encounters." And since one acts differently, the circumstances develop differently, and the world arises as a different place for that individual, and through how they are, around that individual. If there is a whole group or a community sensing, understanding, and acting differently, then the world for each of them is again profoundly different as the social medium is itself changed according to the shift in premise, belief, and action.Given this, I think the extended vision (which makes the metaphor of height appealing) does not result from height and distance, but rather results from a shift in a manner of looking that ultimately results in new worlds to live in.

The opening of a new world does not diminish the intellectual achievement of developing, articulating, and pursuing the ramification of ideas in such a new world. It is in the latter tasks that the generation of the world is instantiated; much like saying that a structure is necessary for the organization to manifest. Manifestation is no lesser a task, no lesser an intellect is required for it, and it too is to be appreciated. If the world is not manifest, it is not there to be lived, and manifestation (in any domain) is something we humans relish in bringing forth, it is a creative act. Yet, the delightful,

---

2.   I will use the word "world" where I could have used "explanatory domain" or "culture" or "conversational net-
      work" but I wish to stress that these are lineages of coherent networks of various manners of sensing, living and
      explaining one's sensing and living.

consensual bringing forth of a rich world is not the same as the gift of the seed for a whole new world for others to manifest, to engage in. I think that when we are gifted with the possibility of living forth such a new world that we appropriately distinguish those who have given us this new "playground" as "giants."

Yet not every such offering is appreciated. Few of the possible, or even of the potentially beautiful and desirable worlds are in fact manifest.

Sometimes the new world that is made possible through the vision of a "giant" is understood by very few, while at the same time the explanations which are generated are accepted as useful in several other lineages of ideas. When this happens the vision offered by the "giant" is neither seen nor understood as it is co-opted into one or more existing lineages as if it were but a detail or a metaphor. What could be a new world with a full set of explanations and understandings with concomitant ways of seeing and acting, is analyzed as if it were a component of some existing, broadly accepted and practised, way of thinking.

This happens in particular when a new underlying premise leads to a new view of some particular phenomenon, with a new explanation of the generative mechanisms which underlie that phenomenon. At the same time the new explanation may also appear suitable from the perspective of a different lineage of ideas, with its implicit set of premises. From the second lineage the new explanation is taken as an extension to what is already seen and known within that set of ideas. However, because premises differ, the set of entailments of notions do not fully match between lineages. Consequently the use of the explanation in the adopting lineage may appear superficial or misleading when considered under the terms of the contributing lineage. We see this happening frequently between disciplines, where the consequences of what is termed "the cross-fertilization of ideas" are both appreciated and scorned. If we were aware that intellectual domains are not simply different locations in the same world, but different worlds between which meanings can be partially mapped but not matched, perhaps we would not be so deeply frustrated.

Fortunately, such assimilation or appropriation does not always take place. Sometimes a group of people becomes mutually inspired by the possibilities, the beauty, the joy of creating a new vision, a new world. When this happens a new field is seen to arise. I think this did happen with cybernetics. The early participants imagined a fullness of understanding grounded in several new notions, including circularity and the observer, and pursued the imbrications of this with depth, perseverance, and intensity.

Yet what these cyberneticians "saw" into existence is now often co-opted into other more popular and perhaps intellectually less demanding lineages of ideas. The attainment of any world other than the one in which one is raised and educated remains daunting, so that new generations of thinkers may not engage adequately with the premises and the praxis which offers the possibility of the dynamic systemic world implicit in cybernetics. If I were to resort back to the metaphor, if we are to stand on the shoulders of the early thinkers in cybernetics, then we would have to expend the energy to climb up there, not look at them from the ground where we stand and think we can see beyond what they saw.

Engagement and consequent manifestation are not the only conditions for the viability of new worlds. Not all new visions lead to worlds that can be populated through the social engagement of others with the ideas that comprise them. Some visions are not adequately connected with the medium of human existence, or the experiences of daily living, including the day to day work in any profession. I claim that if a vision is to be robust enough to generate a whole coherent world, it must be beautiful. By "beautiful" I refer to a fundamental coherence, implicitly with the network of relations which comprises the biosphere, though in practice simply with all that we "sense," both as an observer and as a living being. What I mean by 'both observer and living being' is both that which we distinguish in language, and that which we encounter and respond to without distinguishing this connection as a "thing we do." To be compelling enough to be lived, a new world of premises, and the lineages of notions which follow from them, must be one in which we are able to explain most of our experiences of living, including our observations in the domains of science, enterprise, governance, etc.

To be viable, that is to actually result in a lived world, a vision must also be enticing. It must draw us out of whatever complacency we have with ingrained habits, or with whatever well-ordered world we have been living forth. New visions are sometimes rendered enticing with promises of new utopian worlds; that is their assumed consequences are presented as the reason for accepting them. Since we cannot know what will arise in a dynamic web of relations, this has led to eventual disappointment, and subsequent caution. Alternatively, attempts to conserve the promised results have led to worlds which demand compliance, or have led to the development of institutions which were intended to assure the vision but instead assured their own existence. A vision that is compelling, not because it promises something, but simply through its beauty, its coherence, internally and with all it touches, does not fall into these traps.

This does not mean that we should ignore a consideration of possible or likely consequences, as not every new world, even if it is coherent, is desirable. I think that a fundamental concern with ethical behaviour arises in this regard. As one either implicitly accepts or explicitly chooses a set of grounding premises and a world of ideas, one also accepts the consequences of living in such a world, for oneself, and for all the others, human and our non-human living cohabitants on this planet. Although we cannot predict all the consequences of choosing a world, we can see the kinds of relationships that are implied. Perhaps the best way of considering the nature of unforeseeable consequences is to consider the emotional dynamics which are inherent in the world which arises. Does the vision include openness, awareness and acceptance?[3] Does it include care for the other? If the emotions of curiosity, care, and

---

3. Specifically love, as distinguished by Maturana, as the domain of those relational behaviours in which the other arises as a legitimate other in coexistence with oneself.

love are conserved in the shape of the world, then the world will continue to shape itself around these dynamics, while leaving its form open. This is in effect an expansion of Heinz von Foerster's well know ethical imperative "act always to increase the number of choices," and this expansion avoids the thorny problem of who distinguishes what are "choices" such that they can be counted.

As I reflect on giants, visions and worlds, another dimension of relevance comes to mind, and this has to do with the appreciation of greatness of the individual who opens the new worlds for us to play in. Even when all the conditions for a desirable new vision are satisfied, even when someone presents a beautiful understanding of how a shift in some fundamental premises generates a more harmonious world, this does not necessarily lead to a new world lived forth by others.

I think the manner of living, of being, of the "giant" who sees and illuminates a new lineage of ideas makes the difference in what is seen by others, and hence in the initial contagion of the ideas. If the giant encourages others, generates space for their independent thinking, of living forth and living in the world they have imagined, then this world is more likely to be sought by others. If this "giant" clearly enjoys the ideas of others, whether they are supportive of, or whether they examine the validity of the implications of the underlying premises, or even operate tangentially, then the world is open to play, and invites participation. On the other hand, if the "giant" insists on being a Giant, insists on being an authority, then some will shun, and others will want to use that authority for their own promotion. In either case the emotions that become associated with the ideas are not inviting ones.

When the lineage of ideas intrinsically includes an open manner of living, and this is evident in the daily living of the person who offers them, then a genuinely inviting and opening space arises. Such a lived vision is likely to be populated, articulated, and become a new world. Heinz von Foerster was a person who lived a beautiful world in such an inviting and caring manner that he appeared to magically conjure up a way of seeing, thinking and living – that is a "world." Many speak of Heinz as a magician. To me it seems that his magic appeared as a constitutive manner of being, not a method or a tool—and I think this was the result of the way he lived forth his particular vision, always with a focus on the wonder and beauty of the world he lived. As Ranulph Glanville said[4] "It's the wonder that makes the magic work. And it's the wonder that Heinz gave us all, all his life."

---

4. posting to the cybcom listserve, 10.5.02

Cybernetics And Human Knowing. Vol. 10, no. 2, pp. 169-178

A (Cybernetic) Musing: In Praise of Buffers

Ranulph Glanville[1]

Not long ago, a colleague of many years asked me a question.[2] He told me of the behaviour of the old lime and horse-hair plaster placed over timber laths that was used until quite recently all over northern Europe as a wall finish. This material has an interesting property: it absorbs and emits moisture, thus helping keep the humidity inside a building within reasonable limits: in other words, it acts as a buffer. What he wanted to know was whether buffers were a topic that had been seriously studied. He assumed they would be part of cybernetics, and, when I heard his question, I immediately replied in the affirmative. I was certain that buffers were part of the area of study of early cybernetics and was sure I had read about them in Ross Ashby's *Introduction to Cybernetics*, for me the subject's essential basic text.

I decided that I'd like to pursue this. Buffers were so clearly cybernetic and yet so surprisingly ignored, that I decided to check back to my sources. I was in for a very big surprise. Opening an electronic copy of Ashby's Introduction,[3] I did a text search and found (to my disbelief) there was no single occurrence of the string "buffer." I was astonished.

The word doesn't appear in the index of my copy of Wiener's *Cybernetics*, or in Bateson's *Steps to an Ecology of Mind*. It's not in the *Cybernetics of Cybernetics* (not even in its parabook). I wondered if I was looking in the wrong culture, but Yelena Saparina's "Cybernetics Within Us" makes no mention. It's not in Pask's "An Approach to Cybernetics." In fact, it's almost nowhere. It's hardly even on the web: the examples in the first 10 pages of a google search seem to concentrate on unplanted strips in forestry (fire baffles), gun recoils, computing uses, and buffer solutions which resist pH change on the addition of acids.

So I looked in the dictionaries. My *Shorter Oxford Dictionary* gives a first date of use of the word "buffer" as 1835, when it referred to what we might now describe as those shock-absorbing dampers, rather like gun recoils, attached to the ends of railway trucks and carriages.[4] It also referred to one of the better-known applications of the idea, the "buffer state." Such states (nations) were proposed to reduce friction between adjoining large nations, being located between them. For instance, after the First World War, making the German land on the West of the Rhine (e.g., Alsace, Saar) into a separate buffer state between France and Germany was seriously considered. The

---

1. The Bartlett, University College London, 22 Gordon St, London WC1H 0QB, UK.
    Email: ranulph@glanville.co.uk
2. Thanks, therefore, to Prof Stephen Gage of UCL for inspiring this.
3. I am profoundly grateful to Alex Reigler, supported by the Principia Cybernetica Project, for putting the whole of Ashby's "Introduction" into electronic form. The full story can be found on the site from which you can download the book in pdf format: http://pcp.vub.ac.be/books/IntroCyb.pdf.
4. There is an earlier, but completely different use of the word, as in the expression "He's an old buffer."

Warsaw Pact countries of the old (twentieth century) order were buffer states for the Soviet Union, and the Korean DeMilitarised Zone works similarly.

Eventually, I looked in Charles Francois's *Encyclopaedia of Systems and Cybernetics* (1997)—which I had reviewed for this journal (1999). His entry under Buffer is concerned with message transmission and particularly comes from the concerns of Information Theory. But, under Buffer Compartment, he has something much more helpful:

> Buffer Compartment
> 'A part of a system which acts as a reservoir for incoming energy, matter or information, such that the inputs enter the rest of the system with smoothed and averaged characteristics.' (T. F. H. Allen & T. B. Starr. (1982). *Hierarchy: Perspectives for ecological complexity.* Chicago: Chicago University Press.)

The quantities of energy, matter or information stored in the buffer compartment are at the free disposal of the system. They can be used by regulatory subsystems when needed. This permits a range of differential responses in a changing environment, an adaptive mechanism sometimes called buffering; and it also opposes wide structural destruction.

From this extraordinary lack of discussion, I learnt two things. Firstly, I was reminded that my memory doesn't always co-incide with other evidence and it's important to check back! And secondly, that I was wrong: buffers have not been a major part of cybernetics.[5] But I believe they should be. And so I propose to start an attempted assimilation here.

The Water Jug

Let me start with a domestic example that shows just how ordinary and everyday buffers are, and introduce an alternative. This will allow me to highlight the main qualities of buffers.

At home we use a water filter attached to a water jug to further purify our tap water. From this jug we fill our kettle. There are two approaches to how to manage this. One keeps the kettle full and the water jug continually recharged. The other empties the kettle, filling it when needed from the water jug, in turn leaving the water jug empty. Often enough, both kettle and water jug are empty and filtered water is not readily available, causing untoward delay in tea making.

These two different approaches can be described in several ways. One of these uses the notion of buffering. The water jug (with filter) is, in effect, a buffer. It takes about 5 minutes to fill the jug through the filter. But as long as it's full or being filled, the kettle can be kept charged, so there's always filtered water to be boiled when it's needed. The water in the water jug is a reserve waiting to be used to refill the kettle, so

---

5. They are, however, frequently referred to and used in computing.

the kettle need never be empty (although the water jug will be while it's being refilled). This arrangement guards the kettle against being empty: it's a buffer.

The alternative is a version of "Just in Time" (JiT) management. Here, we should be able to predict our needs a little before they occur, and act on this prediction. We would be able to have filtered water in the jug Just in Time to be poured into the kettle, which we would turn on so that the water was boiling at the instant we needed it. This requires an acute sense of timing and an ability to plan ahead, rather than being able to react/respond to events as they occur. And it means there are no further, unanticipated possibilities—there is less possibility of improvising.

Our domestic example demonstrates two things. Firstly, that buffering can be a help; and secondly, that there are other approaches, which (as we shall see) form a constellation of related ideas, a Thesaurus. Such approaches include antithetical ones, such as JiT. This is what I will explore in the remainder of this paper.

Definition

Let us start our exploration with a definition to help us focus. I propose the following:

> Buffers are stores which use either space (a water reservoir) and/or time (a holding period for the settlement of accounts) to modulate the effects of variations in the flow of whatever it is the particular system handles—e.g. water, money, information—particularly by smoothing out extreme behaviours.
>
> They are in use in many natural and designed systems including computer systems. They are sometimes called dampers (as in, for instance, (car) shock-absorbers, that is dampers on springs).

Buffers iron out differences and smooth out bumps. They absorb, hold and then (later) release in such a way that the effects of extremes are reduced/alleviated: they smooth variation and reduce variety. (Thus, planet Earth is a buffer and moderates climate induced temperature swings. This is why the coldest times of year do not co-incide with the shortest days.)

It will be seen from the above that buffers are common enough (even though I have been so singularly ineffective at finding much information about them)!

They are essentially conservative. The greatest of all buffers is, perhaps, the homeostat: homeostatic systems (including human beings) accommodate vast differences in their environments while remaining, themselves, within a narrow band of accepted and stabilising states/behaviours. The effects of these differences is accommodated within the system so that its behaviour remains more-or-less constant (as, for instance, our body temperature).

Flooding

As a first example, let us consider flooding.

A few years ago, the river channel of the Rhine was so full that large parts of Holland were in danger of imminent inundation. Many people had to be evacuated as the waters rose to within a couple of centimetres of the top of the dykes.

Last (northern) summer, large parts of central Europe were subject to appalling floods. A vast area of China was as close to flooding as Holland was those few years earlier.

And, of recent years, Britain has been visited by a whole string of floods which, while not as large or lethal as those of central Europe and insignificant in comparison to others, cause repeating chaos (for they strike again and again in the same places). At the moment of drafting this paper there were 130 flood warnings in the UK.

There are many reasons for these (near) inundations. The one which is of interest here is the removal of water meadows by the canalisation of rivers. Canalising rivers contains them and controls them. No longer are potentially desirable lands on which, for instance, expensive housing could be built wasted as water meadows. Because the path of the water is controlled by containment, they can be built on. The case in Holland is even more dramatic. A vast part of what is now that country was, once, a variety of extreme (submerged) water meadow!

While there are many factors in such flooding (which I am not competent to discuss or evaluate), one factor is undoubtedly the exchange by which canalisation has replaced the buffer of "soft" banks—water meadows—which, acting as both a sponge and a potential shallow lake, absorbed the excess water, giving it up to the river later, when the flow was low. These water meadows served a purpose. They were buffers. Where there are such meadows, flooding is accommodated and the consequent destruction is minimised. The lack of such water meadow buffers contributes greatly to the damage floods may cause.

There is frequently a beneficial side-effect of using water meadows to buffer us against the destructive effects of flooding. Often the ground so flooded is wonderfully fertile once the waters have receded. In the case of the Nile, a vast civilization was made possible. And then there are those further immensely valuable side effects such as beauty in the landscape and delight in our hearts.

But there are other side effects, too, resulting from the removal of water meadow buffers, which are not so good. The canalisation of rivers has changed where floods happen. In place of the regularly flooded water meadow (traditionally not described as flooded), there is now a new, though perhaps less often flooded, regular flood area. And often this turns out to be the centre of a town.

Markets

A second example comes from the operation of markets. Until recently, the London stock market ran with accounting periods of a fortnight. What this meant was that all bills were settled at two weekly intervals. Stocks and shares bought were paid for then, and the funds from stocks sold became available at these fortnightly points in time. If stocks in the same company were bought and sold within this period, only the difference (profit or loss) was paid. The system worked on trust and was associated with the expression "An Englishman's word is his bond." Anyone who cheated and was caught was drummed out of the stock exchange and would never be allowed back. I have met people who, 60 years on, are not forgiven. They never will be.

The effect of this accounting procedure was to vastly reduce the movement of funds. All accounts were squared up at these fortnightly intervals. This is a buffer. But there was another buffer. Because funds did not come available, and the market worked with a sort of delay, there was a reduced tendency for the markets to suddenly shoot off to the extremes. Panic trading was quite genteel by today's standards. Vast sums of money were not seen to be being moved, so the effect of positive feedback was kept in check. Neither computers nor punters went on Gadarene rampages!

All this changed with the introduction of the real time market brought about by electronic communication and computer dealing (in effect, more or less a JiT system). This meant that the experts believed that they could model the behaviour of the market better, react accordingly at great speed, and thereby play the margins (for instance) to greater profit. The result has been markets where instability and rapid escalations have been common. If they are less common now it is because the computer models and responses are more sophisticated. The market has moved from the relative security of a buffered system to a system of immediate controlling responses; reaction effected without delay.

Stafford Beer touched on this most movingly in his Richard Goodman Lecture, "Fanfare for Effective Freedom," where he talks about the destabilising effect of changing from traditional (time delayed) management to real-time management (Beer 1975).

Another example like this might be email, encouraging immediate communication where instant communication based on immediate responses may be misleading (and may lead to great swings in understanding and emotion). The fact that once an email is sent the sender has washed his hands of it yet can fret about it waiting in the addressee's mailbox just increases the trauma.

Buildings

A third example comes from architecture and building.

At the start of the 1970s it became currency to talk of buildings as environmental filters.[6] By this was meant that buildings protect us from the undesirable external environment (this was before understandings of sustainability were what they are today). Thus, windows gave us acceptable light levels within buildings, as well as allowing a controlled amount of fresh air to enter (in effect, a wind filtering device). A building clearly protects us from rain, thus filtering that out too. It also acts to prevent heat gain and loss.

---

6. My former boss, Geoffrey Broadbent, tells me that this concept arose in discussions around 1970. An account was written up by Hillier et al. (1972).

Heat is an interesting case. Preventing heat loss and gain is normally managed through insulation. Insulation comes about through the structure of the material that divides the interior of the building from the exterior. It used to be mainly a matter of thickness (and mass), though now-a-days it's becoming more a matter of improved thermal performance, generally achieved by making materials that are more and more vacuum-like.

In the case of massive materials, the effect is of a buffer. These materials work as storage heaters: they absorb heat when it's hot outside, but lose it to the inside to keep it warm over the cold nights. During the course of the year they also have an effect: in the summer they keep the inside cooler, in the winter warmer.[7] (This is a faster version of how the Earth acts as a temperature buffer for us.)

Many ecological houses work on this principle. They have a heat store (usually a pit full of boulders) which soaks up the heat generated during the day to release it slowly over the night. By circulating air through this store they can keep the inside of a building warm when it's cold outside, and vice versa—without much further energy requirement. The relative constancy of temperature in the ground—regardless of weather conditions—is a major factor in providing the constant temperature conditions needed for making and storing e.g. great wines. Thus have buffers benefited humanity in the most sophisticated way!

Reservoirs

A final example from the physical world is the use of mountain reservoirs to power electricity generating plant when demand is high. At times of low consumption, electricity is used to pump water up into a reservoir, often in the form of an artificial lake in a mountain range. When demand is high, the water is allowed to flow down again, powering turbines that generate extra electricity as and when required. The mountain reservoir is a buffer designed to alleviate the excesses of demand.

In reverse, the same happens with power sources that are unreliable. Renewable sources such as wind, tide, wave and solar generation peak according to natural phenomena, not our requirements. A buffer is needed between supply surges and actual demand.

Non-Physical Buffers

Buffers do not have to be physical. There is evidence that there are mental and emotional buffers, too, as well as social ones. Buffering is used to regulate the flow of traffic in cities. Most storerooms are buffers. There are all sorts of other examples, just as there are all sorts of counter examples and related phenomena. But there does not seem to be, at least in the realm of cybernetics and systems science, a central study of buffering.

---

7. Buffering by heavy construction is not the only factor at play here.

A Research Programme

It would seem, therefore, that there is a clearly distinguished gap in our knowledge, which concerns buffering. Buffers are valuable, and part of a range of ideas that fit together as complements and contrasts. Though it might be argued that buffering is not efficient (it's certainly not fast reacting — that's the whole point), buffers give us a good, steady performance and, very often, some delightful side effects: and who is to say that any measure of efficiency should ignore these side effects? Therefore, I would like to call for a major research programme into buffering (together with related concepts).

Such a research programme would consider the following.

Firstly, how buffering works. Clearly this involves the use of time delays to cancel the extreme effects of swings either by using up what is stored in the buffer (and then replenishing it), or by allowing positive and negative to even out. There are certainly models of these processes already well developed in engineering and hydrology which may port to other disciplines — or may not. However, any research programme into the cybernetics of buffering would need to take into account non-mechanical systems in which humans are part of, or even the whole system. There are almost always humans in cybernetic systems, and many of their interactions are mental and/or emotional. The point is that the notion of a buffer has potential over the widest of ranges of application.

Secondly, there are common characteristics in such models.[8] It is important to consider these. If my definition above (or any other) is accepted, experience tells us that we will discover surprises in it. It is important to consider not only the effect of buffers on the systems they buffer, but also how they do this: their modes of action. This includes looking at different types of buffer: for instance the water meadow/sponge is quite different to the homeostat, the first being essentially passive and potentially offering a side benefit (fertile land); the second being active and applying actions internally to redress the balance. Breakdown conditions, in particular, are critical. Buffers break down. Think of the overheating of the homeostatic system that is the human body that can be caused by disease, which in turn can lead to death — in our terms, the ultimate breakdown. It is important to understand the conditions under which this is most likely to happen.

Thirdly, buffering, as indicated above, is a notion connected to other notions in some kind of network of relations. Some of these concepts are antithetical (e.g., buffer vs JiT, for instance); some related (e.g., buffer and filter). The appropriate way of thinking is not just in terms of similarities. For this reason I suggest using a Thesaurus type of arrangement, in which related concepts are placed as thesis, antithesis and at points between.[9]

---

8. which is why they can all be thought of as buffers.
9. Unfortunately nowadays many a Thesaurus just deals in synonyms and near synonyms. But Roget's intention when he developed the first Thesaurus was to show the relationship of ideas across the full range, and the antithetical word was as much part of all his entries as the synonymous ones.

Fourthly, and another reason for the Thesaurus proposal, is the exploration of the values of buffers and related concepts, in particular regarding their potential ranges of application, and thus benefit. It is important to know not only what the rival yet complementary concepts are, but the conditions under and circumstances in which one or another is likely to be more helpful.

Buffering and Cybernetics

It is possible that the connection between buffering and cybernetics is not clear from the above. As a conclusion to this piece, I shall indicate the connection.

Cybernetics is concerned with control. In early cybernetics, the concern was to show how to control systems effectively. This is the major concern driving Wiener's book, and what is embodied in Ashby's "Law of Requisite Variety." A little later, interest expanded to include the limits of what is controllable. This was also, above all, down to Ashby, who applied Bremmerman's constant to show that many systems are, in principle, uncontrollable. Later still, it became apparent that control in a circular system exists only between the components (and not by one of another).

Buffering is one way we deal with systems we cannot control, for whatever reason. We can consider the opposite of buffering as control. We remove buffers that we have used, historically, when we come to believe that we can build adequate models that allow us to effectively control (buffers cope with a lack of variety). This is precisely what (first order) cybernetics sets out to do and is one reason it is so important to understand the limits to the controllable So we channel water to replace the wasteful use of land that we come to see water meadows as being. Buffering is a strategy that allows us not to force control when we can't make it work. In effect, buffering is an approach to the dissolving of problems: given time, they go away and everything evens out.

I am suggesting that, if history tells us anything, it tells us we cannot be sure of our models. Therefore, we should be careful. But I have also argued in this journal that there are benefits in being out of control, that is, in living with unmanageability (this is the cybernetics of non-control). Buffers support us in gaining these benefits. We should be careful of rationalising them away when they can allow us to benefit from unmanageability. Nor should we forget the potential for beneficial side-effects.

And we, in cybernetics, should consider control not as a single notion, but, Thesaurus like, as a range that contains synonyms, and moves from thesis to antithesis. And, at the antithetical end to control, where we will find buffering, we also find, strangely, that buffering is a sort of anti-control without a controller. It would be interesting, also, to examine where the limits to this sort of anti-control lie.

References

Beer, S. (1975). Fanfare for Effective Freedom. In S. Beer, *Platform for change*. Chichester: John Wiley and Sons.
Francois, C. (1997). *International encyclopaedia of systems and cybernetics*. Munich: KG Saur.

Glanville, R. (1999.) A (cybernetic) musing: Encyclopaedias and the form of knowing. A celebration of Charles Francois' 'International encyclopaedia of systems and cybernetics: A sort of self-referential work of reference.' *Cybernetics and Human Knowing, 6* (1).

Hillier, W. R. G, Musgrave, J. E. & O'Sullivan, P. (1984). Knowledge and design. In N. Cross, *Developments in design methodology*. Chichester: John Wiley & Sons. (Reprinted from W.J. Mitchell(Ed), *Proceedings of the EDRA 3/AR8 Conference: Environmental design research*. Los Angeles: University of California, 1972)

Appendix: definitions of the term "Buffer."

Random House Dictionary, 1971

Buffer

(2) any device, material, or apparatus used for a shield, cushion, or bumper... (3) any intermediate or intervening shield or device reducing the danger of interaction between two machines, chemicals, electronic components, etc.... (5) any reserve moneys, negotiable securities, legal procedures, etc., which protect a person, organisation. or country against financial ruin (6) one who protects and shields another from petty matters or the brunt of anger or criticism... (8) Computer Technol. an intermediate memory unit for temporarily holding computer data until the proper unit is ready to receive the data, as when the receiving unit has an operating speed lower than that of the unit feeding the data to it... (10) Chem. a. any substance or mixture of compounds that, added to a solution, is capable of neutralising both acids and bases with out appreciably changing the original acidity or alkalinity of the solution... (12) to cushion, shield or protect (13) to lessen the adverse effect of; ease.

Buffer state

a small state lying between potentially hostile larger areas.

International Encyclopedia of Systems and Cybernetics, (Charles Francois) 1997

Buffer

A device introduced into a communication system to allow asynchronous communication.

L. Brimm comments: "A buffer preserves message sequences. The buffer discipline is as follows:
-The sender may always send a message
-The receiver may always receive a message, provided the medium is not empty
-The order of receiving messages is equal to the order of sending messages." (1992 p135)

Buffers allow for serialised and ordered communication, avoids bottlenecks and, to some extent, overloads in communication channels.

Buffer Compartment

"A part of a system which acts as a reservoir for incoming energy, matter, or information such that the inputs enter the rest of the system and smoothed and averaged characteristics." (T. F. H Allen & T. B. Starr, 1982, p. 263)

The quantities of energy, matter, or information stored in the buffer compartment are at the free disposal of the system. They can be used by regulatory subsystems when needed. This permits a range of differential responses in a changing environment, a mechanism sometimes called buffering, and it also opposes wide structural destruction.

Shorter Oxford Dictionary, 1993

Buffer

1835. Mech. A mechanical apparatus for deadening the forces of a concussion, as fixed at the front and back of railway carriages, etc. Extended also to contrivances which sustain without deadening the concussion.

Buffer State

a neutral state lying between two others and serving to render less possible hostilities between them.

Merriam Webster's Collegiate Dictionary (on Encyclopaedia Britannica site)
Main Entry: **1. buff·er**
    Pronunciation:'b&-f&r
    Function:*noun*
    Usage:*often attributive*
    Etymology:*buff,* v., to react like a soft body when struck
    Date:1835
    1: any of various devices or pieces of material for reducing shock or damage due to contact
    2: a means or device used as a cushion against the shock of fluctuations in business or financial activity
    3: something that serves as a protective barrier: as **a: BUFFER STATE b:** a person who shields another especially from annoying routine matters **c: MEDIATOR** 1
    4: a substance capable in solution of neutralizing both acids and bases and thereby maintaining the original acidity or basicity of the solution; *also*: a solution containing such a substance
    5: a temporary storage unit (as in a computer); *especially*: one that accepts information at one rate and delivers it at another
    - **buff·ered** /-f&rd/ *adjective*

View from Rattlesnake Hill.
Frank Galuszka. Oil

Cybernetics And Human Knowing. Vol. 10, nos. 3-4, pp. 179-181

TRUTH IS WAR: Conversations with Heinz von Foerster

A review of *Wahrheit ist die Erfindung eines Lügners — Gespräche für Skeptiker*, by Heinz von Foerster and Bernhard Pörksen[1]

Ole Thyssen[2]

When I stayed in California in the autumn of 1992, I had prepared a small detour to a remote place – Rattlesnake Hill in Pescadero. Here lived a man whose work I had read and used and whom I had a great desire to meet. His production was not large and consisted mostly of small delicately elaborated papers. Some of them were published by his friends in a book with the ambiguous title *Observing Systems* (1984).

High up in the green mountains lived Heinz von Foerster together with his paralyzed wife, who he took care of due to her serious illness. This was the end of the line for a man born in Vienna in 1911 in a milieu comprising persons like Gustav Klimt, Egon Schiele and Ludwig Wittgenstein. He was educated as a physicist and survived the Second World War in Berlin by faking an Arian descent, a step which was necessary because he had close Jewish family members. In 1949, he left Europe and went to the US, where he joined the inventive and multidisciplinary circle created by persons like Warren McCulloch, Margaret Mead, Gregory Bateson and Norbert Wiener. The atmosphere was, according to von Foerster, "friendly and characterized by intensive and fearless creativity." No sterile criticism, but fun and understanding.

Von Foerster's contribution consists above all of what he, somewhat coquettishly, calls his "small Foersters"—sentences which he worked over again and again, until everything superfluous was cut away and they were purified to small crystals in which thinking can reflect and start reflection. His force is not big epistemological constructions, and by scrutinizing his theses it is easy to conclude that the many small crystals do not easily combine to one large diamond. Von Foerster died in 2002. In his later years, he did not write much, and very often, he used interviews as a ways of presenting his ideas. In the mid-90's, the German journalist Bernhard Pörksen interviewed von Foerster, the conversation continued and is now presented as another interview with von Foerster.

That truth is the invention of a liar is such a crystal, which von Foerster cut by himself, only to realize that Nicolas von Cues had anticipated him half a millennium

---

1. Published by Carl-Auer-Systeme Verlag, 1998. Price: 25.50 euros.
2. Dept. of Management, Politics and Philosophy, Copenhagen Business School. Email: thyssen@cbs.dk

earlier. The point is that if there were only truth, the truth would not be worth speaking of. Only the lie, the counter-concept, throws truth in relief.

A point of departure for von Foerster is the stubborn and troublesome insight that even if we experience "a fragrant and colorful and sonorous world," the external world can only be observed on the basis of sensual irritations located in the observer. We construct the world out of the impressions, which our sensory organs are able to receive. But what releases those impressions we do not know and cannot know. Von Foerster remarks that if you stimulated a nerve cell with a drop of vinegar, it would perhaps trigger a sense of color, and if you affected the tongue with a small electrical shock, it would perhaps trigger a sense of vinegar.

On the basis of an ongoing stream of sensory experiences we make calculations of what is constant, for example by changing perspective. In this way, a stabile world is created out of unstable processes, which allows von Foerster to conclude that an object is "a competence in our nerve system." When observations repeat themselves and not only relate to the external world, but also to themselves, the result is not chaos. Repetition leads to experience, that is, to a sufficient stability. Out of chaos emerges spontaneously an order, which is robust enough to allow expectations. Only it is not the external world, but the observer who guarantees this order.

The basic principle is *circularity*—not just observations, but also observations of observations. It is no coincidence that von Foerster was part of the circle, which developed the idea of cybernetics.

Out of this constructivism von Foerster does not draw skeptical conclusions. His only conclusion had its background in his experiences with the Nazi regime: that truth is a horrible word. The same conclusion was reached by another from the same circle as von Foerster, namely the Chilean biologist Humberto Maturana, based on similar experiences with Pinochet: truth is war! Whether this statement itself is true is an interesting question, which the two gentlemen do not show a keen interest in discussing.

Instead von Foerster claims that constructivism leads to responsibility and fellow feeling. He gives name to a principle, the principle of relativity, which states that what is right for two parties individually only can be accepted if it is right for both of them together. Instead of attacking the problem of truth directly, von Foerster makes an ethical evasion and asks if trust is not more important that truth.

The deconstruction of the concept of truth opens, according to von Foerster, an "epistemological Schwitzerland" with a marvelous diversity. His ethical principle states that you should act in such a way that the number of possibilities increases – and because he himself is such a generous person, he does not test whether this principle throws the door wide open for every kind of evil. But perhaps the answer is hidden in the principle itself: that evil *is* to reduce the possibilities of other persons.

When Bernhard Pörksen, the journalist who performs the long interview with von Foerster, challenges the principle and even undermines it, von Foerster is not embarrassed or self-opinionated, but claims that he "enjoys the way you put my ethical imperative *ad absurdum*." To him, it is a liberation to open for the whole spectrum of possibilities and "become free as a bird." Whether this should be called intellectual laziness or emancipation from the dictatorship of reason will not be discussed here.

Von Foerster denies that he is a constructivist and instead calls himself a Viennese. He is ready to be surprised and to risk all prejudices. Labels and schools irritate him, because they lead to clubs, which again leads to war and catastrophe. Therefore he stresses the fundamental ignorance of man. And therefore he wants to replace the linear causality with the parable, the metaphor and the narrative, which accepts that man is not a trivial machine reacting on a specific input with a specific output.

Pedagogically it means that it is "filthy" for a teacher to ask a question if he knows the answer. Also in this domain, the important thing is to increase, not to diminish the number of answers.

By now it should be obvious that von Foerster is not presenting a ready-made system, but instead makes probes and openings, a shower of mental arrows, which in a Socratic way may irritate the established body, whether it be body of the state or the intellectual body.

Cybernetics And Human Knowing. Vol. 10, no. 1, pp. 183-188

Understanding Systems: Conversations on Epistemology and Ethics[1]

A Review of the book by Heinz von Foerster and Bernhard Poerksen[2]

Ranulph Glanville[3]

Ever since (some 30 years ago) I first came across Heinz von Foerster, the man and the academic/author, I have been waiting for him to write a book. Not just a book, but the book in which he would collect together all the various strands of his immensely rich work. And for years he disappointed me. I am sure I am not alone in this!

Nevertheless, various people had a go at getting something book-like published, notably the (no longer obtainable) generously assembled *Observing Systems* compiled and edited by Francisco Varela.

Von Foerster steadfastly downplayed the value of his work and his own contribution. I think he has liked to portray himself more as a ring master rather than a performer: and he has certainly managed to orchestrate conditions so that others have been enormously enabled in their own work. Just to take one example, the Biological Computer Laboratory (BCL) at the University of Illinois can be looked on as a glasshouse in which the talents of many were appreciated and developed—from the already distinguished (including Ashby, Beer, Günther, Loefgren, Maturana, Pask and Varela) to students who came to be current significant masters of the field of cybernetics (Umpleby and Weston, for instance).

Even interviewing von Foerster has only lead to him discussing his own work in moments of temporary lapse while under extreme pressure. I know this, for I spent a week interviewing him ten years ago, only to find the camouflage still largely intact (although I did eventually manage to oblige him to spend one begrudging session on his work).

So it seemed, to me at least, that my hope for "the book" was a lost cause. There would never be the general, co-ordinating statement, the coherent assembly, the simple account by the master himself made available in one place and in one neat package: it would be left for us to read and to construct our own realities

---

1. Kluwer Academic/Plenum Press, New York, Boston, Dordrecht, London, Moscow; and Carl-Auer-Systeme Verlag, Heidelberg. Price, from Carl-Auer Systeme Verlag, 25.5 euros plus postage. The price quoted at Amazon.com in the USA (the only web source bookshop I have been able to find that has this book on its lists) is U.S $68.
2. Translated from the German by Karen Leube.
3. CybernEthics Research, U.K. E-mail: ranulph@glanville.co.uk.

(interpretations) from what we understood. And I could appreciate this position, even while I hoped against hope for more guidance and the presentation of an (already) integrated whole.

And then, about five years ago, a different strategy was brought to bear. During the 1990s, von Foerster was at last discovered at large in the German speaking world. Suddenly he was feted in Germany and Austria (peaking when he was given the freedom of the City of Vienna in 2001; and through the establishment of the von Foerster Society and Archive at the University of Vienna, together with the von Foerster lecture), in his home town, where he had previously been largely ignored.[4]

There was an unexpected side effect that arose out of this. Suddenly there was a number of (younger) German speaking intellectuals who wanted to converse with von Foerster in German (most of his revolutionary cybernetic work having been written in English), and who were prepared to put in many hours studying his published work with a fresh eye. They came to his home in California to speak with him on his balcony, to walk in the forests and on the Pacific shore, assembling from the conversations a number of books in which von Foerster does, at last, talk generally of himself and his work and world view. I know of three such collaborations. One, with Monika Broecker, exists also in a draft English translation. Another, with two (unrelated) Muellers who run the von Foerster Archive, is currently only in German. And a third, with Bernhard Poerksen, which now appears in English and is the subject of this review.

This book, the particular outcome of this process which I am considering here, is named *Understanding Systems*. Although this title contains an enticing ambiguity, it is not the title von Foerster had in mind. He wanted the book to be called "Truth is the Invention of the Liar." The reversal that his preferred title presents, and the consequent jolt of awakening and puzzlement, is typical von Foerster. It's a shame that the publishers couldn't accommodate his wish.

What is this book *Understanding Systems* about? When I started reading the book, and was composing possible reviews—or, at least, approaches—in my mind, I wondered about giving the traditional and normal paraphrase. As I read I began to withdraw from this idea. Of course, all the usual von Foerster suspects are there: self-organisation, trivial and non-trivial machines, constructed realities, the lack of meaning in communication (à la Pask), the cybernetics of cybernetics, cybernetics and ethics,[5] responsibility and choice (and our determinations), memory without record and so on.

But there are two problems with summarising (and then commenting, possibly even arguing against). Firstly, the presentation is, as is usual in von Foerster's papers, unusually terse, dense, to the point—in two words, in Heinz's "inimitable English." This is a book of wide-ranging yet lean interviews, although interviews in which both

---

4. There were, of course, notable exceptions: Niklas Luhmann and his school, and artists such as Trash Treasure, in Aachen.
5. Naming my company CybernEthics Research was a tribute to von Foerster, though I did not realise it was also a quote!

the protagonists and those who make up the story they are developing are forcefully present. So, in a sense, it's already a summary. Secondly, at the heart of the book is an attitude that is inclusive, individual, and which argues against inappropriate reduction and inappropriate definition. By the latter, I refer to both von Foerster's dislike of labelling and being categorised, and the "inter-disciplinary" nature of his work, especially at the Biological Computer Laboratory, which he founded. I have placed "inter-disciplinary" in inverted commas because he argues strongly against the use of this term also. As he says, inter-disciplinary studies require expert knowledge of several disciplines: what he's talking about is the limitations of useful boundaries, the importance of not being bound (restricted) and, hence, non-disciplinary studies.

An important way in which von Foerster demonstrates the power of his ideas is as a debunker. The book is full of attacks ridiculing received wisdom and familiar and favourite ideas that von Foerster shows to be absurd or sentimental. He does this through the application of a rigorous logic that he uses to show absurdity. Generally, he does this with charm and a deftly light touch. Here are just four examples (in my paraphrase).

- We cannot speak about the certainty of death. At the moment a very considerable percentage of those who have been born are still alive.
- We have freedom to decide (ourselves) exactly when a matter is undecidable.
- Our individuality means we are all connected.
- Truth is the invention of a liar.[6]

It is through this debunking of the absurd that von Foerster shows the vigour of his thinking and its importance to us not only in science, but in our every day conduct of our lives.

I should like here to make a comment on the languages used by von Foerster. The language history of von Foerster's writings has always interested me.[7] On his arrival in the USA, speaking no English, Warren McCulloch had him made editor and secretary of the Macy Conferences. This amounted to a crash course in English. The resultant use of language was exquisite. Perhaps von Foerster's progress in English was similar to that of Samuel Beckett in French, who used French so that he would write with more care and precision.[8] To my mind there is a fluidity in English which allows the sort of thinking (a type of sloppy thinking, quite often pun-like and exploiting ambiguity) that permits the breaking of conventional boundaries, which is what was required for the sorts of concepts that von Foerster developed in cybernetics. German gives a sort of legalistic precision, when called upon to do so, which English does not manage so well. The quality of a mind that grew up speaking German and

6. Bringing to mind George Bernard Shaw's "All Great Truths begin life as lies."
7. I have always thought that the rather strange German of Ludwig Wittgenstein was an intuitive attempt to write German as if it were English. When I suggested this to Heinz, he agreed with me.
8. Von Foerster was my doctoral examiner. The main memory I have of the actual exam was his corrections of my English text, specially the spelling. I am a native speaker. What he suggested were genuine improvements!

then had to shift to English can be very powerful. I think von Foerster was a case in point. No matter how true or false this view may be, his groundbreaking work was written in English. It is as though he had to make a different space to do it in. But then, late in life, he could return to his native German and express his thoughts with a different type of clarity, for most of what he "wrote" in his last decade was in German. Perhaps this is an irrelevance, but I think not. This book, *Understanding Systems,* even in its English translation, shows an easy exactitude and precision that is extraordinarily clear, delightful and remarkable. The book, although often terse, is always somehow populated with people and with ideas.

There is another facet of the book I think is important: biography. I don't want to confuse the story with the teller. But, as von Foerster would be the first to point out, there is no story without a teller. Through the tales of his life, many aspects of von Foerster's ways of thinking and acting become ever more apparent. For instance, the importance of magic (not only that the world is magical, but in how magic (conjuring) works as the creation of a world by interaction of the magician and the audience);[9] the human valuing and sustaining of difference (including a story of how he and his wife Mai sustained a Jewish couple in Nazi Berlin); and the significance of communication (von Foerster eavesdropped on the discussions of his parents' circle of artists and intellectuals in Vienna during his early childhood in Vienna and, after the second world war, acted as a radio journalist on scientific and cultural matters, interviewing many important and interesting people). Von Foerster comes across as a very social person who enjoys the interchange of meeting others. Many who read this review will have met him, and of those, many will have visited him at home. Yet there must also be those who have not had this opportunity. In this book, I hear his voice. It's not just that I can hear him speaking, that accent, that intonation, the infuriating habit of speaking very quietly and fast when he's saying something important; but also the person. I am lucky to have known Heinz for a long time, and (I believe) fairly well. For me this book brings me into his presence again. I imagine it will do this for all who have met him. For those who haven't, it does have his presence and so, perhaps, gives an opportunity to meet this fascinating and lovely man.

Finally, it would not do if I were to fail to mention the real magic that von Foerster tells us of in this book. I mentioned this as the key to his work in the obituary I wrote for this journal. Von Foerster wants to re-open our minds to wonder. And, for him, the first wonder is that we have to make the choice on how we will make our universes. This is the deep mystery from which all others follow: it is up to us. Since we cannot know without us being there to do the knowing, the choice is ours. There may or may not be other things that contribute to this choice (deciding which is again our choice), but we cannot escape making that choice. And that is cause for wonder, as is the resulting outcome of our choices. We cannot know whether there is a Mind

---

9. This review was completed shortly after von Foerster's death and was intended for publication in an earlier issue of *Cybernetics and Human Knowing.* My commemorative paper in this issue, "Machines of Wonder and Elephants that Fly through Air," was written after this review.

Independent Reality. But we can chose to act as if there were, or there weren't: that is our choice. More than anything, von Foerster wishes us to wonder with astonishment and awe at who we are and what our experience is. This position derives from his assertion "My doctrine is not to have a doctrine."

I have spoken with a number of others who have read this book. One comment I find interesting is that it is very hard to understand (because, I think, of its density). I did not find this so: to me it was delightful and clear, and we sailed, Heinz, Bernhard and I, with our many shared references and people, through a most beautiful seascape almost without effort. I put this down to that famous remark of von Foerster's "uncle" (Nonnonkel) Ludwig Wittgenstein, who in the introduction to the Tractatus remarks that perhaps his text will only be understood by those who have already had these thoughts (I paraphrase). This book can be seen as the summary of the intent of the "project of second-order cybernetics." To those who were lucky enough to be able, early, to find the concepts, constructions and understandings of second-order cybernetics, this book will, I believe, be instantly clear and fluent. To those who have not, it may be a little harder. But the rewards (including later reading it fast) will be enormous.

I recommend this book not only to the cybernetics and systems community, but to anyone. In fact, if I could think of someone I would not recommend it to, I'd be certain to recommend it to them — and, then, to me. But there appears to be a snag. I have looked for this book on the web, and the only place I found it was at amazon.com and in the publisher's listings. It may be difficult to obtain. But please do try to obtain it. I have recently managed this by contacting the publishers Carl-Auer Systeme Verlag directly via the Internet.

And I want to thank the self-effacing Bernhard Poerksen, whose name has scarcely featured in this review, for the immense, and immensely valuable, effort he put into understanding Heinz's thought so that he could structure both the interviews and then the organising of them into a book, that is so redolent of "the essence of Heinz," and which brings him to us so clearly.

After this, I'm looking forward to reading the other collaborative texts. Can they be as good?

Reference

Foerster, H. von. (1980.) *Observing systems* (compiled and edited by F. Varela). Seaside, CA: Intersystems.

The Lama and the telescope

Back in 47 some lamas left their Tibetan heaven.
They sailed down the Ganges over the Pacific to the South American Andes.
Here they met the wise men of the West.
Together the slowed down their hearts and put their minds to rest.
One day came a messenger of no hope.
He said, soon they will build a giant telescope.
Then came a bulldozer and mechanical toys.
You could here the ghost of Galileo screaming in the noise.
The lama went to the construction sight
to complain about the loss of the light.
The astronomers said he saw a black hole eating a red giant's face,
millions of galaxies racing to the same place.
On the large scale he could see the human form,
Long and thin held together by gravity and magnetic spin.
It had a long finger stretching out over millions of light years,
Pointing to some thing it loves, or fears.
With the new telescope, I can see if it can laugh or cry tears.
The lama said I'm going away to leave you.
I want to say goodbye.
Maybe a machine can see God in the sky?

Bill Schiffer
The cosmic flower,
Christiania, Copenhagen

Cybernetics And Human Knowing. Vol. 10, nos. 3-4, pp. 189-194

Plein Air Painting on Rattlesnake Hill

Frank Galuszka[1]

The last time Christina and I came to paint on Rattlesnake Hill, it was one o'clock on a late August afternoon. We visited Heinz in the house, and he went off for a nap. We agreed that we would show him our paintings when he woke from his afternoon rest at three thirty or four. It was typical perfect summer weather, and we carried the easels, canvases and paints further up the hill. We made our way more cautiously than in past visits as the path had been reclaimed by the poison oak Heinz had successfully kept in check by daily sweat and toil for over twenty years.

Once he told us that he put in two to three hours a day of heavy yardwork. Mostly this time was devoted to clearing poison oak to which Heinz was famously immune. Its red color spilled over surrounding hills in some seasons like lava. Christina and I speculated about the beneficial effect of this strenuous work on Heinz's mood and on his impressive physique. Certainly his characteristic vibrant state of mind was neither entirely due to genetic luck nor to his philosophy of life. His endorphins were also teased into play by a habit of robust physical activity, and, until a succession of small strokes brought mortality to his front door, Heinz was to be encountered not behind a desk or in a laboratory, but jumping off his tractor and pulling from his hands the scarred rawhide gloves of a cowboy.

Heinz explained that there were indeed rattlesnakes on Rattlesnake Hill, and coyotes and a bobcat, and deer. The house, designed by his architect son, Andreas, was constructed according to Heinz's wish from materials available at the local hardware store. This strategy insured there would be minimal delays as the family, like pioneers, built the house, Mai herself wielding a hammer. The house is up a steep gravel drive from Eden Road, and overlooks the memory of a nudist colony that had long ago been defeated by poison oak and had left only the name of the road. The house is close to the top of the hill, which narrows into a ridge at a certain elevation. There are two principle views, one looking east from the living room and deck toward forested hills that reminded Heinz of Austria, and another which looked west across a narrow valley to a low range of meadowed hills that were pure California and concealed the Pacific. It is the view to the West that Christina and I painted most.

We made the effort to begin and complete each painting in the afternoon before the light changed. This approach to painting is called *plein air* painting, or, as Monet called it, painting *sur le motif*. Plein air painting flourished in nineteenth century France with the invention of equipment such as portable easels and paints in lead tubes, and with the laying of rail lines which permitted artists speedy travel from city

---

1. Professor, Baskin Visual Arts, University of California, Santa Cruz, Santa Cruz, CA 95064.
Email: frgalusz@cats.ucsc.edu

to country and back. Outdoor painting had been pioneered by British professional and amateur painters who used portable watercolor supplies to document tourist locations.

The origin of this kind of painting is generally traced to Albrecht Durer's sketches in watercolor while journeying to Italy in the 15th century.

The aim of the *plein air* painting is to paint out of the experience of the unique present moment. The landscape, with its shifting color and light, gives poignancy to the present. but to create out of the experience of confronting an outdoor place where confluences of natural forces—geological, biological and meteorological— predominate and include the artist as part of a totality. It is this totality, and the conflict between inclusion by nature and differentiation from it that is the subtext of each such painting.

The Valley Below
Christina Waters, August 8, 2002. 8 x 17" Oil on panel

Art ringed Heinz's world. His bookshelves contained a prodigious collection of artbooks and catalogs ranging from Tantric art to Aristede Maillol. In the house hung an abstract painting of luminous beads in space, a surrealist image of nested eyes and thorns, a late Renaissance portrait of a lady, a painting of Our Lady of Guadalupe supported by an angel, A Magritte poster, some framed Egon Schiele reproductions, as well as things closer to his heart: his mother's Seccessionist watercolors and a remarkable representation of a World War I Italian prison camp painted by his POW father out of dyes extracted from kitchen scraps: potato skins, spinach and beets. This subtle, precise and moving painting had been done by Heinz's father to mail to his wife in a letter intending to show that, all in all, his incarceration could have been under worse circumstances. On the coffee table were always stacked new books and magazines. Among them one day was an Oskar Kokoshka catalog from a current Guggenheim Museum retrospective. On the cover was a vibrant *jungenstijl* Garden of Paradise. "That is my MaMa!" Heinz said proudly, pointing to Eve, for his remarkable mother had not only been a feminist and footballer, but Kokoshka's classmate in the academy of art and his model as well.

It seems wrong, a betrayal even, to call the man Heinz von Foerster by the name "Heinz von Foerster." His unflagging effort to see through the eyes of every *other* that entered his life, sparked an automatic intimacy that dispatched formality. He was almost universally referred to only as "Heinz" by those who had met him. This informal "Heinz" suggests both his unique stature and the shared affectionate familiarity of those around him.

Over his lifetime, Heinz transformed from archetypal prodigy into archetypal grandfather. By the time of his last years, he had become not only mentor, but grandfather to many, and, in his company, many who loved him felt for the first time the dimension of a relationship they had failed to appreciate fully when they were younger and their biologically given grand dads were still alive.

By the time I met Heinz in the mid 1980's his days of scientific acuity had somewhat subsided, but he was still a magician, an inventive rhetorician, a compelling apologist for his life's work, a raconteur, expert schmoozer and adept politician, gluing together professional and social situations with wit, charm, generosity and a nimble anthology of stories, insights and paradoxes. He was always pulling strings, engineering outcomes. More than once, over tea, Mai matter-of-factly warned visitors about the charmer who sat to her left, "Heinz is a steamroller."

It is a topic of controversy as to whether Heinz was a "guru" or not. Mai flatly insisted that Heinz would "not have permitted it." Yet experience suggested otherwise. People came from far and wide to see him. Sometimes people came with questions, looking for his view on one thing or another. He would meet neighbors, visitors, pilgrims, students and interviewers with equanimity, generosity and enthusiasm, sometimes, near the end, at the expense of his physical comfort and well-being.

Heinz clearly possessed an attractive mystique in which who he was and what he said were impossible to separate, He worked on the international scene in promoting cybernetics, through his support of the journal *Cybernetics and Human Knowing*, the American Society for Cybernetics, and by giving his name and advice to various enterprises meant to ensure the endurance of the field which, in the United States at least, seemed in danger of eclipse due to its accumulated achievements which were busily spawning fields of their own.

And yes, all the way until his nineties Heinz was a steamroller too. Long after I had ceased to be president of the ASC, Heinz would find a moment in every lunch, tea and meeting to promote his pet projects. It would go something like this: "Without a journal a society is just a club..." followed by "... The ASC needs a monograph series. It could be issued occasionally, each number would be the same size and would fit on a shelf together...." Always the designer. And always the self-publisher. Heinz created countless books, from scrupulously chronological photo albums to copies of his own monograph series of precious pamphlets made from eight and a half by eleven inch paper folded and stapled with color coded covers.

Beneath the living room, beside his Mesozoic Atari computer was his printing press—one of the hardest-working little photocopiers of all time. If, in the course of a conversation, anyone expressed a wish or need for this paper or that, he would go straightaway downstairs to work retrieving or producing it, there on the spot. He said he had learned never to put anything off. Because of this, the past and the future converged vigorously on the Now for him, and even in his last days he would say that he gave little or any thought to his past, arguing that his life had been so marvelous that meditating on the past would make him depressed as he saw it in contrast to the "now" of decline.

"The Heinz-machine is kaput" he announced with humor, explanation and apology, regarding his accumulating infirmities, conceding that, in old age, for one as vigorous as he, the mind and body, though not split, seemed determined to part company.

When Christina and I walked up the hill to paint the view west of Rattlesnake Hill where the Pacific lies just behind the soft hills on the western side of the valley, we talked, as we always did, about how this might be the last time we painted here, and how precious it was to be here, how precious Heinz was for us and for so many other people, and about how incomprehensible or at least how idiosyncratic he was, about habits, his and ours, about the landscape itself- what it meant to us, what it meant to Heinz and to Mai.

I had first painted this landscape on a visit ten years earlier. I painted his orderly woodpile and the landscape beyond it to learn something about the man, by acting so as to see what he saw, by trying to "see through the eyes of the other."

Later in his life, it was a dropped piece of firewood that fell on his toe as, recovering from a stroke, his will to resume his chores outpaced his strength. This hurt toe refused to heal and ultimately led to Heinz losing his foot to a surgeon, and led too to his admission that his famous positive attitude was slipping into depression now and then as his independence was finally undeniably challenged, as he needed to ask for someone to help him with simple tasks he had taken for granted, such as getting a book down from a shelf.

In the mid to late nineties when Heinz could still tour the property with Mai or with a visitor, often a lady, on his arm, climbing and descending well-memorized slopes cunningly if no longer with youthful agility, pointing out the site of one anecdote, then another, with sweeping gestures of his free arm. Christina and I visited for conversation in those days and, ostensibly, for purposes of completing ongoing ASC business. If we were part of a large group, we'd go down the hill for an early afternoon lunch at Duarte's tavern in the town. At Duarte's Heinz recommended the Chilean sea bass and the ollalieberry pie. He drank a glass of white wine and a bottle of Callistoga water. There was good cheer and even merriment there. Everyone knew him and the waitresses loved him. The happiest I ever saw Heinz was a Duarte's, beaming blissfully between his two grand daughters.

More and more often we would meet in the late afternoon, at four o'clock, for tea.

Once Christina interviewed him indoors for *Cybernetics and Human Knowing* while I followed his instructions, painting his beloved anomalous "crazy tree" for him, and this painting was exhibited for some time, leaning against the woodburning stove, like some others of our paintings, which we would occasionally leave behind for him and Mai to see if, at the end of our painting session, he was still napping. When we came Christina and I would bring Mexican wedding cookies, *pfeffernuese* or an apple strudel from Beckmann's Bakery in Santa Cruz. Sometimes a bottle of chardonnay. Often we would arrive with another guest or two, or bring some students from the U.C.S.C. who were anxious for *darshan* with the legendary cybernetician. They inspected the wonders of the house: Andreas von Foerster's cross-section of a bowl of spaghetti, Heinz's designs of table and lamp, the elegant and simple house itself, dangerously low beams over the upper floor library, complete with prime editions of *Minotaur* and *Flair*, reproductions of Egon Schiele's watercolors on the walls, an extravagant feather and a twisted bright lump of magnesium, a piece of space junk that had set a tree on fire when it fell from the heavens above California onto the eastern slope of Rattlesnake Hill. The collection of Damon Runyon pulp novels from which the von Foersters, upon arriving in New York, had learned idiomatic American speech. A William Wegman bedroom "supergraphic," Wegman being just one of Heinz's unexpected students. The stuffed rabbits in the bedroom, assembled in honor of "Uncle Cornelio." Heinz's jazzy collage mural of 60's Vogue models and Mercury astronauts. His amazing and impeccable filing system. His grand office. His archaic computer.

These young students, interested in ecology, design and cybernetics, looked forward to lively and enlightening conversation on these subjects. But Heinz also talked about art: of the affinities of Second Order Cybernetics to surrealism, particularly Magritte, of his success in training engineering his students to detect forged Vermeers more effectively than those students trained by the art history department. Infirm as he was, Heinz maintained a relentless social schedule. His popularity never waned. Getting a date to see him, even in his last months, seemed nearly as arduous as arranging to see the Pope. In 1999 he started to complain of sudden fatigue that would overwhelm him only minutes after one of his typically explosive and enthusiastic hellos had convinced visitors who arrived from great distances that their pilgrimage to his door was more than worth the effort.

Christina, in her pink sweater, and I, in an orange baseball cap, fell into the category of "local visitors." We negotiated a plan by which we could see him and visit as frequently as we would like.

As Heinz was happy that we painted on Rattlesnake Hill, we arranged that we could paint there whether he could see us or not. This way he wasn't encumbered by the obligation to entertain us, even an obligation to be awake or even at home. This worked out well. We demonstrated that we were true to our word and would visit with him for only fifteen or twenty minutes before carrying our equipment up the hill to set up the easels in a patch of shade overlooking the vertiginous view.

By the time of our last paintings last August, Christina and I had reduced our palettes to a few key colors. We packed all the necessary equipment into a long maroon bag that could be carried easily to the site. The last view I painted from Rattlesnake Hill was much the same as the one I first painted there ten years earlier. Now, in the encroaching poison oak, lizards darted. Many of them had lost their tails.

Was this the season, I wondered, for lizards to lose their tails? I considered Heinz's favored two-dragon ourobouros, and how essential tails are to *ourobouroi*.

Both Christina and I did good paintings. We talked, as we had each time we came to paint in the last years, that this might be the last time we would do this. It was. Subsequent visits were tenderer, and without easels. Heinz's health was taking downturns, and then, as if by magic, upturns. I remembered his canny endorsement Bateson's "all men are grass" revision of Aristotle's syllogism, and his conclusion about fifteen years earlier that one could choose to disbelieve Aristotle's grim sentence "all men must die." As he himself had not died, Heinz mischievously speculated, he might live forever.

Given Heinz's recurring resurrections, it seemed sometimes that he might have been right. He might indeed live forever. But even among the most vital of us, the eternal moment of our existence drops out of sight to those around us when our body fails beyond a certain degree. "While we live we are immortal," Maturana said. So it was with Heinz, who chose immortality daily throughout his mortal life.

View from Rattlesnake Hill
Frank Galuszka, Summer, 2000. 20 x 16" Ink

Cybernetics And Human Knowing. Vol. 10, nos. 3-4, pp. 195-196

Recollections of Heinz von Foerster, a rhetorical genius[1]

Klaus Krippendorff[2]

On a cold day between Christmas and New Year 1961, in search of a place to study, I met Heinz in his office at the Biological Computer Laboratory. I knew of him through a network of designers who, like me, were interested in issues that conventional curricula did not address. Heinz greeted me, a total stranger, with the enthusiasm usually reserved for an old friend. To my surprise, he knew of the place where I had came from (the Ulm School of Design, an avant-garde institution now extinct but reproduced everywhere - much as cybernetics is now), and he suggested that I come to the University of Illinois to study with W. Ross Ashby. This short encounter enrolled me into cybernetics and defined my intellectual focus for years to come.

Heinz was an amazing orator. He used the language of mathematics to ingeniously demonstrate the profundity of simple ideas. In 1974, now a professor of communication, I organized an American Society for Cybernetics (ASC) conference on cybernetics in society at the University of Pennsylvania. He had just finished teaching his famous course on the cybernetics of cybernetics and brought a carload of students from Urbana to Philadelphia. He was the key note speaker, of course. I can still see him addressing the audience with his usual Viennese charm: "Ladies and Gentlemen." Calling our attention to the axiomatic phrase "Anything said is said by an observer," he named it Humberto Maturana's Theorem Number One, and suggested a "modest" extension: "Heinz von Foerster's Corollary Number One: 'Anything said is said to an observer'." In a stroke of genius, by changing only one two-letter word, he shifted our epistemologic attention from Maturana's acts of observation to acts of communication and proceeded to show that such acts entail responsibilities that we must not transfer to others.

Heinz accomplished rhetorical feasts like that often and with the ease of a magician: asking questions that others had not thought of; turning conventional beliefs into puzzling opposites; leading his audiences to consider alternative ways of thinking - always moving recursive constructions of human activity into the center of the conversations. Heinz' greatest strength undoubtedly was his ability to encourage others to be audacious as well, to have the courage to ponder radical questions. Doing this was his cybernetics and it has now become ours.

---

1. Originally published in German as: Krippendorff, K. (2003) Rhetorische Geniestreiche. *Lernende Organization, 11*(February), 59-60.
2. Gregory Bateson Term Professor for Cybernetics, Language, and Culture, The Annenberg School for Communication, University of Pennsylvania. E-mail: kkrippendorff@asc.upenn.edu

We stayed in touch by phone, exchanged papers, and met at many conferences and on his beloved Rattlesnake Hill. For the last couple of years, he was not well, he told me. But as a second-order cybernetician, this did not prevent him from applying his own principles to himself and carrying on against all medical predictions, always positive, curious, interpersonally engaged, fascinated by new ideas, and excited about even the smallest accomplishments. The last time I saw Heinz was in June 2002, with a friend. He greeted us with his characteristically animated, "Hello," inquired about our plans for the forthcoming cybernetics conference in Santa Cruz, asked about the people in our lives, wanted to know of any breakthroughs, and showed us the latest books about him. He was full of live and present against all odds.

Reading interviews of him or transcripts of his talks, those who knew him cannot but help hearing his exuberance, sensing his energy, and enjoying his playful juggling of ideas— even through translations. We will miss him, but his voice will continue to be heard.

10th Macy-Conference on Cybernetics, Princeton, 1953. Heinz von Foerster sitting far side, second from the right (photographer unknown)

Cybernetics And Human Knowing. Vol. 10, nos. 3-4, pp. 197-201

The Man in the Room Across the Hall

Cornelia Bessie[1]

I was a teenager, living on the top floor of my parents' house in New York, when I was told that there was going to be a visitor, the friend of friends of my family, living in the guest room across the hall.

There appeared, straight off the plane, a vibrant, fascinating, slightly frightening man. He spoke no English, my German was rudimentary, but I soon recognized that this was like no one I had ever known. He was a scientist, I had met only people concerned with the arts. He had an old-world courtliness that extended even to a female teenager, and he exuded a *joie de vivre* and a sense of fun that captivated me instantly. In just a few days I would realize that I had met a great teacher, a person who would teach me more profoundly than anyone I would ever meet. Of course, I didn't know then that this was the start of a friendship that would last without interruption for 60-odd years and would cover every aspect of my life; intellectual, emotional, ethical, artistic.

He proposed: if I would start teaching him English, he would introduce me to science. Done. We began lessons. Cybernetics, what's that? In just a few days I made the first important decision of my life: there was a better education at home than at school, and I stopped going to school. So this scene: every morning a worried Heinz appeared at my door, "Don't you think you should go to school today?" (He was no more a morning person then than he was later) Me: "No." "What will your parents say?" "They won't know if you'll bring up a couple of pieces of toast from your breakfast." He couldn't imagine a house where the parents didn't know if their kid was at school. I knew I was perfectly safe.

So it went till he was due to give a lecture at Princeton. I took him to the station, very apprehensive about his still small store of English. He smiled, "But I'm not going to speak English, I'm going to speak science." Aha. Another door opening.

I think that shortly thereafter he would go to meet Warren McCulloch, who had been responsible for getting him to America, having read the only scientific paper (on memory) Heinz had published at that time. And soon McCulloch would be responsible as well for making him secretary of the Josiah Macy meetings—that will be the quickest way for him to learn English, he said. New names now appeared on my horizon: Norbert Wiener, Margaret Mead, John von Neumann, Gregory Bateson and more. I began to have some inkling of why these people were important, and what they thought and wrote as Heinz came home tired and exhilarated.

---

1. Cornelia Bessie has been in book publishing for over 40 years. She has been involved with Freeman Dyson and Peter Medawar, Anwar Sadat and Mikhail Gorbachev, and many European and American authors. She is now co-publisher of Bessie Books. 296 Joshuatown Road, Lyme, Connecticut 06371.

I went back to school and Heinz went to the University of Illinois and got a job. Not long thereafter Heinz grew very excited. Mai and the boys were coming. "You'll love Mai," he said, "I had to go to those universities to learn what Mai knew at birth." I began to have an idea of what a close harmony between a man and a woman could be. A dyad, somebody would call it later.

The years went by, we talked on the phone, he sent me the papers I might understand, sometimes he came to New York. I went to various universities and started to work in book publishing. Thanks to Heinz's initial grounding in showing me how a scientist's mind works I would be involved in publishing some science for the general reader: Peter Medawar and later Freeman Dyson, among others.

In 1960 there was another milestone in our friendship. A phone call explained: the Navy was funding a conference at the University of Illinois to be called Principles of Self-Organizing Systems. Heinz had been given a certain number of invitations, people he could have brought in from anywhere, scientists from very different disciplines, to present papers they were currently working on. When he had invited the people he wanted he had one invitation left over, and it occurred to him that there might be an interesting translation problem between man and machine that someone whose business was language might see from a different angle than the scientists. Would I come? I was thrilled, frightened, determined not to shame his generous invitation. I knew I couldn't give myself an education in sophisticated science in a few months, but I thought that if I could learn the basics of their language I might be able to follow.

So I began to read, and after a while I phoned Heinz, reading list in hand. "This is what I've read, what else should I read?" A peal of laughter from the other end of the line. "Stop," he said. "You'll understand the first-rate minds, one always does, and the rest don't matter." A sentence that has stayed with me ever since.

The clear June days of that conference were to change my life. I had always had such a mental block about numbers that I had failed Math 1 twice. But here, to use the new lingo, the payoff for comprehension was so great that I suddenly found myself understanding—and retaining—concepts that were really far beyond my reach. I had help. We were all seated around a horseshoe-shaped table, with the speaker at the open end. Time and again a tall bearded man would pad up behind me and write a sentence or an equation on my notebook, whispering "Understand this and you'll understand what he's saying." He seemed to know, magically, when I was lost. That was the beginning of another dear and wonderful friendship, Warren McCulloch.

I was so excited and thrilled by what I was hearing that such mundane matters as sleep and food quite vanished. (In fact, we were all so keyed up that on the last day of the conference one of the participants, who was also a doctor, walked around giving us all vitamin B12 shots.) The conversations went on into all hours of the night. I was living on an adrenaline high, and I learned more, I think, in those few days than in several years of college, and many of those interests have lasted to this day.

There were also friendships made during those days that went on and on. Gordon Pask, who in my mind was not born of woman: there must have been a clap of thunder on a heath somewhere and there stood a small man in a crumpled black suit with a triangular haircut, looking just as he did for all his life, following ideas to the outer edges of the thought of his day. Ross Ashby, who explained to me one night about eohippus: the day the little animal had changed from thinking "nose up" (boughs) to "nose down" (grass) and thus had become the ancestor of one of man's truest friends. Stafford Beer, then the management guru of his time, talking about the vagaries of corporations, some of which has a hollow echo at this time. People talking about neural nets, brain functions, order and disorder—I won't go on, the scientific contributors will do this better than I could. One of the first things I learned was that this group of people were in some ways strangely familiar. There was some proximity to the kind of artistic thought that I knew. These were searching, investigative minds, just like writers or painters. Often they scooped ideas out of the blue and then looked for a logic to validate them. They knew the importance of accidents and mistakes. It seemed to me as though they could be divided into people who looked through microscopes in order not to see the world as a whole, and people who saw the world in all its complexity.

Now the important—and difficult—part. What makes me say that the person who came to live on the top floor of that house on 58th Street influenced, changed, my life more than any other one person?

Heinz loved to quote his uncle Ludwig Wittgenstein to the effect that ethics could not be talked about, ethics are implicit. In other words, one lives ethics, one does not describe them. By the same token, the effect of a life-changing teacher/friend is probably best shown by a series of vignettes, remembered sayings, small insights. Disjointed perhaps, but giving a more accurate picture than a more orderly presentation might do.

First, an attitude that was at the basis of every aspect of his life, from the mailman to his students, his colleagues, his family. One must always be open; the other is always interesting, a person, not a function. Charm there certainly was, but this was not charm, it was the quintessence of true courtesy, a welcoming of the world. This openness made him a good scientist, (it is quite easy to find what one is looking for, but very difficult to discern the unwanted or unsuspected—or in Heinzspeak, the blind spot does not see what it does not see) but it also had a human effect—it is why the postmistress in Pescadero lights up when Heinz is mentioned. The most casual acquaintances seemed to sense a "specialness" in this man, not the effect of a wonderful mind, but the effect of an ethos that welcomed. "Dancing with the world" was a notion that delighted him.

One of his favorite descriptive words in German was "lustig." He translated this into English as "funny," which is not quite the same thing, but then Heinz's English was his own. "I met this funny man," I would often hear on the phone. Often what this would turn out to be was somebody whose seriousness was not heavy or somber or self-important. A sense of play was very important. Play—pushing around notions, admiring beautiful women (all his life he subscribed to Vogue because he liked to look at the girls), building something strange in the middle of the night, finding just the right drawing for the cover of a paper—these were an important part of life, and pursued with the same intensity as the more "serious" things. On my desk there has stood for fifty-odd years a box called "the young lady's cursing set." There are six hand-carved expletive stamps, under them two ink pads, and because it's Heinz, at the side two rolled kleenexes for cleaning up. Very handy for some manuscripts.

Making a woodpile with Heinz was a learning experience: until the logs were exactly—but exactly—lined up the job wasn't finished.

He lovingly cut paths across the poison oak and scrub on Rattlesnake Hill so that visitors from all over the world could be walked across his beloved acres, on Fifth Avenue to the Coffee House (a clearing with benches) to the solar shower or to the Ilse bench where the view was glorious. I once accused him of trying to Schoenbrunnify his patch of California when every twig on the path had to be removed. But it was all essential Heinz: play, esthetics, loyalty to the people you love.

Perhaps the most important lesson that Heinz taught so many of us is the hardest to write about: he was a living example of how to love: Mai, of course, first and foremost, and passionately for seventy-odd years; his sons, his grandchildren, his friends, his students. To quote Phaidros, via Heinz, "much has been written about specialized topics, but who discusses an inter-disciplinary problem as, for instance, love?" Heinz didn't much discuss it, he lived it. Once, when the remarkable dyad he and Mai lived was in the air, he reminded me that their terrible war years began their union, a time when trust, loyalty, and closeness were literally life and death matters. He has talked and written about loyalty and commitment, although those rather dry and abstract notions don't begin to describe what one saw. Passion, perhaps, is the word that comes closest. If Heinz loved you as a friend he loved you unreservedly. Which didn't mean he did not see your flaws. But the love was unswerving. There was no criticism of his sons, his family, his friends. Yet with a clear-eyed view of who they were. Perhaps, Uncle Ludwig, love is even more implicit than ethics, and cannot be described. But for many people Heinz and Mai were a touchstone for the art of love. "To open a space for the other" as Maturana said.

Heinz's sense of play was infectious. It even infected Walt Kelly, father of Pogo. Heinz once wrote a tongue-in-cheek paper on overpopulation, where he posited that the end of the world would be Friday, November 13th, 2026 (before or after lunch? asks Pogo) when there would be no more room on earth for all of us. So on December 8th, 1960, Pogo asks, "Does that mean that too many people is bad for humanity, or that too much humanity is bad for people?" I don't think Heinz ever answered.

I have not touched on thoughts that have instructed my life. "Always act so as to increase your number of choices." The difference between talking about a problem and talking about how to talk about a problem. The different forms and meanings of a self-organizing system. The whole notion of causality, of circularity. The notion that memory is not storage but recreation. (Is this whole little paper a demonstration?) "The only person you can change is yourself." I could go on with this for pages. Heinz talked a lot about trivial and non-trivial machines. Perhaps as near a summation as I can find is that he was the least trivial human being I have ever known.

Heinz once gave a course at the University of Illinois called Heuristics. The word comes from the Greek heuriskein, from which comes heurika! or eureka! in English. It was what Archimedes called out in the bathtub when he noticed that bodies are lighter in water—eureka, I have found it. All his life Heinz led us to eureka moments, large and small; about love, life, philosophy, science, play, physics, family, fun, the real, the false, and how to continue down the path.

Heinz and Mai von Foerster, 1962, at the International Design Conference, Aspen, Colorado (unknown photographer)

Cybernetics And Human Knowing. Vol. 10, no. 2, pp. 202-203

Growing up with the BCL (and before)

Tom von Foerster

I hope the notes below will be useful, despite my not having had much of anything to do with electron tubes, cybernetics, cognition, constructivism, or family therapy, the fields with which Heinz has been associated with. Perhaps because I was also trained as a physicist but am now only peripherally associated with physics, my career has paralleled Heinz's to a slight extent, but this does not give me any greater insight into Heinz's ideas and their impact in their fields than the average physicist manqué. Nor can I say that I had any influence on Heinz's work at all, except by being part of the social matrix in which he operated. Heinz always emphasized how much his family and early life influenced him, especially since it included such figures as GretheWiesenthal and Ludwig Wittgenstein, but I think that he was always clear about operating within a social context that included many layers of intimacy, of emotional connections, and of intellectual collaborations. And in this set of layers, the immediate family always figured prominently. There was never any question, no matter what I (or Johnny or Andy) did or said, that Heinz and Mai would support us in any important decision we reached. When Mai's mother at one point complained that the tree of us did not show enough gratitude to our parents, Heinz joked that no gratitude was needed, he'd had his fun and was now paying for it. Omi was scandalized, but I think the three of us knew that the emotional and intellectual bond between our parents and us did not need ostentations of gratitude, that the mutual debts were too deep for that.

My earliest consistent memories date from Vienna, shortly after the end of the War. At that time, Heinz was a very rare presence in our lives, since he held down two jobs to keep the family together. However, that meant that the times we did see him for more than a few minutes were causes for great play and celebration. Thinking back on it now, I realize how much effort Mai must have put into the family while also keeping up with her freelance writing jobs. But at the time this was not at all apparent. Already then she was the quiet center that held things together without seeming to do anything special at all.

After we moved to the US, Heinz was a much larger presence in our lives, challenging us, leading us on, supervising our education. We could always count on him to provide deep insights, but also considerably more work, if we asked him a question. But it was Mai who helped us with our homework every day and who answered our personal questions. She would understand what it was we needed to know and why, and would try point us to the most reasonable solutions. Already while we were in grade school, we were encouraged to join in dinner-table conversations not only with family and friends, but also with the colleagues, graduate students, or visitors to his lab whom Heinz brought home. We learned early on that the interesting adults were not really very different from ourselves, and that the adults who insisted that they were adults were not really interesting (nor to Heinz and Mai either).

As the Electron Tube Lab became the Biological Computer Lab, the outside visitors became more and more frequent and more and more interesting. Having Warren McCullough advise you on your senior essay is a memorable experience, as is having Oliver Selfridge and Jerry Lettvin give demonstrations on the best way to use palmistry for picking up girls.

Although, of course, I could not have said so at the time, I think that the uniform message in our entire upbringing was to respect other people, no matter what their status, or age, or color—and concomitantly, a contempt for people who did not behave accordingly. Being rude to waiters, or dismissing children as childish, or undergraduates as immature, simply because of their status, was as good a way as any not to be included in the future. Although Heinz has been clearly associated with this attitude toward others because it became a central part of the philosophy that he taught, it was, I think, Mai who contributed even more to that moral code—and who provided much of the generosity toward those who did matter, who were respected— that characterized the household. It was, after all, she who baked the 90 fruitcakes a year that went all over the globe at Christmas-time—and which were, unlike most fruitcakes, prized (and eaten) by the recipients.

View From Rattlesnake Hill
Frank Galuszka. Oil

Cybernetics And Human Knowing. Vol. 10, no. 2, pp. 204-205

Growing up in the von Foerster family

Andy von Foerster

At first, my family was Tommy and Mai. My oldest brother, Jonny, had been sent to live with my grandmother in rural Germany. I don't remember Heinz being around. Not that he wasn't; all I remember is that, when he WAS around, it was a really big deal. When we immigrated to the United States and arrived at the dock in New York, peering down into the crowd from the ship, Mai, Jonny, and Tom could pick him out, I couldn't.

I remember always having the sense that Heinz' family was important, in a way that transcended money. There were photo albums of Heinz doing unimaginable things: handstands on ladders on rooftops, performing as a magician, scaling vertical rock walls in the Alps. Ancestors were city planners, artists, political activists and military officers. Heinz spent his youth with philosophers and titled aristocrats, at castles and at the opera.

My brothers and I were learning these things as we were growing up in a small university town in a flat agricultural area in the Midwest. Cornfields stretched for hundreds of miles in every direction. At least, the University had some Viennese faculty, and one close friend at the Music School put on opera performances with graduate students. Heinz worked hard, and rapidly ascended the academic ladder. Mai got my brothers and me to school, took care of the family finances, and put a hearty, tasty dinner on the table 365 days of the year (we never ate out).

Heinz would close himself into his office at home after dinner and work until maybe two in the morning, getting up at around ten o'clock. We saw him at dinner and on weekends, when the family would work on projects, or go on outings with Heinz' sister Erika (Rikki) and her husband, Peps. Heinz also took a vacation every year, the entire month of August, until the beginning of the Fall semester, after Labor Day. We would go on month-long camping trips, joined by Rikki and Peps, and sometimes other friends for part of the time. These were wonderful times of exploration, discovery and loafing. We would try to find isolated places, because nudity was an important part of Heinz' enjoyment of the outdoors.

Another thing about Heinz was that he was a big risk-taker. Heinz always took huge intellectual risks, proposed or defended unpopular ideas, and supported the underdog. We had photographic evidence of his rock-climbing and of daredevil acrobatic stunts. Heinz always took huge intellectual risks, proposed or defended unpopular ideas, and supported the underdog. Later, he could continue to do this because he knew Mai would always keep the home together while he buzzed around, sticking his nose into places. Jonny and I adopted more of the ignore-the-risk attitude than Tom did. We would drive to Colorado during semester break to go skiing, for example, and camp in a tent in the parking lot of the ski area. I left home and college aged eighteen, and got married in San Francisco at age twenty. Jonny died in a motorcycle crash at age twenty-five, passing a truck on a dusty road in Africa.

For Heinz, who came from generations of iconoclasts, to have Mai, who, although intelligent and adventurous, was at least not *a priori* opposed to having things done in a conventional way, must have been liberating. He could always check with her to see how far off base he was. We've all seen it: Heinz all over the place, and Mai, a solid, loving rock.

Bedside rabbits and books

Rattlesnake Hill

April 99

Transfinity

666 said the moon child.
Ride with me and your hidden devils can get wild
To get back on the homμe path, you might need reason, or a little math.
If you want to be a mathematical hero, begin with a point, and a zero.
With one you get some, and the possibility of unity.
Two leads to the pair and square,
Angles that are right create height.
Three makes perspective, and the cube,
Now look at the next higher dimension in a telescopic tube.
With four you can enter the time door.
Entropy won't let you go from now to before.
Lines of time end in death,
But this is a shadow of the next dimensions - light and breath.
Time is also rotation, circulation and duration measured by infinity to the infinite power,
And now we stand on a transfinite tower!
Has logic become phantasy?
You might need intuition to return to reality!

Bill Schiffer
The Cosmic Flower
Christiania
Copenhagen, Denmark

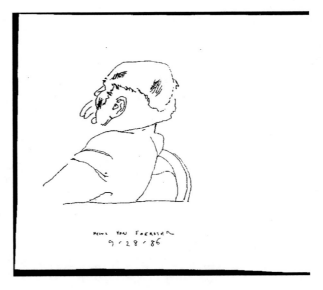

HEINZ VON FOERSTER
9·28·86